Essentials of Interviewing

Essentials of Mental Health Practice Series
Founding Editors, Alan S. Kaufman and Nadeen L. Kaufman

Essentials of Interviewing
by Donald E. Wiger and Debra K. Huntley

Essentials of Outcome Assessment
by Benjamin M. Ogles, Michael J. Lambert, and Scott A. Fields

Essentials of Treatment Planning
by Mark E. Maruish

Essentials

of Interviewing

Donald E. Wiger

Debra K. Huntley

 John Wiley & Sons, Inc.

ISBN: 0-471-00237-2

Printed in the United States of America.

10   9   8   7   6   5   4

CONTENTS

Series Preface   vii

One   Overview of the Mental Health Interview   1

Two   The Intake Interview Process   13

Three   Factors Affecting the Quality of Information Received   35

Four   Establishing Rapport: Mainstream and Special Populations   61

Five   The Biopsychosocial Assessment   90

Six   Suicide Assessment   118

Seven   Diagnostic Interviewing   137

Eight   The Mental Status Exam (MSE)   167

Nine   The Report: Incorporating Diagnostic Information with Mental Health Services   191

Appendix   Overview of Selected *DSM-IV-TR*™ Diagnoses   199

References   211

Annotated Bibliography   217

Index   219

About the Authors   229

SERIES PREFACE

In the *Essentials of Mental Health Practice* series, our goal is to provide readers with books that will deliver key practical information in an efficient and accessible style. The series features books on a variety of critical practice topics, such as interviewing, treatment planning, and outcomes assessment, to name a few. For the experienced professional, books in the series offer a concise yet thorough overview of a specific area of expertise, including numerous tips for best practices. Students will find here a prioritized assembly of all the information and techniques that must be at one's fingertips to practice knowledgably, efficiently, and ethically in today's behavioral health environment.

Wherever feasible, visual cues highlighting key points are utilized alongside systematic, step-by-step guidelines. Chapters are focused and succinct. Topics are organized for an easy understanding of the essential material related to a particular practice area. Theory and research are continually woven into the fabric of each book, but always to enhance the practical application of the material, rather than sidetrack or overwhelm readers. With this series, we aim to challenge and assist readers engaged in providing mental health services to aspire to the highest level of proficiency in their particular discipline by arming them with the tools they need for effective practice.

This text is written to provide an additional perspective of clinical interviewing than what is typically presented in introductory texts. In addition to the nuts and bolts of basic interviewing skills, the interview requirements of third party payers and accreditation agencies are covered in this text. The major strengths of this text lie in learning both the client-oriented relationship skills and the practical skills needed to obtain and document diagnostic information required by accrediting agencies such as the Joint Commission on Accreditation of Healthcare Organizations (JCAHO) and the Commission on Accreditation of Rehabilitation Facilities (CARF), and third-party payers.

Chapter 1 provides an overview of what is required in a mental health interview. Chapter 2 covers topics such as the *DSM-IV-TR*™, medical necessity, confidentiality, and time management. Chapter 3 includes interviewing techniques, such as building rapport, and effective listening skills necessary to help gather valid information. Chapter 4 considers the needs of special populations such as children, older adults, people with disabilities, and clients from diverse cultural backgrounds. Chapter 5 teaches the multifaceted areas to cover in a biopsychosocial assessment and how to integrate this information into treatment. Chapter 6 provides training in suicide assessment, identifying risk factors, and ethical/legal considerations. Chapter 7 details the diagnostic interview from a *DSM-IV-TR*™ perspective. Chapter 8 covers the Mental Status Exam. Chapter 9 provides a sample psychological report. This text is intended for use as a supplementary graduate, or upper level undergraduate text, and for therapists desiring to improve their client relationship skills and to enhance their proficiency in designing their interviews to fit third-party requirements.

Alan S. Kaufman, PhD, and Nadeen L. Kaufman, EdD, Founding Editors
Yale University School of Medicine

Essentials of Interviewing

One

OVERVIEW OF THE MENTAL HEALTH INTERVIEW

A comprehensive mental health interview is the cornerstone of obtaining an accurate diagnosis and providing on target treatment. It is the first step in determining the scope of services a client may receive. The interview is a crucial point in establishing trust and rapport with a client, so that the client will feel comfortable sharing vulnerable aspects of his or her life. Additionally, the clinical interview is designed to collect sufficient information to make a diagnosis, determine the level (setting, frequency, intensity, duration) of treatment needed, and develop a treatment plan. Without the interview, there is a lack of information with which to conduct services aimed at treating specific problem areas. The initial interview is required by virtually all third-party payers and accrediting agencies.

Prior to conducting the interview, it is common to collect biopsychosocial information (Chapter 5), which summarizes the client's past and current behaviors, background, health, and previous treatment. The information collected helps identify areas to emphasize during the interview. The client's strengths, needs, abilities, and preferences (SNAPs) are incorporated in all aspects of treatment.

The interview may be conducted by an individual mental health professional or by a multidisciplinary team. The person interviewed may be seen for a number of reasons such as individual counseling services, employment screening, marriage and family counseling, determination of competency to stand trial, disability determination, chemical dependency evaluation or treatment, need for medications, inpatient hospitalization, and several others. *Essentials of Interviewing* focuses on obtaining information for a *DSM* diagnosis and mental health treatment.

It takes little training to ask the client questions and obtain information. However, significant training, experience, and supervision are needed to develop the skills necessary to put together the appropriate information in a meaningful way.

Maloney and Ward (1976) state that there are two distinct methods of conducting an assessment. The *psychometric perspective* relies on standardized procedures and objective tests that compare the client to a reference group by means of statistical analysis. However, this perspective fails to consider an individual's distinctive features, strengths, or weaknesses in the context of everyday life or specific environmental variables. The *psychological assessment approach,* on the other hand, emphasizes the client's specific strengths and weaknesses. It focuses on the art, rather than the science of interviewing. Today, typical clinical practice incorporates each of these methods. This text incorporates aspects of both methods, but does not provide training in psychological testing.

Information gathered during the diagnostic interview serves several purposes beyond that of helping the therapist formulate a clinical diagnosis. Generating a clinical diagnosis is a usual procedure in mental health treatment and required by third-party payers; however, the diagnosis alone provides little clinical information other than assigning the name of a disorder, its corresponding classification number, and diagnostic characteristics. For example, clients assigned the same mental health diagnosis may function at notably different levels and require varying types of care ranging from periodic counseling sessions to extensive inpatient psychiatric treatment. Although typical funding sources require a *DSM-IV-TR* (Diagnostic and Statistical Manual of Mental Disorders, Fourth Edition, Text Revision; American Psychiatric Association, 2000) or an ICD-10 (International Classification of Diseases, Tenth Revision; World Health Organization, 1997a, 1997b) diagnosis to qualify clients for reimbursement, additional clarifying information is needed to provide the proficient delivery of mental health services. A diagnosis alone does not indicate the onset, frequency, duration, or intensity of symptoms and impairments. Without this additional information, determining the medical necessity of mental health treatment is, at most, tentative. Further, it does not define the client's strengths, which will ultimately aid the client in treatment.

The interview itself is a delicate balance of empathy and empirical data collection. Empathy serves clients by providing a sense of understanding and assurance that the problems they face are manageable and that help is on its way. C. R. Rogers (1975) adds that empathy involves being sensitive and in the moment to the changing meanings and emotions of the client. It also means the therapist must temporarily live in the client's life without making judgments. Empirical data supplies the therapist with the necessary information to validate a diagnosis and plan a course of action based on specific client needs. Behavioral data, in itself (such as test results), can be an important element of diagnostic assessment but is often meaningless without integrating the interview material.

The client may experience an unusual combination of both comforting and unpleasant emotions during the interview. While hope may be instilled, difficult material may also be presented. As topics change frequently during the interview, emotions may change rapidly. An effective therapist understands how to provide support and understanding while at the same time following up on information that is necessary to implement the most therapeutic treatment plan.

ROLE OF THE INTERVIEWER

An effective clinician in mental health interviewing must know much more than how to arrive at a clinical diagnosis. The three broad areas of necessary skills include (a) interviewing skills such as establishing and maintaining rapport with the client, (b) diagnostic skills such as knowledge of psychopathology and mental health diagnoses, and (c) documentation skills such as knowledge of current third-party requirements in report writing and treatment planning.

A review of literature by Meehl (1954, 1965) compared the accuracy of clinical judgment to actuarial or statistical methods in which the same data were available for each method of assessment. Results indicated that statistical methods yielded more accurate predictions than clinical judgment alone. Several subsequent studies (e.g., Gold-

> # DON'T FORGET
>
> ### *Skills and Knowledge Necessary for Successful Interviewing*
>
> **Interviewing Skills**
> (Skills and knowledge of relationship building and information collecting)
>
> +
>
> **Diagnostic Skills**
> (Skills and knowledge of psychopathology and *DSM-IV-TR*)
>
> +
>
> **Documentation Skills**
> (Skills and knowledge of third-party requirements and report writing)

berg, 1965; Wiggins, 1973) confirmed Meehl's results. As clinical methods follow more standardized procedures, more accuracy is obtained.

Due to the objectivity required in diagnostic interviewing, the clinician must remain focused as to the purpose of the interview. If the interview resembles a counseling session, there may be initial apparent benefits to the client, but ultimately, the client suffers, because most third-party payers require that specific diagnostic information be gathered in the initial session. That is, further sessions may not be authorized due to inadequate documentation in the initial interview.

If any of the above-mentioned interview skills are lacking (i.e., interviewing, diagnostic, or documentation), the validity of the interview may be compromised. For example, the most empathic therapist, without sufficient expertise in psychopathology or the *DSM-IV-TR,* may be helpful and encouraging to the client in the interview session but provide little or no empirical diagnostic information to the insurance company. In such cases, it is likely that a client who may need mental health services could be denied by a third-party payer due to inadequate documentation. Likewise, an expert in psychopathology, with few skills in rapport, may not adequately connect with the client; thus, the client may not disclose some important information. Again, this could result in services being denied by a third-party payer. Adequate documentation is also paramount. The adage, "if it isn't written down, it doesn't exist," has never been truer. Further, in today's managed-care environment, a therapist lacking in knowledge of specific types of information required in the initial interview could result in a denial of services.

The most important question for the interviewing clinician to answer is the *referral question,* or the reason for the referral. The course of the interview and the type of report will specifically address that issue. Although most mental health interviews focus on determining the need for mental health services, others are meant to provide clarity or understanding of the client for other reasons (e.g., competency to stand trial, disability determination, educational services, custody evaluation, employment).

Traditional psychotherapy began with an insight-oriented perspective in assessment and treatment. However, modern standards of assessment, including the *DSM-IV-TR* classifications, derive from a medical or symptoms orientation model. Othmer and Othmer (1994) state that each method (insight and symptoms orientation) can be integrated. Insight methods focus on resolving unconscious conflicts by bringing them into consciousness. This model attempts to explain signs, symptoms, and behaviors, whereas a medical model classifies specific symptoms into groups of diagnoses. The medical model orientation focuses on specific symptoms that treatment will aim to reduce or alleviate.

It is possible that two clients with similar problem areas and symptoms could receive different diagnoses, or different conceptualizations of the problem area, depending on the background of the person conducting the interview. Therefore, standardized procedures in interviewing are needed to avoid therapist bias. While the insight-oriented clinician may provide helpful interpretations of the client's behavior and psychological processes, the medical model focuses on specific current observable problem areas and symptoms.

In the initial sessions, it is necessary to formulate a diagnosis and collect sufficient background information about the client in order to provide a clinical hypothesis. At this point, the form of treatment may range from behavioral to cognitive to insight-oriented. That is, the treatment does not have to coincide with how the initial information was formulated. Treatment follows a theory; however, the interview should be atheoretical.

MEDICAL NECESSITY

Today's most widespread decisive factor for receiving (or being denied) third-party payment for both physical and mental health services is called *medical necessity*. The term comes from the medical model, which holds that medically necessary services are those that must be performed for the patient to recover in a reasonable time period. Sabin and Daniels (1994) point out that this is based on treatment of sickness and injury but not on services for people who are "suffering from life."

In the mental health field, medical necessity is determined when services are needed for the client to return to or attain adequate adaptive functioning. Mental health services that are viewed as helpful but not necessary may not be eligible for third-party payment. Thus, throughout the entire interview the clinician must keep in mind the need for collecting information to document medical necessity. Demonstrating medical necessity of services is crucial from the standpoint of being reimbursed for treatment. Many clients cannot afford the high cost of mental health care; therefore, documentation indicating medical necessity can make the difference between receiving or not receiving care. Nevertheless, it is clearly unethical to charge an insurance company for services that are not medically necessary solely to receive payment. Other payment arrangements (e.g., sliding fee, time payments, pro bono services, referral to nonprofit agency) may be considered for nonmedically necessary counseling services.

In the physical health field, an example of medical necessity would be someone breaking a leg and needing to have it set and placed in a cast. Without the procedure, the person would likely suffer increased pain, no progress, complications, or other regressions. Medical necessity in treating mental health problems is parallel to that in treating physical health; unnecessary treatments are not covered by insurance payments. For example, although cosmetic surgery, such as a face-lift, might be helpful to the client in many ways, it is not necessary for physical functioning. If the patient desires the services, he or she must cover the cost. Different insurance companies have different criteria about what procedures are covered by their policies.

Likewise, mental health concerns fall on a continuum of medical necessity (see Rapid Reference 1.1). The standard of which services are covered varies among third-party payers. If the client will most likely get worse, regress, or likely not return to adequate or premorbid functioning without counseling, the interview information must clearly provide supportive evidence. Some mental health services, such as coping with current stressors, may be covered, but only a limited number of sessions are approved for payment. Significant mental health problems, such as those requiring hospitalization or intensive outpatient treatment, are commonly covered mental health services.

As the degree of medical necessity increases, the level of care and number of sessions increases proportionately. Other factors that increase include length of stay, level of clinical expertise required, support needed, and client's level of vulnerability and risk. The person conducting the interview must carefully assess the level of care needed. Recommending too many or too few services can create problems. Overprescribing treatment is not only unnecessary, but it leads to overspending funds, which ultimately cause insurance premium increases and may possibly lead to fewer services being available to those who

Rapid Reference 1.1

Degrees of Medical Necessity

Not Medically Necessary	Moderate Level of Medical Necessity	Significant Level of Medical Necessity
Services are helpful. With or without treatment, the client or patient is able to function within normal limits.	*Services are important.* Client will function better with treatment; however, current functioning may not be significantly impaired.	*Services are crucial.* Without treatment, client is likely to decline or fail to attain an adequate level of functioning.

Impairments

Little or no impairment (e.g., due to condition rarely misses work or school, usually gets along well with others).	Moderate impairment (e.g., missing more work or school than average, beginning to withdraw from friends).	Significant impairments (e.g., not in touch with reality, withdrawing from most or all social contacts).

Medical Examples

Elective cosmetic surgery Hair implants Gold dental caps	Infertility treatment Allergy treatment Contact lenses	Major surgery Broken bones Chemotherapy

(continued)

Mental health examples

Personal growth counseling	Mild/moderate depression	Hallucinations
Psychoeducational services	Behavior problems	Paranoia
Relationship counseling	Outpatient treatment	Inpatient treatment
Adjustment issues	Suicide attempt	

Third-party payment

Rarely paid by third parties because of lack of functional impairments or significant distress.	Some services covered. Lesser number of sessions covered depending on the degree of impairment documented.	Services covered. Additional services covered with continued documentation of medical necessity.

Corresponding Approximate GAF Scores

100	90	80	70	60[a]	50	40	30	20	10	1

[a]GAF of 60 is a common minimum criterion for receiving third-party benefits, but it may vary. GAF scores are a 1–100 rating scale described in the DSM-IV-TR of the client's Global Assessment of Functioning.

need a greater level of help. Under-prescribing treatment is never in the client's best interest because it increases the probability of relapse and decreases the probability of the client's attaining an appropriate level of adaptive functioning.

> ## CAUTION
>
> If the therapist does not document that services are medically necessary, third-party payers typically have the right to take back payments already paid to the therapist. Even when services are critical, if the documentation does not provide adequate evidence, the need for services will not be substantiated. The burden of proof is on the clinician, not the client, or third-party payer, to demonstrate that services are necessary.

Shortly after the initial interview the clinician will file either a written or verbal (over the telephone) report describing the client's condition to the client's insurer. The clinician conducting the mental health interview therefore must develop concise writing and verbal skills to properly portray the client's condition. The quality and specificity of the report directly influence the type and the number of services the client is authorized to receive. Another reason for keeping an accurate and readable report is that other sources, such as other professionals, the client, or third-party payers, may request client information at some point during or after treatment has taken place. If these requests meet the client's consent for disclosure requirements, this information must be easily comprehensible to these parties.

It is the task of the interviewer to provide examples of functional impairments, significant distress, or both, in the client's life. They must further clearly document or provide evidence that without mental health treatment, there will not be improvements in a reasonable time period, or that there will be deterioration in functioning. Although a client might have significant mental health and functional impairments, if it is not clearly empirically documented, third-party payment for services could be denied. The denial would stem from the clinician's lack of proper documentation, rather than the client's lack of impairment. It is clearly the clinician's duty to provide accurate documentation of the material assessed during the interview. Therefore, a mental health interviewer must carefully evaluate medical necessity as part of the assessment process. Diagnostic and interviewing skills are necessary but insufficient.

Putting It Into Practice

Example of Documenting Medical Necessity

Mary is seeking counseling services due to experiencing a severely depressed mood since she was turned down to be in the pre-med program at her college. She has had an unwavering desire to be a physician all through her life. Therefore, she describes the rejection as "traumatic." Prior to receiving the notice, she had a B average in college and rarely missed any classes. Since she received the notice six weeks ago, she has missed over 50% of her college classes. She received a letter from the dean stating that she is in danger of not passing any of her courses this term. Over the past three weeks, she has increasing symptoms of social withdrawal, irritability, increasing thoughts of death, a 5% weight loss, lack of sleep, feelings of hopelessness, and severe dysphoria. She is in need of intensive outpatient counseling; without such services, further decompensation is predicted, and suicidal potential is increased due to her current feelings of hopelessness.

Teaching Point: *Documenting medical necessity must clearly describe specific problem areas that are impairing the client's daily functioning, as well as how the impairment is related to mental health concerns.*

CHAPTER SUMMARY

1. A psychometric perspective of interviewing relies upon standardized procedures, whereas a psychological assessment approach focuses on individual behaviors.

2. The diagnostic mental health interview goes far beyond simply arriving at a diagnosis.

3. Therapists should be competent in interviewing, diagnosing, and in documentation to meet the needs of the client, the profession, and third parties.

4. Third-party payers require a *DSM-IV-TR* Axis I diagnosis, and services must be medically necessary to be covered for payment.

5. The interviewer must be qualified in at least five areas, including (a) establishing and maintaining rapport, (b) knowledge of psychopathology and mental health diagnosis, (c) knowledge of current third-party requirements, (d) expertise in treatment planning, and (e) excellent communication skills in both verbal and written areas.

6. Standardized interview procedures help provide adequate commu-

nication between professionals and provide consistency in the information received from clients.

7. In the relatively little time allowed for a mental health interview, data must be collected from a wide range of domains in the client's life.

🦅 TEST YOURSELF 🦅

1. **Which of the following statements best depicts a statement representing the psychometric approach to mental health assessment?**
   (a) "My experiences suggest that the diagnosis is a depressive disorder."
   (b) "The client appears to be depressed."
   (c) "Test results suggest depression."
   (d) "The *DSM-IV-TR* suggests depression in this case."

2. **Which of the following is not an intended procedure of the initial client diagnostic interview?**
   (a) Providing psychotherapy
   (b) Attaining a diagnosis
   (c) Establishing rapport
   (d) Assessing suicide risk

3. **Medical necessity is best depicted in which of the following statements?**
   (a) "John needs counseling. He doesn't seem to be his old self anymore."
   (b) "Sally is physically ill. She should get a complete checkup."
   (c) "Without counseling Bill's mental health will continue to decline."
   (d) "Bill will be less anxious after ten psychotherapy sessions."

4. **Although counseling solely for personal growth may be _____, it is generally not considered to be _____.**
   (a) brief, helpful
   (b) good experience for beginning therapists, therapeutic
   (c) medically necessary, cost effective
   (d) helpful, medically necessary

5. **It is the client's job to demonstrate to a third party that services are medically necessary.** True or False?

6. **Crisis counseling is usually medically necessary.** True or False?

(continued)

7. **Describe how it is possible for a therapist to provide excellent counseling services but be consistently denied for providing mental health services after the initial interview.**

8. **Describe the relationship between medical necessity and functional impairments.**

Answers: 1. c; 2. a; 3. c; 4. d; 5. False; 6. True; 7. If a therapist does not clearly document the need for services, further services will not be authorized. 8. When a mental health disorder leads to functional impairments, services are considered medically necessary.

Two

THE INTAKE INTERVIEW PROCESS

BEFORE THE INTERVIEW BEGINS

Conducting a diagnostic mental health interview is not parallel to a mechanic's diagnosing what needs to be repaired in an automobile engine. It is not necessary to tactfully and empathically persuade the automobile to disclose information about why it is no longer functioning adequately. Similarly, the personality and personal belief systems of the mechanic have nothing to do with the repair. Unlike a therapy client, the engine can be hooked up to monitors and may even be taken apart for a visual inspection if necessary. An automobile does not malinger, become defensive, or dwell in denial. The engine is not able to be a part of its own repair or healing process. Nevertheless, both the mechanic and the therapist must be ethical in providing the appropriate level of services that most efficiently serves the recipient. That is, just as a broken spark plug does not warrant an engine overhaul, problems coping with in-laws do not warrant three years of psychotherapy.

A comprehensive mental health diagnosis, on the other hand, is significantly dependent upon the client's cooperation, the clinician's skills, and the therapeutic relationship. Clinicians must exercise careful awareness of how their backgrounds, experiences, and current emotional state can influence countertransference, type of treatment, length of treatment, and definition of the client's problem areas. Other factors such as payment issues and other agency requirements may also affect the course of treatment. Likewise, mental health diagnosis is no more accurate than the information the client is willing to disclose. Establishing good rapport can enhance the quality (and quantity) of information the client shares with the therapist.

Neither the clinician nor the client has unlimited time available for the interview. Most insurance companies pay for 1 or (at most) perhaps 2 hr for the diagnostic (also called *assessment* or *intake*) interview (coded 90801). Although it may be convenient to have additional time, the reality of being paid for about an hour requires that the interview be time-efficient. One should learn to conduct the procedures discussed in this text, except the written report, in this time period (1 to 2 hr).

A clinician well versed in psychopathology, the *DSM-IV-TR,* and interview techniques should be able to obtain adequate information within the time constraints. Students typically require about 3 hr to conduct a thorough interview, but with increasing experience and ongoing supervision, the learning curve decreases the interview time. Morrison (1993) estimates the following percentages of time for the various aspects of the mental health interview:

15%	Chief complaint and free speech
30%	Pursuit of specific diagnoses; asking about suicide, history of violence, and substance abuse
15%	Medical history, review of systems, family history
25%	Personal and social history; evaluation of character pathology
10%	Mental status evaluation
5%	Discussion of diagnosis and treatment with patient; planning next meeting

CAUTION

Due to time restraints, therapists must be particularly time efficient when conducting the diagnostic interview. In most cases, third-party payers will reimburse for either 1, 1.5, or (at most) 2 hr for the initial interview. Although this session may be therapeutic as a result of empathy and rapport development, its primary purpose is to gather data, not to conduct therapy. If an insurance company pays for only 1 hr for the diagnostic interview (code 90801), and the interview is not completed, the additional time must either be paid for by the client or conducted free of charge. An ethical therapist will not bill for individual therapy (code 90806) if the bulk of the interview is still collecting diagnostic information, rather than conducting therapy. Auditors routinely review charts to determine whether the billing code matches the content of the session.

NOTE TAKING DURING THE INTERVIEW

The initial interview has two primary goals that are common to all schools of thought: (a) establishing rapport, and (b) collecting and documenting information. If rapport is not established, the client might not return for services, or be emotionally prepared to disclose information. Written documentation is considered crucial because it is the only evidence of the client's condition. Documentation must meet the requirements as requested by the agency in which services will be rendered, by third-party payers, by the mental health profession, and by accrediting agencies. When notes are not taken during the session, important material will likely be missed. Some therapists are reticent to take notes in the client's presence for fear that rapport will be compromised. Morrison (1993) suggests that therapists point out to the client, before the session begins, that they will be taking notes and make sure that it is all right. Time is saved and there is less distraction when key words and phrases are noted rather than written down in complete sentences for every notation. Some therapists prefer to audiotape or videotape, although client permission must always be obtained first. Keep in mind that this practice is time-consuming because the therapist must listen to the material from the interview a second time in order to gather information for the report.

The clinician can build rapport and gather accurate information by learning how to take notes in such a way that the client feels positive about the experience. This is easily accomplished when the therapist's nonverbal behaviors suggest that it is important to write down what the client is saying. The theme of "you and what you say are important" goes a long way in eliminating any client objections to note taking.

A therapist who makes eye contact with, expresses interest in, and demonstrates positive regard for a client can incorporate note taking as another means of showing interest in the client. If eye contact and attention to the client are sacrificed due to excessive note taking, rapport will be decreased. Interview forms that contain several checklists of behaviors and symptoms significantly reduce the amount of material that needs to be written down. Clients' feelings must be respected when sensitive information is disclosed. Some information can be written in a nondescript manner, whereas other information, such as validating a diagnosis, symptoms, stressors, and impairments, should be detailed.

Putting It Into Practice

Let the Past Be the Past

A client appeared for an evaluation for counseling due to depression. She disclosed a long history of alcohol and cocaine dependence, plus several hospitalizations for suicidal behaviors. Because her chemical usage was recent, it was important to include a CD (chemical dependency) evaluation, a thorough suicide-risk assessment, and a differential diagnosis of her depression.

Toward the beginning of the interview her employment history was requested. Her demeanor quickly changed from talkative to reserved, embarrassed, and upset by a seemingly neutral question. She went on to say that no matter where she goes, people find out about her involvement in prostitution several years ago, adding that she has lost a number of jobs after her criminal record was obtained. In her mind, the interview was now another document declaring her as a prostitute. She was relieved and thankful when the interviewer told her that this information would not be included in the notes or the report. Her level of trust for the therapist and depth of self-disclosure increased considerably at that time.

In this case, a notation such as "history of several poor decisions" and a few examples, excluding prostitution, were sufficient to get the point across and not degrade the integrity of the client. Her record included a number of impulsive and self-destructive behaviors that coincided with her reason for requesting services. Prostitution was no longer a problem behavior; only other people's perceptions of her due to her past were damaged. Simply knowing that she was sensitive to her past behaviors was clinically significant information. The therapist's acceptance of her as a fellow human being in the interview session was, in itself, therapeutic.

Teaching Point: *The most important client information to include in the notes and report is material documenting the presenting problem, which is legally required to be in the records. The therapist-client relationship either can be enhanced or destroyed when the interviewer writes down specific information that deflates the client or exacerbates concerns that are irrelevant to the presenting problem.*

ETHICAL CONSIDERATIONS

Every national and state association of the mental health professions has a code of ethics, or subscribes to a recognized code. Ethical codes typically cover realms such as confidentiality, informed consent, therapist-client relationships, competencies, standards of care, and documentation. The following areas must be considered at all times in the initial interview.

CONFIDENTIALITY

The confidentiality of information shared between a therapist and client is recognized by the United States Supreme Court (*Jaffee v. Redmond,* 1996). Although various states and jurisdictions may interpret the law from different points of view, under normal circumstances others are not privy to this information. However, there are several circumstances and gray areas in which confidentiality is not always upheld. Specific policies and procedures must be developed for dissemination of information for each of the following areas, as presented by Wiger (1999). These areas either are covered by law or can be problematic if not communicated to the client in advance.

1. Duty to warn and protect
2. Abuse of children and vulnerable adults
3. Prenatal exposure to controlled substances
4. Death of the client
5. Professional misconduct
6. Court orders/IRS/other government mandates
7. Guardianship of minor or other person
8. Collection agency involvement
9. Third-party payer involvement
10. Medical emergency
11. Case consultation
12. Research

INFORMED CONSENT

Clients have a right to be part of the decision-making process. Accreditation agencies require that clients take an active part in the formulation of the treatment plan and discharge goals. Therapists should make information about their credentials, qualifications, theoretical stance, and specialty areas readily available to clients. Other information such as how to contact the therapist, limits of confidentiality, billing procedures, cancellation fees, length of sessions, fees, how emergencies are taken care of, and estimated duration of treatment are typically provided to clients.

Both the benefits and risks of entering treatment should be explained to each client. In most clinical settings, it is common to display the credentials and

Putting It Into Practice

Example of Client Notice of Confidentiality Statement

Client Notice of Confidentiality: The confidentiality of patient records maintained by the center is protected by federal or state law and regulations. Generally, the center may not reveal to a person outside the center that a patient attends the program or disclose any information identifying a patient as an alcohol or drug abuser unless: (a) the patient consents in writing, (b) the disclosure is allowed by a court, government, or IRS order, or (c) the disclosure is made to medical personnel in a medical emergency.

Violation of federal or state law and regulations by a treatment facility or provider is a crime. Suspected violations may be reported to appropriate authorities. Federal or state law and regulations do not protect any information about a crime committed by a patient either at the center, against any person who works for the program, or about any threat to commit such a crime. Federal law and regulations do not protect any information about suspected child (or vulnerable adult) abuse or neglect, or adult abuse from being reported under federal or state law to appropriate state or local authorities. Health care professionals are required to report admitted prenatal exposure to controlled substances that are potentially harmful. It is the center's duty to warn any potential victim when a significant threat of harm has been made. In the event of a client's death, the spouse or parents of a deceased client have a right to access their child's or spouse's records. Professional misconduct by a health care professional must be reported by other health care professionals, in which related client records may be released to substantiate disciplinary concerns. Parents or legal guardians of nonemancipated minor clients have the right to access the client's records.

Clinical records may be available to health providers in cases of medical emergencies. Records are available to the client's third-party payers, managed care, case reviewers, and for clinical consultation or supervision. When fees are not paid in a timely manner, a collection agency will be given appropriate billing and financial information about a client, not clinical information. Client data of clinical outcomes or research may be used for program evaluation purposes, but individual results will not be disclosed to outside sources. My signature below indicates that I understand, and consent to, the above Client Notice of Confidentiality and have been given a copy of my rights regarding confidentiality. I permit a copy of this authorization to be used in the place of the original.

X_____   _____

Client's (or Guardian's) signature   Date

Teaching Point: *Confidentiality of records is never simply an assumption. The clinician must clearly provide the legal requirements of confidentiality to the client and obtain a signature showing that the client has been informed of these rights.*

competencies of each therapist, as well as provide clients with various hand-outs such as typical clinical procedures, patient's bill of rights, and grievance procedures. Wagner, Davis, and Handelsman (1998) found that when consent forms are well written and personable, it enhances the client's impression of the therapist. Clients should be given an adequate amount of information to determine reasonably whether they desire to receive the treatment suggested.

Although there may be situations in which the client may not have the mental autonomy to make informed choices (Faden & Beauchamp, 1986), all clients should be treated as if they are capable until there is contrary evidence (Haas & Malouf, 1995). The explanation delivered to the client must be given in terms that can be understood.

THERAPIST-CLIENT RELATIONSHIPS

To achieve the most effective, unbiased treatment for their clients, therapists behave in a professional manner. An effective therapist is able to draw the line

Putting It Into Practice

Dual Relationships: A Case of Good Intent, but a Bad Idea

A therapist was asked by a close relative to conduct a psychological assessment as part of a custody evaluation. The therapist asked his supervisor for permission to conduct the evaluation for a relative and was clearly told not to proceed due to the dual relationship. About 2 years later, the supervisor read in a state professional publication that ethical charges were filed against the therapist by the ethics board for conducting an evaluation for a relative. The therapist's defense was that he was aware of inappropriate behaviors by his relative's spouse; therefore he believed that positive results in the evaluation for his relative could prevent future child abuse by the client's ex-spouse. He stated that his motive was to protect the child involved in the custody battle. The ethics noted this as an ethics violation with specific concerns that the therapist did not identify the client as a relative and misrepresented results as if the client was previously unknown to the therapist.

Teaching Point: *Never conduct an assessment or treatment service that involves a dual relationship in which objectivity is compromised. Good intentions are no excuse for violating ethical principles. The reward for being a nice person could be license restriction, suspension, or revocation.*

between emotionally connecting with the client and having a personal relationship with the client. Dual relationships such as conducting business with the client for exchange of services, socializing with a client, or having any form of a sexual relationship with a client may lead to loss or suspension of licensure and significant legal, ethical, and malpractice issues.

Dual relationships are not a black and white issue. Not all dual relations may be risky or inappropriate. The degree and potential problems of the relationship should first be considered. For example, an evaluation should not be conducted for a friend, relative, or business associate. However, a casual acquaintance poses less of a threat. When a possible dual-relationship issue presents itself, the therapist should seek and document consultation obtained. In addition the therapist should explain how the decision about whether to provide services or make a referral is reached.

COMPETENCIES

Therapists must work within their professional competencies, not only in conducting therapy, but also in performing assessments. Larger clinics that are nationally accredited or hold certain managed-care contracts routinely require each therapist in the practice to demonstrate clinical competency in all areas of service they perform. In a typical clinical setting, therapists are granted clinical privileges in specific areas when they demonstrate that they have sufficient education, supervision, experience, and proficiency to provide clinical services for a target population. Mental health clinics should make available to clients the competencies of each therapist and let them know whether a case is being supervised. Therapists in solo practice settings should take extra precautions to receive consultation and supervision.

Psychological testing is often employed in the initial assessment. A therapist is not automatically qualified to use or interpret psychological tests. Without adequate training and supervision in each test a therapist uses, there is an increased chance of misinterpretation or misunderstanding of test scores. Computerized test results are never intended to be used as the sole means of reaching a diagnosis. Typically, results are based on statistical fit rather than incorporating client variables. Misuse of computerized psychological test interpretations may lead to ethical problems (Matarazzo, 1986). Groth-Marnat

Putting It Into Practice

Clinical Interview Information Outweighs Testing

A newly licensed therapist conducted a psychological evaluation. His credentials required supervision by a licensed doctoral level clinician. The therapist's first supervisory session consisted of signing off on a psychological evaluation. His report summarized the results of four psychological tests and concluded with a diagnosis based on test results. The report did not validate client behaviors, impairments, or DSM-IV-TR symptoms, and only test results were used to make the diagnosis. The resulting supervision consisted of training the therapist how interview information is of primary importance to giving the diagnosis and must be clearly documented; testing simply confirms, clarifies, or provides additional information.

Teaching Point: *Although psychological testing may be helpful in confirming diagnostic conclusions or impressions, it is not meant to be the primary evidence in making a diagnosis. Diagnoses are based on individual behaviors and symptoms. Tests are based on statistical averages of the behaviors of large groups of people. They do not account for individual circumstances, environment, history, background, culture, or other idiosyncratic differences.*

(1990) states that a computerized test interpretation alone will be less accurate than when individual behaviors are considered.

INFORMATION GATHERING IN THE INTERVIEW

No matter how directive versus nondirective, or structured versus nonstructured, an interview may be, the same basic information must be obtained. The specific style or theoretical orientation affecting the information gathering is not as important as what information is collected. A clinical diagnosis is best obtained by integrating several types of clinical information that have been collected through multiple means. The fewer sources of information available, the fewer perspectives are available in understanding the client. Most clinicians attempt to gather information from a wide range of sources. Although all potential information is not available for every interview, the wider the perspective, the clearer the picture is of the client's needs. The six most common sources of client data include (a) the clinical interview, (b) clinical observations, (c) records from other sources, (d) testing, (e) biographical information,

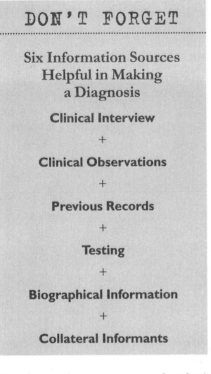

and (f) collateral informants. This text focuses on providing training for items a and b, and provides examples of integrating the information in items c–f.

Although multiple sources of information provide the widest range of background material, this can lead to a greater possibility of receiving information that conflicts with other data. Information received from other sources such as family members can be quite helpful in assessing malingering, exaggeration, withholding information, poor insight, denial, resistance, and other hindrances to gathering valid client information. Morrison (1995) points out that permission to talk to others or obtain information from other sources must be obtained from the client before engaging in this form of data collection. In such cases, the clinician cannot ignore information that does not fit in with his or her hypotheses. Inconsistencies in clinical information are quite common and must be evaluated ethically and competently. Although it may seem convenient to leave out conflicting information for the sake of simplicity, it may be that the information left out is the most crucial.

Data collection is a continuous process throughout the course of treatment. Although third-party payers have different billing codes for the diagnostic interview (code 90801) and individual therapy (code 90806), diagnostic information is received and revised on an ongoing basis throughout treatment. Billing codes are based on the intent and content of the session. Generally only one diagnostic session is allowed in billing. The remainder of the sessions are billed for actual therapy. If, during therapy, new diagnostic information is discovered, the diagnosis must be revised. It is acceptable to change a client's diagnosis when new information warrants the revision. Any change in diagnosis must be documented in the client's file and reported to the third-party payer in subsequent billings.

SHARING INTERVIEW RESULTS

Clients have the right to know the results of the clinical interview. However, there are ethical principles to consider. It is common practice to weigh the benefits and risks of sharing all of the clinical results with the client. Clients are entitled to the results of the interview unless it may prove harmful.

There may be cases in which all information is shared with the client, except information that might be harmful or countertherapeutic. Such information might best be presented in a manner that is inoffensive. For example, it might be more tactful to say to a client, "You tend to approach the world differently than most people," rather than, "You might have schizophrenia." Until sufficient information is gathered, it is best to provide general rather than specific hypotheses in potentially volatile situations. Results and explanations must be presented to the client at a language level that the client can understand.

PREVIOUS DIAGNOSES: HELP OR HINDRANCE IN FORMULATING THE CURRENT DIAGNOSIS?

Previous diagnoses are generally very helpful but occasionally can be a hindrance to pinpointing the current diagnosis. Clinicians may be tempted to endorse a previous diagnosis because supplying a different diagnosis may imply disagreeing with the previous therapist or rocking the boat. A change in a clinical diagnosis also may contraindicate the client's current medication regime. Further, the therapist may doubt his or her judgment when planning to change a client's diagnosis. When changing a diagnosis, the clinician must take special precautions to demonstrate clearly that the symptoms that validated the previous diagnosis are no longer prevalent. All diagnoses must be made based on the client's current endorsement of symptoms, not simply because a client was previously diagnosed with a particular disorder. (Rapid Reference 2.1 lists a number of reasons that one client may receive differing diagnoses from different therapists.)

⎯Rapid Reference 2.1

Possible Reasons That the Same Client Could Receive Different Diagnoses From Different Clinicians Over Time

1. Multiple disorders, but not all initially detected
2. Incorrect, incomplete, or conflicting previous or current information obtained (which may be the result of any of a number of reasons, such as poor rapport or discomfort)
3. Personality disorders exacerbated by Axis I-type symptoms
4. Discrepant cyclical behaviors that are observed at different points in the cycle by different clinicians or observers
5. Effects of using (or abstaining from) alcohol or drugs
6. Medications: effects, level of compliance, changes, interactions, side effects
7. Changes in levels and types of environmental stressors lead to different reactions
8. Organic or physical factors affecting psychological condition
9. Therapist's expertise, experiences, and theoretical stance
10. Level of client insight, exaggeration, or denial
11. Malingering or secondary gain
12. Actual change in the diagnosis

Dealing With Previous Diagnoses

Knowing clients' previous diagnoses can be very helpful in tracking the course of their disorders. Behavioral and emotional concerns over the years often provide beneficial therapeutic information about how a client reacts to treatment, conflicts, and stress. However, it is easy to be swayed by a client's previous mental health diagnosis. Therapists' preconceived notions about the client due to the previous diagnosis may overshadow, or at least influence, the interview. Imagine interviewing three clients with the same background information for mental health services. The only differences in their files are different diagnoses of (a) Adjustment Disorder, (b) Pedophilia, and (c) Paranoid Schizophrenia. Therapists would most likely have different preconceptions, reactions, and expectations of these three clients simply because the previous diagnosis is different.

Because mental health treatment can lead to successful results, a previous diagnosis may no longer be valid or applicable after successful treatment. It is not uncommon for clients who have seen several therapists and experienced an array of symptoms to have been diagnosed with different disorders over time. Additionally, diagnoses may change within a relatively short period of time depending on the severity of the stressors and the client's coping skills. Previous diagnoses should serve as guidelines of previous behaviors but should not be assumed as a current diagnosis. Although some diagnoses tend to be chronic (e.g., Mental Retardation, Schizophrenia, Bipolar Disorder), others can be acute (e.g., Adjustment Disorder; Major Depression, Single Episode).

A structured interview format is one of the best defenses against being swayed by a previous diagnosis. To best help a client and future readers of a psychological report, after a diagnosis is made, clearly explain the diagnosis by verifying the *DSM-IV-TR* symptoms and providing examples of how the client is being impaired due to the effects of the disorder.

Commonly, a clinician reports a previous diagnosis that is currently not prevalent by stating the diagnosis and adding *Prior History* (e.g., ADHD, Prior History). This method of documentation is most often used to provide historical information about the client. It may indicate that the diagnosis has evolved from one to another.

When the clinician is reasonably assured that the diagnosis existed in the past, as in previously treating the client or previous records, a qualifier of *In (full or partial) Remission* (e.g., Major Depressive Disorder, In Full Remission) may be used. It implies a stronger level of confidence in the diagnosis that was made the past than does Prior History. The term *remission* means that the symptoms existed in the past but now are in the process of alleviating (In Partial Remission) or are no longer prevalent (In Full Remission). Such a designation sometimes suggests that currently the client may be functioning adequately, but that certain conditions such as ending therapy, increased stress, or returning to an adverse environment may trigger previous mental health symptoms. The more time that passes in which the symptoms are in remission, the less reason there is for even mentioning the diagnosis. For example, if a client was previously diagnosed with Posttraumatic Stress Disorder (PTSD), then received significant treatment in which symptoms were alleviated several months later, it is common to provide a diagnosis of PTSD, In Full Remission, at that time. If the client has continued not to experience symptoms several

Putting It Into Practice

Misdiagnosing a Client Based on Previous Diagnoses

A client, age 48, who has lived in various group homes for the past 30 years, was referred for a periodic psychological evaluation. A review of records indicated consistent previous diagnoses of Mild Mental Retardation and Schizophrenia. Psychological testing and a review of adaptive functioning confirmed Mild Mental Retardation, but the diagnosis of Schizophrenia has not been validated in his records since originally diagnosed approximately 30 years ago.

A review of his current behaviors and treatment indicated no meds for Schizophrenia or any behaviors suggesting delusions, hallucinations, paranoia, mental confusion, or any symptoms suggestive of a thought disorder. Further interviews with the client, his caregivers, and family revealed that no one remembered why he had been diagnosed with Schizophrenia. Nevertheless, the diagnosis remained in his medical records as if it were still applicable. Finally, one family member recalled that at age 18, he objected to being institutionalized for Mental Retardation, and became quite upset and irrational. It turned out that he had not taken his insulin for an unknown period of time. Medical and psychological issues quickly developed which led to an admitting diagnosis of Schizophrenia due to psychotic symptoms. The diagnosis prevailed in subsequent evaluations. In this case, what should have been diagnosed as an adjustment disorder or possibly organic factors, causing behavioral and mental health symptoms due to lack of insulin, led to a diagnosis of Schizophrenia based on incorrect or incomplete information. Although no such behaviors followed him once he stabilized on his insulin and enjoyed the freedoms allotted him in a supportive group home and employment enclave, the diagnosis of Schizophrenia prevailed.

Over the next 30 years, his various residential providers received additional funding due to his dual diagnosis. In fact, when the diagnosis was not supported in his most recent evaluation, his providers were disgruntled to say the least. Their most common objection was "He's always had that diagnosis . . . it just doesn't go away after 30 years."

Teaching Point: *When a client is interviewed, it should not be assumed that previous diagnoses are accurate. All previous diagnoses should be ruled in or ruled out. Current evidence must be demonstrated to continue a previous diagnosis. Reconfirming an incorrect previous diagnosis to avoid rocking the boat can be quite harmful to the client.*

years later, it may no longer be productive to continue assigning the diagnosis. As time progresses, the distinction between "no diagnosis" and "diagnosis in remission" becomes blurred.

Effective mental health treatment is intended to alleviate areas of impairment, distress, or both. A primary goal of mental health professionals is to help people return to premorbid or adequate functioning. Continuing to list a diagnosis in clients' files that can no longer be validated suggests a belief that recovery has not or cannot take place. Similarly, in the medical field, if someone breaks an arm or leg, the diagnosis is dropped after healing has taken place. A physical health record might mention the previous injury, but when healing takes place, the diagnosis does not remain active. Although it is not uncommon for someone to declare after several years of abstinence, "I am a recovering alcoholic," it would be unusual to claim to be still recovering from depression if after a similar time span that person has been restored to adequate adaptive functioning and no longer experiences significant symptoms of depression. It is possible, however, that he or she may be more prone to depression than someone without the previous diagnosis.

Many clients experience an alleviation of symptoms with medications. However, when they discontinue medications, symptoms return. Thus, their

CAUTION

Common Errors Related to Mental Health Diagnoses

1. Clients with the same diagnosis do not necessarily function at similar levels. Therefore, much more than the diagnosis should be documented.

2. A diagnosis, in itself, does not imply the level or type of care needed. Therefore, specific client needs must be documented.

3. If medical necessity is not documented the client may be denied services by a third-party payer. Therefore, specific problems in functional impairments must be documented.

4. Although counseling may be helpful, it does not imply medical necessity. Therefore, it is important to explain to the client that services are not necessarily covered by a third party.

5. Spending too much time counseling in the initial session can lead to lack of diagnostic information received, possibly depriving the client of future services. Therefore, it is important to stay on target.

diagnosis can be followed by the term *med controlled* (e.g., ADHD, med controlled).

A *provisional* diagnosis suggests that a diagnosis is prevalent but that more information is needed to fully validate it. (This is similar to a Rule-Out diagnosis.) Information such as another opinion, testing, a review of additional records, observations, or information from collaterals is needed to amend a provisional diagnosis to a full diagnosis. (See Rapid Reference 2.2.)

≡ *Rapid Reference 2.2*

Common Specifiers to Diagnoses

1. **In Full Remission** (e.g., Panic Disorder with Agoraphobia, In Full Remission): The diagnosis was once given, but symptoms and impairments have not been prevalent for a specified amount of time.

2. **In Partial Remission** (e.g., Panic Disorder with Agoraphobia, In Partial Remission): The diagnostic criteria were previously met, but some symptoms have alleviated; thus, full criteria are not currently met. It may also mean insufficient time has passed with alleviation of symptoms.

3. **Provisional** (e.g., Panic Disorder with Agoraphobia, Provisional): The clinician is reasonably confident that the diagnosis is present, but more validation of symptoms is needed for a full confirmation of the diagnosis. There is a higher level of confidence than in a Rule-Out diagnosis. The diagnosis is generally accepted as prevalent.

4. **Rule Out (R/O)** (e.g., R/O Panic Disorder with Agoraphobia): The diagnosis is possible or probable, but either sufficient questions have not yet been asked or a moderate amount of information is needed in the future to validate the diagnosis. Without further validation, such as testing, a second opinion, or further review of records, the diagnosis is generally not accepted as prevalent.

5. **Prior History** (e.g., Panic Disorder with Agoraphobia, Prior History): Previous records indicate assignment of the diagnoses. It suggests that criteria for the diagnosis does not still exist.

6. **Med Controlled** (e.g., Panic Disorder with Agoraphobia, med controlled): Due to the client's compliance with medications, symptoms and impairments are in remission. It is likely that without medications, symptoms would recur.

Note: The above specifiers are commonly used in clinical practice. Other specifiers for specific diagnoses are included in the *DSM-IV-TR*. The *DSM-IV-TR* also includes several other common means of describing diagnostic uncertainty and means to exclude other diagnoses.

THE INTERVIEW AND THE *DSM-IV-TR*

The diagnostic interview, in most cases, is based on the *DSM-IV-TR,* which provides specific guidelines for determining mental health diagnoses. Methods of confirming mental health diagnoses have evolved over the years, from being based primarily on clinical judgment to requiring endorsement of specific symptoms and impairments that identify differential diagnoses combined with clinical judgment. The scientific method of testing the evidence with an objective standard departs significantly from traditional means of making a diagnosis. Each edition of the *DSM* is updated based on empirical research designed to more aptly differentiate between the hundreds of mental health disorders.

Until recently, mental health disorders were primarily defined by specific symptoms experienced by the client. That is, if the client or significant observers endorsed certain symptoms, a diagnosis was given. It did not take long to realize that symptoms are necessary but not sufficient to warrant a diagnosis. Both symptoms and impairments or distress are necessary.

Proponents of the medical model introduced the term *medical necessity,* which deemed that mental health services are considered medically necessary if the client is not likely to return to an adequate level of functioning in a timely manner without mental health intervention. A related term, *functional impairments,* identifies various aspects of the client's life that can be impaired due to a mental health condition for which services are medically necessary. Examples of functional impairments include those that are social, occupational, academic, legal, and so on. The threshold for making a diagnosis is whether the client is suffering from functional impairments as the result of a mental health condition, not simply endorsing the existence or nonexistence of symptoms. Therefore, to validate a mental health diagnosis, the clinician must first match the client's symptomology with the *DSM-IV-TR* criteria and provide evidence of functional impairments due to the mental disorder.

THE *DSM-IV-TR* MULTIAXIAL CLASSIFICATION SYSTEM

The *DSM-IV-TR* endorses a five-axis diagnostic system. Each axis provides important diagnostic, physical, environmental, and functional information about the client. This biopsychochosocial information helps individualize the client's level of functioning in several domains of the client's life. In the past, clinicians tended to spotlight clinical disorders; however, increased attention has focused on the other four axes. Although not all clinicians use the five-axis system, it is the most common standard.

Axis I	Clinical Disorders
	Other Conditions That May Be a Focus of Clinical Attention
Axis II	Personality Disorders
	Mental Retardation
Axis III	General Medical Condition
Axis IV	Psychosocial and Environmental Problems
Axis V	Global Assessment of Functioning Scale

Axis I: Clinical Disorders

Mental health diagnoses, excluding mental retardation and personality disorders, are included on Axis I. Almost all third-party payers require an Axis I diagnosis as the minimum prerequisite for payment of services. Each diagnosis has a specific name and number assigned to it. It is not uncommon for a client to have more than one Axis I diagnosis. The primary (or principal) diagnosis should be listed first when more than one diagnosis is given.

Clinicians should become familiar with the names and classification numbers of the major diagnoses. Although there are several hundred *DSM-IV-TR* diagnoses and variations of diagnoses, a given clinician never encounters many of them (due to clinical specialties). However, mental health clinicians typically memorize the classification numbers of the most common diagnoses.

Axis I disorders also have V-Code Diagnoses in which the focus of treatment is geared more toward problems with relationships. V-Code diagnoses are rarely covered by third-party payers.

Axis II: Personality Disorders and Mental Retardation

Although personality disorders and Mental Retardation in themselves are not typically covered for services by third-party payers, they represent significant concerns about the client's adaptive functioning. Mental retardation is diagnosed prior to age 18, whereby the client's IQ and adaptive functioning are two or more standard deviations below the mean. Personality disorders indicate significant maladaptive personality patterns. They are often exacerbated when the client is under stress and are more pervasive than Axis I disorders. In addition, maladaptive defense mechanisms are placed on Axis II. When both an Axis I and an Axis II diagnosis are given, and Axis II is primary, it should be denoted Primary Diagnosis.

Axis III: Physical Conditions and Disorders

Axis III records the client's current medical condition in areas that are potentially relevant to (whether by causing, maintaining, or exacerbating) a mental health disorder. Only those physical conditions that relate to current mental health problems are noted. When there is a clear causal connection, in which the mental disorder is due to a general medical condition, it is coded as such on Axis I (e.g., Mood Disorder, Due to Hypthyroidism; the hypothyroidism is noted on Axis III).

Axis IV: Psychosocial and Environmental Problems

Axis IV describes current stressors in the client's life. All stressors, whether positive or negative, that affect the client's condition should be listed. Life changes, such as marriage, job changes, residential moves, and so on, may be positive events, but the changes they incur may lead to mental difficulties adjusting.

It is common to incorporate the stressors into the client's treatment planning and after-care planning. Treatment may focus on coping with, accepting, eliminating, or alleviating stressors. The *DSM-IV-TR* groups problem areas into the following areas: (a) primary social supports, (b) social environment, (c) education, (d) occupation, (e) housing, (f) economic status, (g) access to health care, (h) legal issues, and (i) other.

Axis V: Global Assessment of Functioning

The Global Assessment of Functioning Scale (GAF) indicates the client's overall level of functioning, considering the psychological, social, and occupational variables. Physical or environmental limitations are not to be considered. The GAF Scale is a 1–100 rating scale, in which the *DSM-IV-TR* categorizes a hierarchy of mental health dysfunction. Ten labels (e.g., 100, 90, 80, etc.)

DON'T FORGET

Things to Remember When Making a Diagnosis

1. The *DSM-IV-TR* requires that the client must be experiencing symptoms and impairments concordant with the diagnosis; however, *DSM-IV-TR* symptoms are necessary but not sufficient to warrant a diagnosis.
2. Evidence of functional impairment or distress is also necessary to make a diagnosis. Impairments are the results of mental health symptoms that prevent adequate functioning in daily activities.
3. Medical necessity is determined when the client's functional impairments require mental health services to assist the client in returning to adequate functioning in a reasonable amount of time.
4. A five-axis classification describes five separate domains in the client's life, providing individualized biopsychosocial information.

with examples are given with descriptive guidelines to provide a description of current global functioning. Numbers between tens (e.g., 67) are based on the clinician's estimate of the degree between the descriptors given in the *DSM-TR*. The GAF scale is used in treatment planning and outcomes measurement (i.e., measuring treatment effects).

CHAPTER SUMMARY

1. Mental health diagnosis has evolved from clinical opinion to a scientific method in which evidence to confirm a diagnosis must be measurable and observable.
2. Today's third-party payers of mental health services require that services be medically necessary to receive reimbursement.
3. Clinicians must be well versed in areas of confidentiality.
4. There are several styles of interviewing. Each has its strengths and weaknesses.
5. It is not uncommon for a client to receive conflicting diagnoses over time and concurrently.
6. The *DSM-IV-TR* is the reference book by which clinical diagnoses are defined. Therapists should be familiar with the symptoms of the major diagnoses and the five-axis diagnostic classification system.

🖋 TEST YOURSELF 🖋

1. **In which of the following situations is a therapist not required to break confidentiality?**
    (a) The client is clearly suicidal.
    (b) A pregnant client is abusing cocaine.
    (c) The client committed a crime 10 years ago and was not caught.
    (d) The client is abusing a mentally retarded adult.

2. **Informed consent is best represented in which of the following statements?**
    (a) "Your diagnosis suggests that you will get better in about 10 sessions."
    (b) "The benefits and risks of your counseling are as follows . . ."
    (c) "The client agrees to come to counseling twice per week."
    (d) "I consent to allow my records to go to my physician."

3. **Rule-out diagnosis is best represented in which of the following?**
    (a) "The client appears to have Panic Disorder, but more information is needed."
    (b) "All criteria for Panic Disorder have been met."
    (c) "The symptoms are similar to an amnestic disorder, but no impairments are evident."
    (d) "The client hasn't used marijuana in over two years."

4. **Which diagnostic specifier is best depicted in the following? "The client has not experienced symptoms of the diagnosis since childhood."**
    (a) Mild
    (b) In Full Remission
    (c) Prior History
    (d) In Partial Remission

5. **A client has a current diagnosis of Major Depressive Disorder from another therapist at a different clinic. Which of the following procedures should be followed by the new intake therapist?**
    (a) Accept the previous diagnosis and begin counseling immediately to save time.
    (b) Begin counseling immediately, but revise it if conflicting information arises.
    (c) Conduct a complete diagnostic interview for all new clients before counseling begins.
    (d) Set up an appointment with the previous therapist to discuss the diagnosis.

(continued)

6. **A psychometric perspective of assessment relies primarily on clinical judgment to arrive at a diagnosis.** True or False?

7. **The presenting problem is the client's description of the problem.** True or False?

8. **Because the *DSM-IV-TR* is a standardized means of communicating diagnostic information, there is little disagreement over client diagnoses.** True or False?

9. **A therapist should never conduct an interview or counsel someone he or she knows in any capacity.** True or False?

10. **It may be in the best interest of some clients not to be informed of all assessment results.** True or False?

11. **Describe procedures you would conduct in the initial interview if the client has a history of a variety of mental health diagnoses.**

12. **Describe both the benefits and drawbacks of taking notes during the interview.**

Answers: 1. c; 2. b; 3. a; 4. c; 5. c; 6. False; 7. True; 8. False; 9. False; 10. True; 11. Clearly rule in or rule out current symptoms of each diagnosis, also including personality disorders. Evaluate situational factors that may change behaviors over time. 12. Benefits: Recording observations as they happen, client quotes, time savings. Drawbacks: Possibly distracting the client or being perceived as inattentive to the client.

Three

FACTORS AFFECTING THE QUALITY OF INFORMATION RECEIVED

The quality of information gathered in the clinical interview is highly dependent upon the interaction of client and therapist variables. While some clients and therapists develop instant rapport, others find difficulty relating in any capacity. The therapist's theoretical background, beliefs, prejudices, and interview style clearly affect the evaluation process, and there are several possible reasons why clients might distort or withhold information. The process of obtaining information from clients is a combination of art and skill.

THERAPIST'S SELF-AWARENESS

The emotion-laden information and topic areas presented from clients can lead to affective reactions from the therapist. Therefore, therapists must be aware of how their beliefs, emotions, and perceptions are affected by client behaviors. It is possible for clients to trigger emotions or behaviors in the therapist that interfere with the counseling process. Self-understanding, or self-awareness, is a crucial element in avoiding factors that could alter a therapist's understanding of the client.

R. Sommers-Flannagan and J. Sommers-Flannagan (1999) distinguish four types of self-awareness in conducting clinical interviews.

1. *Physical self-awareness* is being aware of one's physical attributes such as gender, physical characteristics, voice and body language. Those higher in physical self-awareness are in touch with how their physical self affects others.
2. *Psychosocial self-awareness* is the perception of how oneself relates to others and how one's psychological, social, and emotional needs in-

fluence one's interpersonal needs. Clinicians who are highly aware of psychosocial needs monitor how their interpersonal needs affect the quality of the interview.

3. *Developmental self-awareness* involves being conscious of how one's developmental history (e.g., previous triumphs, problem areas) may affect the therapist's perception of information received by the client. Therapists high in developmental self-awareness carefully monitor how their means of relating to people affects their reaction to clients during the interview.

4. *Cultural self-awareness* is being cognizant that one's own culture may have different norms, expectations, and mores than others. Therapists increase their cultural awareness through reading, exposure to other cultures, self-examination, or other means to uncover lack of information or blind spots.

Although it is not necessary for therapists to have personally suffered through a client's mental illness or to have lived amongst the client's culture to provide therapeutic services, it is important for the therapist to be cognizant of his or her own personal issues, strengths, weaknesses, prejudices, and belief patterns. It is not unusual for a therapist to exhibit a defensive pattern in reaction to a client's behavior, but it is not helpful to act upon such feelings or thoughts. Therapists should be in touch with the here and now aspect of their own feelings. The therapist's own emotional baggage will never assist in the therapeutic process. If the therapist experiences reactions that get in the way of providing effective therapy, it is best to refer the client out and get some professional help for addressing these issues to decrease the likelihood that they will impact future clients. It is also helpful to discuss concerns with colleagues and get feedback as to the degree to which the therapist's issues affect therapy.

The school of thought or theoretical stances emphasized in the therapist's training significantly affects the level of self-awareness emphasized in therapy. Training that emphasizes insight is perhaps the most stringent in providing early and continued insight into the therapist's feelings, beliefs, and role in the process of therapy. Cognitive therapists focus on awareness of thought patterns that may distort the therapist's view of the world. Behaviorists focus on punishments and rewards that may influence behavior. Regardless of their theoretical background, all therapists must take precautions that nothing about them adversely impacts the client's progress. When the therapist is not aware of how his or her personal traits, beliefs, ongoing emotional concerns, current mood, and life situations can affect the quality and direction of therapy, clients may receive treatment from a distorted point of view and the effectiveness of therapy is significantly compromised.

Traditionally, mental health training has included a therapeutic component in which graduate students must be in mental health treatment at some point in their training, or are required to be in self-growth groups. Some graduate programs incorporate this experience in selected coursework, such as an experiential group therapy course, in which being an active group member and leader is incorporated into the course. Some programs have discontinued experiential therapy courses due to a fear of a dual relationship with the instructor. Cavanaugh (1990) notes that therapists are models of behavior, and if they do not demonstrate psychological health, they become part of the problem rather than part of the solution. You can only lead someone as far as you have traveled yourself, and thus, some writers believe becoming fully functioning

DON'T FORGET

Common Areas in Which a Therapist's Attributes Adversely Affect Both Assessment and Therapy.

1. The defensive therapist has problems listening to feedback from the client.
2. A rigid therapist does not allow the client to be different than the therapist.
3. A therapist's mental health issues are often diagnosed in the client.
4. Therapists might impose their level of morality upon clients.
5. A therapist's family background and current family concerns may influence relationship counseling.
6. The therapist's view of mental illness may affect progress in therapy.
7. A therapist's mood at the time of the session may significantly affect treatment.
8. A therapist's view of other cultures and ethnic groups may affect expectations in treatment.
9. A therapist, currently under significant stress (e.g., financial, marital, occupational), may not provide positive support, may not be attentive to what the client is saying, or may appear stressed during the therapy.

should be an objective for therapists as well as clients (Carkhuff & Berenson, 1977).

TRANSFERENCE AND COUNTERTRANSFERENCE

The interpretation and quality of information received during the interview are influenced by the relationship between the therapist and client. Statements that are not meant to have any overtones or hidden meanings may be interpreted otherwise based on this perceived relationship. Overly positive or negative feelings and beliefs about the client or therapist unduly influence the evaluation. For example, a patient who is viewed as difficult by one therapist may establish excellent rapport with another. In this situation, Steiger and Hirsch (1965) warn not to refer to a patient as a "difficult patient," but rather to examine the doctor-patient relationship, which may be difficult. In such cases, either the problem areas must be dealt with or a referral to another mental health professional must be made.

Transference involves the client feeling toward the therapist or experiencing the therapist similarly as he or she has toward someone else from his or her infantile past (Laplanche & Pontalis, 1973). The client may transfer feelings, such as rejection, acceptance, love, or need for approval from others, based on unfinished business in the past. A client with a need to please others may overendorse symptoms simply because the therapist asks questions about various problem areas. Another client, who does not trust authority figures, may provide minimal information. Transference may lead to resisting giving information, consciously or unconsciously or providing inaccurate information.

Countertransference takes place when the therapist experiences feelings toward the client that are similar to feelings he or she had toward a significant person in his or her past. The therapist may hold back asking certain questions or guide the interview in a different direction by focusing on areas less relevant to the therapeutic interview but of interest to the therapist. Countertransference may also influence feelings experienced toward the client such that the emotional experience is more related to the therapist's past than to the current client's behavior.

Smith (1986) warns that clinicians must carefully monitor countertransference feelings such as anger and anxiety toward suicidal clients, because their clin-

ical judgment may suffer. Also regarding suicidal clients, Maltsberger
(1988) states that countertransference may lead to the therapist feeling
great empathy for the client and thus
pain in acknowledging the client's
hopelessness. The therapist may then
minimize the problem to alleviate

> **DON'T FORGET**
>
> Transference and countertransfer-
> ence are commonplace in therapist-
> client relationships. The issue is not
> whether it takes place, but rather,
> how it is handled.

dealing with his or her emotional pain. Therefore, the clinician may not adequately assess the situation, leaving the client more vulnerable to risk.

RESISTANCE

Clients may consciously or unconsciously avoid disclosing information for
several possible reasons. Morrison (1993) describes ten areas in which clients
may demonstrate resistance:

1. *Tardiness.* Although tardiness is not common during the initial interview, it may increase with subsequent sessions due to resistance.
2. *Voluntary behaviors.* Gestures such as poor eye contact or constantly
   checking the clock may be an indication of difficulties with the
   topic, or resistance.
3. *Forgetfulness.* Increased responses such as "I don't know (or remember)" are convenient for the client to avoid responding.
4. *Omissions.* It is difficult to detect when the client leaves out information, therefore the use of collateral informants may be helpful.
5. *Contradictions.* Information that doesn't match previous information given by the client is difficult to integrate.
6. *Changing the subject.* Changing the subject is often an indication that
   the client wants to avoid the
   topic.
7. *Exaggerations.* When clients
   brag or exaggerate their ac-
   complishments, it may be a
   means of covering up their
   problem areas.

> **DON'T FORGET**
>
> Therapists should not take client re-
> sistance personally or view it as re-
> jection. The client is resisting thera-
> peutic variables, not the therapist.

8. *Diversionary tactics.* Behaviors that take away from the focus of the session such as asking to use the restroom, changing the topic, and chitchat may be indicative of resistance.
9. *Silence.* Although not always representative of resistance, some clients may not respond to questions.
10. *Hesitation.* Although subtle, slight hesitations before responding may suggest resistance.

MALINGERING

Malingering is the purposeful fabrication of signs and symptoms of a physical or mental disorder. It is most common when the client may either gain something or avoid a punishment by feigning symptoms. Diagnosing malingering is extremely difficult since it is hard to distinguish between responses accurately reporting a serious condition and responses exaggerated to indicate a serious condition. Morrison (1995) warns to suspect malingering in the following situations: (a) when there are legal problems or prospects of financial gain, (b) Antisocial Personality Disorder, (c) the patient's story does not match that of collateral informants or other known facts, or (d) the patient is not cooperative.

Psychological tests have been used to detect malingering in certain populations. Some of these tests have scales to detect malingering built into them, such as the Minnesota Multiphasic Personality Inventory–2 (MMPI-2; Butcher, Dahlstrom, Graham, Tellegen, & Kaemmer, 1989; see Fruch & Kinder, 1994; Gaies & Kinder, 1995), the Wechsler Memory Scale–III (Wechsler, 1997b; see Iverson, Slick, & Franzen, 2000; Mittenberg, Azrin, Millsaps, & Heilbronner, 1993), and the Personality Assessment Inventory (PAI; Morey, 1991; see Morey & Lanier, 1998).

Another use of psychological tests to detect malingering is to interpret standardized tests (although developed for another purpose) by examining how the scores or pattern of scores differ between malingerers and nonmalingerers. A few examples of this approach have been used with the Reliable Digits Test (see Greiffenstein, Baker, & Gola, 1994), which uses the digit span of the WAIS-III (Wechsler, 1997a) both forward and backward, to detect malingering in a neuropsychiatric population, as well as the Wisconsin Card Sorting Test (see Bernard, Mcgrath, & Houston, 1996; Suhr & Boyer, 1999), the Trail

Putting It Into Practice

Example of Malingering

A man applied for disability benefits, stating that he was "crazy" because he hears voices. None of his medical records indicated any history of psychoticism or any mental health disorder. While waiting for his appointment, he talked with a few people in the waiting room, holding a seemingly normal conversation. When he was called in for his evaluation his demeanor changed dramatically.

Although he was able to take a bus to the interview independently, he presented himself as being extremely confused and dysfunctional. For example, when he was asked to count by twos, he recited the alphabet. He also stated that his best friend is the president of the United States. During the interview, he held an occasional conversation with his invisible friend. When he was asked to repeat three words after 5 and 30 minutes, he confabulated new words each time. Further, when he was asked to repeat any number of digits forward and backward, he never provided a correct answer. Often, after providing an unusual response, he made comments such as, "See, I'm crazy." The interviewing clinician suspected malingering.

The client continued to state that he hears voices, but described them quite vaguely. In an attempt to more clearly rule out malingering, the therapist then asked the client if he sees a red light with green spots in his head seven seconds, every time, before he hears voices. The client responded, "Oh yes, it's always a red light with green spots, seven seconds before the voices come ... How did you know that?" The interviewer further inquired if he sees a green light with yellow spots 30 seconds after the voice goes away. He adamantly declared that he sees these colors and spots within the suggested time frame. For the next several minutes he discussed the voices and spots without even being asked about them any further.

In this case, the client could not remember even one word or any numbers he was asked to repeat. However, when the clinician made up fictitious characteristics of a disorder with fairly elaborate symptoms, the client remembered each of them throughout the remainder of the interview, believing that it would verify his diagnosis of "being crazy." Other conflicting factors, such as exhibiting extreme confusion, but being able to take a bus to an address where he had never been before, provided further evidence of malingering. In addition, he was not receiving any mental health treatment or counseling, nor were there any records available to validate a previous mental health diagnosis or treatment. The only records available showed that he had a significant criminal record. There would have been financial gain if he had succeeded in this poor attempt at malingering.

(continued)

> **Teaching Point:** *Anyone can suspect malingering, but providing empirical evidence is usually difficult. It is one of the most difficult diagnoses to give, because it almost always alienates the client from the clinician. Making the diagnosis, in effect, is a statement to the client that untruthful information was presented, possibly leading to negative consequences for the client. Therefore, when it is suspected, one must provide clear examples of discrepancies in observations, records, and client statements. Evidence must be provided that the contradictions are not simply evidence of a mental health disorder, rather than malingering. Malingering must be validated by empirical evidence, not just a gut feeling. Clearly back up the diagnosis, because there is a good chance that the person or agency who made the referral will want to discuss the case in detail.*
>
> *Because there is always an element of uncertainty in making a diagnosis of Malingering, some clinicians prefer to give the diagnosis as Rule Out Malingering or to make it a provisional diagnosis rather than make the full diagnosis. However, this procedure often leads to placing the burden of proof on someone else, rather than having to go through the difficult procedures of validating malingering. Beginning clinicians should immediately consult a supervisor when malingering is suspected.*

Making Test (Ruffolo, Guilmette, & Willis, 2000), and the Rey Auditory Verbal Learning Test (Bernard, 1991; Binder, Villaneuva, Howieson, & Moore, 1993).

Finally, there are psychological instruments designed solely for the purpose of detecting malingering, such as the Structured Interview of Reported Symptoms (Sirs, Rogers, Bagby, & Dickens, 1992), the Structured Inventory of Malingered Symptomatology (see Edens, Otto, & Dwyer, 1999), the Validity Indicator Profile (Frederick, Crosby, Wynkoop, 2000), the Miller's Forensic Assessment of Symptoms Test (Miller, 2000), and the Wildman Symptom Checklist (Wildman & Wildman, 1999).

INTERVIEW QUESTIONS:
IS STRUCTURE A HELP OR HINDRANCE?

There are inherent dangers in being either too structured or nonstructured in posing interview questions. Spitzer (in Skodol, 1989; LaBruzza, 1994) describes three styles of conducting the diagnostic interview: (a) the "checklist," (b) the "smorgasbord," and (c) the "canine." In addition, there is another interview style noted in this text termed the "butterfly."

The checklist interviewer asks rote, computer-like questions, with the em-

Putting It Into Practice

....

Examples of the Checklist, Smorgasbord, Butterfly, and Canine Approaches to Interviewing

(*Note:* These approaches are not intended to represent counseling styles. They represent the means in which diagnostic information is collected to validate a diagnosis and demonstrate that services are medially necessary. They represent only a sample of the questions that would be asked of the client.)

I. Checklist Approach

Therapist: "Are you depressed most of the time?"

Client: "Yes."

Therapist: "Have you been depressed over two weeks?"

Client: "Yes."

Therapist: "Do you have any pleasure in your life?"

Client: "No."

Therapist: "Is your appetite either high or low?"

Client: "Yes."

Therapist: "Do you have thoughts of death or suicide?"

Client: "Yes."

Therapist: "Do you have problems sleeping?"

Client: "Yes."

Therapist: Diagnosis: Major Depressive Disorder

The interview continues with interrogations aimed at validating a diagnosis. No more in-depth information is gathered other than endorsement of symptoms.

2. Smorgasbord Approach

Therapist: "Do you have problems with anxiety or worrying too much?"

Client: "No."

Therapist: "Do you have problems with depression?"

Client: "Yes."

Therapist: "Do you ever hear voices?"

Client: "No."

Therapist: "Are you paranoid?"

Client: "No."

Therapist: "Do you have alcohol or drug problems?"

Client: "Sometimes."   (*continued*)

Therapist: Diagnosis: Depression

The interview continues asking a little bit about several problem areas, with no follow-up of specific areas that are endorsed.

3. Butterfly Approach

Therapist: "How are you feeling?"

Client: "Thank you for asking. I just don't feel right."

Therapist: "You seem upset about something."

Client: "Yes, there are so many things I want to talk about."

Therapist: "I'm glad that you are willing to talk about your life."

Client: "I just want to get this load off my back."

Therapist: "It seems like a heavy load you're carrying."

Client: "Believe me, no one understands ... things aren't coming together."

Therapist: "Tell me about the load you're carrying."

Client: "Everything wrong just falls on me ... no one else takes what I have to take."

Therapist: "It sounds like you are really down on life right now."

Client: "You've got it, doc."

Therapist: Diagnosis: Depression

The session goes on with much empathy and rapport building, but the quality of diagnostic information suffers. If a third-party case manager asked for specific DSM-IV-TR symptoms and impairments in an effort to approve additional sessions, little or no evidence would be available, thus services would be denied.

4. Canine Approach

Therapist: "Do you have problems with anxiety or worrying too much?"

Client: "No, not at all."

Therapist: "Have you been feeling depressed?"

Client: "Yes."

Therapist: "How long have you felt depressed?"

Client: "About three months ... I've never been depressed before this ... Now I feel empty inside."

Therapist: "Was there an event or situation that brought on the depression?"

Client: "Yes, I was diagnosed with Multiple Sclerosis. I don't know what's going to happen to me now ... everything is changing."

Therapist: "Have you experienced any weight loss or gain? Tell me about it."

Client: "Oh yes, I've lost over 20 pounds since I was diagnosed ... I just don't feel like eating or doing anything anymore. Nothing feels good to me."

Therapist: "How else has it affected you?"

Client: "I just can't take it any longer ... I have no hope ... I can't even sleep at night ... It's not fair."

Therapist: "Have you experienced any suicidal thoughts or behaviors? ...Tell me about it."

Client: "Sometimes, I just feel like taking a bottle of pills. I don't think I'd ever do it, but what good am I to anybody anymore?"

Therapist: "How has this affected various areas in your life, like work and your relationships with others?"

Client: "They gave me a three month leave of absence at work ..." "I avoid everybody ... I'm too ashamed ... I just hide out at home and sleep."

Therapist: Diagnosis: Major Depressive Disorder, Single Episode

The interview continues both exploring specific symptoms and impairments of problem areas endorsed and ruling out areas that are not problem areas. It goes beyond yes/no questions, allowing the client to express needs and concerns, which leads to increased rapport and a valid diagnosis with sufficient specific client information. Of course, features of the butterfly approach would be helpful to establish rapport.

Teaching Point: *There are several interviewing styles.The clinician must be aware of both the strengths and limitations of each approach. One does not have to be locked into one style.*

phasis on gathering data. The interview abounds with yes/no type questions in an effort to endorse symptoms that warrant making a diagnosis. Although the approach may be technically correct, it is abrupt, rather than flowing. The relationship with the client is not as important as formulating the diagnosis in this approach. Smorgasbord interviewers ask a little about everything, but fail to explore the depth of specific, significant clinical issues. It is like the jack of all trades but master of none. Both the checklist and smorgasbord interviewer are weak in integrating information. The butterfly approach provides a beautiful flow of information in darting from one topic to another, lightly touching various topics, but seldom dwelling long enough on one topic to be of any help diagnostically. The approach is quite soothing to the client, thus aiding the relationship. However, it is so abstract and non-diagnosis oriented that when the chart is reviewed, there is little evidence to validate the diagnosis. Although emphasis is clearly client-relationship oriented, it provides little data for treatment. This approach may be helpful in counseling, but it does not reach the goal of the diagnostic interview's purpose. The canine interviewer, like a dog, first sniffs out all areas, then digs deeper in areas where the bone (clinically significant information) is buried. This approach incorporates the strengths of the other approaches.

STYLE, STRUCTURE, AND THE INTERVIEW PROCESS

Style of Individual Questions and Responses

It is common to refer to individual interview questions as either open-ended or closed-ended. *Open-ended* questions allow for individual, variable responses and cannot be answered with a yes or no response. They invite clients to open up, rather than simply providing a yes/no or brief, factual response. Questions will result in answers that reveal how the client thinks, feels, and acts. Many open-ended questions begin with words such as who, what, when, where, how, and why. *Closed-ended* questions do not encourage the client to elaborate or supply more information; that is, their responses are fixed. They can be extremely useful and save time, but are associated with three potential problems: (a) Clients may feel interrogated if you rapid-fire a series of closed-ended questions at them; (b) clients who are not very verbal will not provide much information; and (c) if you start with closed-ended questions, clients may get the idea that you will initiate the whole process and that their role is only to respond when questions are asked (Hutchings & Vaught, 1997).

Scissons (1993) distinguishes between open- and closed-ended questions: A closed-ended question demands a specific answer, whereas an open-ended question does not seek to elicit a specific response and allows for the client's interpretation of the question. Both open- and closed-ended questions are quite useful in eliciting the quality of client responses being targeted. In addition to open-ended questions, there are four levels of questions and responses that aid in providing specific information.

Interview Responses to Open-ended versus Closed-ended Questions

Open-ended (variable-response) questions allow the client to answer in a nondirected, often lengthy manner, whereas closed-ended questions solicit a brief (fixed) response. For example, the request to "tell me how you feel" will elicit a significantly different response than will asking "Are you depressed?"

Open-ended questions allow the client to express the answer in a number of ways that may or may not be on track clinically; however, they may also be the better method to help the client express areas of concern. Closed-ended (fixed-response) questions more quickly help the clinician make a diagnosis, but could seem cold and uncaring if not presented tactfully. Closed-ended questions do not allow for an array of responses; the possible responses are typically answers such as yes, no, or brief (factual) information.

Structure of the Series of Questions

Nonstructured Sequence: Going with the Flow

Nonstructured interviewing does not rely upon lists of prepared questions; rather, inquiries vary considerably, based on the individual client's concerns. The specific questions asked may differ significantly from client to client depending on the client's responses and the therapist's theoretical orientation. A greater level of therapist expertise and experience will ensure that the line of questioning elicits the information needed in each case. Staying on target involves asking appropriate follow-up questions based on the answers provided to previous questions, rather than relying on a formulaic interview process. Nonstructured interviewing is more apt to pick up on the idiosyncrasies and uniqueness of the individual (Groth-Marnat, 1990). Also, the level of rapport is likely to be higher than a structured interview.

However, if different questions are asked of different individuals, or if they are asked different types of questions at different points in time throughout treatment, there is less certainty that equivalent diagnostic standards are being applied. For example, if a clinician who happens to have a specialty in anxiety disorders interviews a client, it is possible that without controls on the interviewing questions and techniques, the diagnostic results may differ from those of a clinician specializing in mood disorders. Further, a clinician with a philosophy that most mental health problems are based on childhood experiences will likely view the client's problem areas differently than one who focuses on the present.

The amount of structure in an interview may be affected by both client and therapist variables. For example, some clients may become upset when presented with a lack of structure or direction. Clients suffering with concerns such as anxiety, social withdrawal, or other factors that may make it difficult to

Putting It Into Practice

Clinicians' Backgrounds Affect Patients' Diagnoses

A case example was presented at a mental health documentation seminar. A fictitious client, obviously suffering from Major Depression, presented with symptoms taken directly from the *DSM-IV-TR*. The symptoms included (a) being depressed most of the time for the past 3 months, (b) lack of pleasure, (c) gaining 15 lbs. unintentionally in the past month, (d) significantly increased appetite, (e) suicidal ideations, and (f) decreased concentration. No other associated symptoms were endorsed. Further, the client exhibited several social and occupational impairments secondary to the depression. The purpose of the supposedly unambiguous example was to teach how to validate a *DSM-IV-TR* diagnosis.

One of the attendees, a specialist in dissociative disorders, stated emphatically that the client was not suffering Major Depression, but rather Dissociative Identity Disorder. Based on his training, specialty, and theoretical stance, the attendee came to a different conclusion using the same diagnostic criteria.

Teaching Point: *Clinicians must be careful not to allow their personal views, backgrounds, and theoretical stances overshadow other information when assigning mental health diagnoses. The client's diagnosis should be independent of these variables. Clinicians should monitor the frequency with which they assign various diagnoses.*

express oneself may find the interview to be anxiety provoking. Such clients may prefer a more direct form of questioning. Therapists from empirically based schools of thought, such as behaviorism, tend to emphasize structured interviews, whereas other approaches, whether psychoanalytic or client centered, lean toward nonstructured techniques. However, most clinicians do not rely on either method exclusively.

Structured Sequence: Sticking with the Program

Structured interviewing formats ensure that all clients are asked the same or a similar core of questions, thus increasing the reliability of the interview. The standardized interview objectively rules in and rules out each diagnostic category for each client served. Diagnostic areas that might have been overlooked because they were not in the client's history or in the presenting problem may continue to be overlooked, although it is less likely than in an unstructured interview format.

A typical structured interview lays out an array of questions that are designed to thoroughly explore all diagnostic categories. The flow of questions from one clinician to another will have more similarities than differences. Differences tend to lie more in the style of the therapist than in the areas addressed. Groth-Marnat (1990) states that structured interviews have many distinct advantages over unstructured approaches, including more psychometric precision and efficiency.

However, if a clinician is too rigid, asking only the questions on the clinical form, the interview may become "canned," not allowing for unusual situations, or client problem areas not included in the form. No clinical form (preprinted questionnaire), in itself, can pick up on client idiosyncrasies and specific observations taking place at the time of the interview. A form should never control the interview—however, it can be a helpful guide in being thorough in data collection. For example, Hutchings and Vaught (1997) discuss *systematic inquiry* as a way of seeking information in an organized manner that uses an open-ended approach. Six general questions can guide a systematic inquiry into almost any problem: (a) who is involved, (b) what is the problem, (c) when does it occur, (d) where does it occur, (e) how do you or others behave in this situation, and (f) why are you concerned.

Putting It Into Practice

Benefits of Questioning in Areas Not Presented by the Client

A client was referred for a psychological evaluation. Previous records indicated a diagnosis of Depressive Disorder NOS, with notations of memory problems. She had received counseling for several years in dealing with depression. During the interview for disability, it would have been convenient simply to ask questions regarding depression due to her history. However, because the interview was structured, questions about symptoms of Posttraumatic Stress Disorder (PTSD) were posed. The client began to cry, noting that no one had ever asked her about the abuse she went through as a child. The previous counseling and diagnosis had not been sufficient to focus on the core of her problems. That is, treatment for PTSD is not the same as treatment for depression. The depression was secondary to the PTSD.

Teaching Point: *The therapist should not assume that the previous records and client descriptions fully explain the problem areas. A comprehensive interview that rules in and rules out all diagnostic categories will often uncover unidentified problem areas.*

CAUTION

Too much structure in interviewing leads to being technically correct but may miss specific client information and diminish rapport. Too little structure may increase rapport, but it is weak in accurately gathering diagnostic information.

The reliability of an interview increases with structure. *Reliability,* in this case, is defined as replicability. That is, when the clinician asks all clients the basic core questions, with the *DSM-IV-TR* as the reference point, it can be assumed that each client is being questioned by the same standard. An interviewer becomes less reliable, psychometrically, when posing very different interview questions to different clients. In such cases, the chance of receiving different diagnoses at different times increases. The *DSM-IV-TR* should be the guide for ruling in and ruling out the various diagnoses, because the diagnosis is based on the *DSM-IV-TR* (or ICD-10). The array of questions asked, therefore, must cover the diagnostic categories in the *DSM-IV-TR.*

A common error in diagnostic interviewing occurs when the clinician does not ask questions beyond the scope of the client's presenting problem. For example, a client presenting with depression may also suffer from alcoholism, anxiety, or a number of other problems; but if the clinician does not rule them in or out, misdiagnosis (or an incomplete diagnosis) may occur.

Combining Structured and Nonstructured Interview Formats

Few, if any, clinicians rely solely on either structured or nonstructured interviewing techniques. Commonly, clinicians will rule out various diagnostic categories using structured techniques, then ask a number of nonstructured questions, based on the individuals needs, during the rule-in process. Combining the two techniques is often referred to as *semi-structured interviewing*. The structured series of questions validates the *DSM-IV-TR* diagnosis, whereas the nonstructured series of questions is directed toward the client's idiosyncratic needs. For example, a structured format might include asking the client whether each of a list of symptoms from a wide range of diagnoses exists. The same categories of symptoms should be ruled in or ruled out for each client. After several diagnostic categories have been ruled out and others have been ruled in, the clinician can change to a nonstructured approach to gather the information needed to clarify the client's specific needs, symptoms, impairments, strengths, weaknesses, and other information necessary for treatment planning and validation of medical necessity for those areas that have been ruled in.

Morrison (1993) suggests that the initial portion of the first interview is most productive using a nondirective approach, which will help to establish rapport, whereas the latter part of the interview will elicit a different type of response with the use of structured questions. Similarly, Maloney and Ward (1976) recommend that the clinician initially ask open-ended questions, monitor the client's responses, then ask more closed-ended questions to fill in the gaps.

An interview that is solely open- or closed-ended and solely structured or nonstructured in its entirety will be thorough in some areas but superficial in others. A diagnostic interview typically utilizes, at some point, each of the four combinations illustrated in the quadrants of Table 3.1. As both the rapport and need for more specific diagnostic information increase and change, the struc-

Table 3.1 The Four-Quadrant Approach to Interview Formats

	Sequence of Questioning	
	Nonstructured (sequence is variable)	**Structured** (sequence is fixed)
Open-ended (response type is variable)	**Quadrant 1:** Therapist gathers general, nonthreatening information. *corresponds with* Clinical Interview Step 1: Establishing Initial Rapport with Client	**Quadrant 4:** Therapist documents impairments caused by the disorder. *corresponds with* Clinical Interview Step 4: Determining Specific Impairments
Closed-ended (response type is fixed)	**Quadrant 2:** Therapist considers major diagnostic categories (e.g., Depression vs. Anxiety). *corresponds with* Clinical Interview Step 2: Assessing the Diagnostic Categories	**Quadrant 3:** Therapist documents impairments caused by the disorder. *corresponds with* Clinical Interview Step 3: Validating Specific Diagnoses

Style of Questions and Responses

ture of the interview is likely to shift among the quadrants. A gradual progression from establishing rapport to soliciting very specific diagnostic criteria will incorporate the strengths of each technique. As information is clarified and as topics change, the combination may shift back to previous quadrants, as needed. Both the therapist's and the client's own style of relating will influence the means by which the information is gathered.

THE FOUR-QUADRANT APPROACH TO INTERVIEW FORMATS

Quadrant 1

In this quadrant, the nonstructured questioning sequence and the open-ended style of questioning intersect. The resulting overall approach is ideal for building rapport and trust, and coincides perfectly with Step 1 of the clinical interview: *Establishing initial rapport with the client.* Later, as rapport develops and the client feels more comfortable sharing information with the therapist, the degree of structure and the nature of the information being sought will change. At this initial stage, however, the flow of information is general. The types of answers provided now will lay a foundation for the gathering of more specific, structured information, which will be needed later.

Examples of questions posed to the client include the following:

"What brings you here today?"
"How did you hear about our clinic?"
"Tell me about yourself."
"Do you have any questions about the interview or the counseling process?"

Note that the client's responses could go in any of a number of directions under nonstructured and open-ended questioning. Neutral questions, such as those in the example, may help elicit important clinical information.

Quadrant 2

Here, the nonstructured questioning sequence intersects with closed-ended (or fixed) responses, yielding an approach useful for determining a diagnostic category. As with Quadrant 1 and Step 1 of the clinical interview, Quadrant 2 works well with Step 2 of the clinical interview: Assessing the diagnostic categories. The lack of "script" makes the interviewing nonstructured may vary due to the suspected diagnosis. Each rule-in and rule-out leads the therapist and client to take a different fork in the road in diagnostic questioning. Yet the style of question is closed-ended, the answers generally limited to yes or no, due to the need to pinpoint the diagnostic category.

Therapist: "Are you experiencing anxiety, worrying, or nervousness?"
Client: "No."
Therapist: "Are you experiencing any problems with depression?"
Client: "Yes, I have been very depressed lately."

Each question answered with a "yes" changes the subsequent questions needed to elicit more specific diagnostic information—in this case, about a potential mood disorder. The questions also vary depending on which diagnostic categories are endorsed.

Quadrant 3

In this quadrant, we have crossed over into the structured questioning sequence column of Table 3.1, but remain in the closed-ended question style row. The result is a fixed set of questions with fixed responses, intended to endorse symptoms related to specific diagnoses. This coincides precisely with the third step in the clinical interview: validating specific diagnoses. Having ruled in or ruled out the general diagnostic categories, the therapist asks the client specific yes/no questions related to the specific diagnoses suggested in the previous steps of the clinical interview. The structure of the sequence of questions is best taken directly from *DSM-IV-R* criteria.

In the following example, assume that several diagnoses have been ruled out (as in Quadrant 2), and the therapist is at the point of testing the validity of a specific diagnosis of Major Depressive Disorder.

Therapist: "How long have you been feeling depressed?"
Client: "At least a year."
Therapist: "How often are you depressed?"
Client: "I'm depressed almost all of the time . . . I rarely feel any joy or pleasure."
Therapist: "Have you had any significant weight changes?"

Client: "I've dropped at least 25 pounds in the last six months . . . I just don't have any appetite at all."

Therapist: "Are you experiencing feelings of worthlessness?"

Client: "Yes, significantly."

Therapist: "Have you had any thoughts of death or suicide?"

Client: "I'm not suicidal, but I often think about what it would be like for my family to be without me."

The therapist continues to validate the diagnosis of Major Depressive Disorder by going through all the *DSM-IV-TR* criteria.

Quadrant 4

In the final quadrant, we find the structured questioning sequence intersecting with the open-ended style of questions. The associated step in the clinical interview is Step 4: validating the client's levels of experienced stress and impairment. The *DSM-IV-TR* and most third-party payers indicate that, although symptoms of a diagnosis may be endorsed, treatment is not considered to be medically necessary without significant distress or impairment. The therapist follows a roughly predetermined structure of questioning, the individual elements of which allow the client to give the individualized, open-ended responses that are crucial in treatment planning.

Therapist: "How are these problems affecting you on the job?"

Client: "I'm missing more and more work. My boss thinks I don't care any more. My spouse has to force me just to get up and go to work. I don't think they'll let me work there much longer. If I don't snap out of this, I'll be out of a job soon."

Therapist: "How were things at work before you felt depressed?"

Client: "I never missed work then. I loved going to work. I felt like it gave me purpose in life. I was the boss' favorite."

Therapist: "How is it affecting your friendships and how you get along with people in general?"

Client: "I've stopped all socializing. I just want to be alone."

Therapist: "How has this changed compared to before you felt depressed?"

Client: "I used to go out with my friends at least twice a week."

As the interview proceeds, the therapist continues to evaluate various functional impairments and the level of distress the client is experiencing.

RULE-IN AND RULE-OUT PROCEDURES

Rule-in refers to a process in which the clinician systematically identifies specific symptoms and impairments that warrant a corresponding diagnosis. For example, if the *DSM-IV-TR* requires that at least four of seven listed symptoms must be prevalent in order to assign a given diagnosis, the rule-in procedure would consist of investigating whether the client is significantly impaired or distressed by at least four of these symptoms. In this case, if at least four of the seven are causing functional impairments that necessitate treatment, and other *DSM-IV-TR* considerations have been satisfied, the diagnosis has been ruled in. In a medical model, treatment is considered effective when the client no longer experiences sufficient symptoms, distress, and impairments to warrant the diagnosis.

The term rule-out is important in clarifying a diagnosis. *Rule-out* is used in the future tense when clinicians suspect that a client is suffering from a particular disorder, but more information is needed for confirmation. For example, a diagnosis of R/O (rule-out) ADHD suggests that the clinician believes ADHD may be the correct diagnosis, but more information (e.g., collateral information, testing, examples of impairments, referral to a specialist, rule-out of medical condition) is needed to fully validate it. Diagnoses preceded by R/O should be resolved by obtaining the necessary information to validate or invalidate them, otherwise treatment planning becomes confusing and problems could arise in third-party reimbursement. In this situation, when a rule-out diagnosis is made, it should later either be ruled in (e.g., confirmed after obtaining additional information) or ruled out (e.g., found to be invalid after obtaining additional information).

Ruled-out is used in the past tense when a client does not endorse sufficient symptomology and impairments to warrant a particular diagnosis. The diagnosis that was suspected to be present in the client has been found to be invalid. When a rule-out diagnosis is made initially, it should later either be ruled in or ruled out. Conversely, when sufficient symptomology and impairment exist, a diagnosis is ruled in. In theory, after a comprehensive diagnostic interview, all diagnoses, except those given, have been ruled out. However, in prac-

CAUTION

When a diagnosis with a Rule-Out (R/O) has been given, be sure to obtain the necessary information in subsequent sessions to adequately rule in or rule out the diagnosis. If the client has only one Axis-I diagnosis that has been noted as a R/O diagnosis but which has been billed to an insurance company as the primary diagnosis, the ethics of continuing to bill under that diagnosis must be considered if the diagnosis hasn't been formally ruled in or ruled out. If an auditor from a third-party payer discovers that insurance payment has been made for a R/O diagnosis, and the diagnosis has not been ruled in in a relatively brief time period, there could be a financial payback to the insurance company for funds received.

tice it is not uncommon to make additional clinical discoveries during the course of treatment that could change the initial diagnosis.

The rule-in/rule-out process is a step-by-step process in which the diagnosis is reached by the following process:

1. *Rule-out diagnostic categories:* e.g., "Not: mood disorder, thought disorder, cognitive disorder, behavioral disorder, etc."
2. *Rule-in diagnostic categories:* e.g., "Client endorses significant symptoms and impairment due to anxiety."
3. *Specific rule-out diagnoses of anxiety:* e.g., "Not phobia, not adjustment disorder, not PTSD, etc."
4. *Specific rule-in diagnosis:* e.g., "Meets criteria for Generalized Anxiety Disorder."
5. *List the specific diagnostic criteria that the client endorses to validate the diagnosis:* e.g., "Client meets criteria for Generalized Anxiety Disorder. She has felt anxious most of the time for the past few years. Symptoms include usually feeling restless, easily fatigued, decreased concentration, increased irritability, and sleep disturbance. Due to the above symptoms, she recently quit her job due to making too many mistakes from 'overworrying,' and she has been increasingly more argumentative, leading to no activities with her friends in the past year. She describes herself as 'a nervous wreck,' and is quite distressed about her increasing level of anxiety, in which panic symptoms are developing." (See Rapid Reference 3.1.)

≡Rapid Reference 3.1

Interview Questions and Rule-In/Rule-Out Procedures

1. Structured interview questions increase the validity and reliability of the interview by assuring that all clients are asked the same range of questions.
2. Open-ended interview questions increase the level of specific client concerns, aiding in specific treatment planning.
3. Rule-out procedures enable the clinician to determine which diagnoses are not prevalent, whereas rule-in procedures help the clinician systematically assign a diagnosis.

ROLE OF TESTING

Testing is an important aspect of obtaining client information. Although not all clinicians incorporate testing, others test most clients. A thorough review of testing procedures is beyond the scope of this text.

Testing is useful in validating a diagnosis and in providing baseline measures of the client's functioning. For example, a test such as the Beck Depression Inventory-II is commonly given to clients at various points during therapy to assess their relative degree of depression as the number of sessions increases. See Wiger and Solberg (2001) for a comprehensive discussion of mental health outcome measures.

CHAPTER SUMMARY

1. Several rapport-building skills and techniques can be learned that will enhance the quality of both the relationship and the level of information attained.
2. The interviewer must be highly self-aware in order to prevent characteristics of the client from influencing how the clinician perceives the information received.
3. Open-ended questions and responses allow for probing specific client concerns, but may miss important material not specifically brought up by the client; closed-ended questions and responses are

important in providing specific information. A thorough evaluation incorporates both methods.

4. Ruling in a diagnosis is the process of asking questions to determine whether a diagnosis is prevalent, while ruling out a diagnosis is the process of determining that a diagnosis is not prevalent for the client.

5. The diagnosis is based on the integration of several types of information such as, (a) Clinical Interview, (b) Clinical Observations, (c) Previous Records, (d) Testing, (e) Biographical Information, and (f) Collateral Informants.

6. Diagnostic qualifiers, such as in (full or partial) remission, provisional, rule-out, prior history, and med-controlled, provide more specific information than simply listing a diagnosis.

7. Because of the similarities between diagnoses, the clinician must have a thorough understanding of the *DSM-IV-TR,* or misdiagnosis is likely.

8. Although it is not difficult to suspect malingering, it is difficult to prove.

9. Ruling in a diagnosis confirms that the client's symptoms meet *DSM-IV-TR* criteria. Ruling it out confirms that *DSM-IV-TR* criteria are not met.

TEST YOURSELF

1. Which of the following best represents the concept of transference?

(a) The relationship transfers from neutral to positive.

(b) The client gets upset whenever the therapist brings up a seemingly unemotional issue.

(c) The therapist is easily upset at the client.

(d) Both the client and therapist fail to respect each other's feelings.

2. Countertransference

(a) can only happen when transference first takes place.

(b) takes place only with new therapists.

(c) is best countered when the therapist is aware of its existence.

(d) is a good indication to end treatment.

3. **Which of the following statements best represents a mental health rule-in procedure?**
   (a) Do you feel down or sad most of the time?
   (b) Do your panic attacks increase in duration when you are anxious?
   (c) How much school did you miss last week because of your problem?
   (d) When you are stressed do you feel uncomfortable?

4. **Client resistance indicates which of the following?**
   (a) The therapist has not performed an adequate job.
   (b) The interview questions are off target.
   (c) Transference and countertransference have taken place.
   (d) The client does not want to deal with the clinical material.

5. **What is the greatest disadvantage of nonstructured interviewing?**
   (a) Important information could be left out.
   (b) Rapport could suffer.
   (c) It is atheoretical.
   (d) It picks up on too many client variables.

6. **When is the most structure needed in a clinical interview?**
   (a) Arriving at a diagnosis
   (b) Developing rapport
   (c) Discussing the presenting problem
   (d) Describing one's mental health treatment history

7. **What is meant by the following statement? "Alcohol Dependence has been ruled out."**
   (a) Alcohol Dependence might be the diagnosis.
   (b) Alcohol Dependence is the diagnosis.
   (c) More must be asked about Alcohol Dependence to determine whether it is the appropriate diagnosis.
   (d) Alcohol Dependence is not the diagnosis.

8. **When a diagnosis has been given previously by an MD, the mental health therapist is required to give the same diagnosis.** True or False?

9. **When a sufficient number of symptoms have been endorsed to define a diagnosis, the diagnosis can be given with reasonable confidence.** True or False?

10. **Medical necessity is a major criteria in determining whether a third-party will pay for mental health services.** True or False?

(continued)

11. **The reliability of an interview increases the more structured and comprehensive the questions posed.** True or False?

12. **Although little or no counseling might take place in the diagnostic interview, how can it be therapeutic?**

13. **Discuss reasons why people would underendorse psychological problems and why others might overendorse psychological problems.**

14. **If the scientific method of attaining information is important, why is rapport, a nonscientific concept, considered necessary?**

Answers: 1. b; 2. c; 3. a; 4. d; 5. a; 6. a; 7. d; 8. False; 9. False; 10. True; 11. True; 12. The empathy, concern, and understanding of the client's problem areas are therapeutic. 13. Underendorse: Not wanting to receive services, appearing healthy, defensiveness. Overendorse: Cry for help, secondary gain. 14. The human touch aspect of counseling is a major aspect for positive change. The scientific aspect helps empirically demonstrate the need for services.

Four

ESTABLISHING RAPPORT: MAINSTREAM AND SPECIAL POPULATIONS

A n accurate and informative interview is necessary for developing a working hypothesis of the presenting problem and possible treatment approaches. However, obtaining this information depends heavily upon the relationship between therapist and the client. Establishing rapport refers to a process and quality within the therapeutic relationship in which the client feels safe and valued enough to share private and personal information. There are several things a therapist might do to establish rapport. They include the following:

THE THERAPEUTIC SETTING

The therapist must take into account what is appropriate for the population he or she serves. For example, young children would be more comfortable in a less formal office that has age-appropriate toys and items of interest displayed (e.g., beanbag toys, building toys, cartoon characters) along with rugs, pillows, beanbag chairs, tables, and chairs of appropriate size for children. Adults, however, would feel more relaxed in a setting that is similar to someone's family room. For instance, comfortable chairs, less harsh lighting, and some homey details like plants and wall hangings would be appropriate.

Along a similar train of thought, the therapist should be aware of his or her attire and how it impacts the relationship with the client. Children are less likely to open up to someone who is formally dressed in a business suit (which connotes an aura of authoritarianism) than someone dressed more casually and comfortably (so that they could sit on the floor if needed and play with the child). However, jeans and a T-shirt provide a message that is too informal and unprofessional, especially for adult clientele. Attire that is too casual might be

DON'T FORGET

Checking Out the Suitability of the Setting

Ensure the client's privacy by paying attention to such things as soundproofing.

Make the setting inviting to your particular client group.

Minimize distractions such as traffic, interruptions, and noise.

Make sure the setting is accessible in terms of handicapped accommodations and transportation availability (e.g., bus lines).

Keep confidential information locked and out-of-sight. If needed, pick up after each client so that no intrusions of your client's style or personality are imposed on the next client.

interpreted by the client as a lack of respect for that client or might indicate the lack of respect the client is allowed to show toward the therapist.

TYPE OF LANGUAGE USED

The verbal communication used between the therapist and client is important in creating a comfortable atmosphere. The therapist is well advised to consider how he or she communicates with the client and how this may influence rapport. For example, overuse of professional jargon can distance the client from the therapist and lead to confusion, misunderstanding, and a sense of the therapist talking over the client's head. The therapist should feel free to use the words of the client as a way of communicating understanding, and establishing rapport.

EMPATHY, CONGRUENCE, AND UNCONDITIONAL POSITIVE REGARD

Carl Rogers' (1961) view of the necessary elements of psychotherapy has withstood the test of time and has been accepted by most approaches to psychotherapy. *Empathy* refers to the ability to see things through the client's perspective. It involves putting aside the therapist's own expectations and preconceptions and closely listening to the client. The therapist may need to gather more information to be sure that he or she has really understood what the client meant, but when this is done with an attitude of genuine honesty, the client will feel appreciated. If you have difficulty in feeling empathy for a particular client, don't try to manufacture it. In that case, attention and appropriate questions convey your interest in the client better than phony empathy (Othmer & Othmer, 1989).

Congruence refers to a genuine, honest presence of the therapist. The therapist is not trying to pretend to be someone he or she is not (e.g., best friend, authoritarian expert, aloof professional), nor is he or she being dishonest when it is necessary to portray a reaction to the client that is not real. Nevertheless, therapists should be aware that clients will recognize whether a therapist is being real or not and that the relationship is compromised by falseness.

Unconditional positive regard refers to a positive way of viewing and thinking about the client. It is both a sincere belief in the positive traits of the client and a respectful attitude toward the client. This does not mean that the therapist accepts everything the client does, such as committing a crime, but the client is entitled to his or her thoughts and feelings and the opportunity to explore his or her behavior in a nonthreatening environment. Other qualities of the

Putting It Into Practice

Concepts of Empathy, Congruence, and Unconditional Positive Regard

Client: I feel terrible, like I should have done something to make my son stop taking drugs.

Therapist: I can see that you are really hurting and feel responsible. (Empathy)

Client: Yes. I blame myself for his addiction. If I weren't so involved in my own little world and career, I would have seen it sooner.

Therapist: I believe that parents do the best they can with what they have. Your level of concern right now shows me that you care very much, so let's see what you would like to do. (Unconditional positive regard)

Note: Congruence is demonstrated when the therapist makes the above statements in a genuine, honest manner.

therapist that are deemed essential for building rapport include warmth, respect, and availability.

Perhaps one of the most valuable skills an interviewer or a therapist can learn is listening skills. Effective listening increases the amount of information the client contributes, and allows the client to vent feelings. Hutchings and Vaught (1997) note that effective listening includes the following:

1. Listening carefully to both what is said and how it is said
2. Avoiding interruptions and allowing the client to complete sentences and ideas
3. Using silence to encourage the client to continue talking, thus giving the client the time and space to verbalize thoughts and feelings that may be difficult to talk about
4. Reflecting and clarifying the client's meaning
5. Asking questions to ascertain important details and work toward solutions
6. Noting similarities and discrepancies in what the client says, how the client says it, and what the client does
7. Eliciting feedback from the client to determine and ensure accuracy of the therapist's perceptions

USE OF THE THERAPIST'S PERSONAL EXPERIENCES

The use of the therapist's personal experiences may benefit the establishment of rapport. It may help the client feel that he or she is not alone (e.g., "even an expert has gone through this") or allow the client to place more validity in what the therapist says (e.g., "the therapist has gotten through this and must know how to handle it"). Keep in mind that you are not doing this to get something off your chest or confess, but to present something helpful that the client can use in a therapeutic way. Finally, know your client before using this tech-

> **CAUTION**
>
> Although discussing the therapist's personal experiences can be a useful technique, do not dominate too much of the session time or do it on a regular basis. Such a practice gives the impression that the session is about working on your problems, not the client's.

nique. Some clients, such as children, may feel too burdened by your personal revelations. Other clients, particularly from certain cultural groups (refer to section on cultural considerations), may view it as an inappropriate display for a professional and lose respect for you.

INITIAL CONTACT

Provide some initial direction in the first session, such as "What brings you here today?" This immediately sets the tone that you will try to be helpful, you care about the client's point of view, and you will provide guidance for the client. Be authentic and honest regarding your experience as a clinician and what you can offer (e.g., "No, I do not have children, but with my understanding and training in psychological principles and your expert input on your children, I believe I can help you."), and provide the client with some hope without resorting to an insincere, "I'm sure it will all work out." Put the client at ease by requesting basic information such as name and what he or she prefers to be called and engaging in small talk about the drive to your office, where they are from, or anything that might be comfortable and familiar to the client (Othmer & Othmer, 1989).

OTHER THERAPIST SKILLS

Don't forget some of the basics of interpersonal communication, which will certainly influence rapport. Maintain comfortable eye contact such that you indicate interest and respect but not an uncomfortable dominance. Because eye contact does indicate your interest in what the client is saying, you should not keep your eyes fixed on your intake sheet or notes. Similarly, maintain an appropriate distance between you and the client. For example, most clients would feel uncomfortable sharing the same couch with the therapist. Touching, other than handshakes or pats on the back or shoulder can be very threatening to clients. The use of humor is a great stress releaser and can enhance rapport if it is done while still showing respect and compassion to the client. Finally, respecting silence can be an important tool that demonstrates to the client that what they have to say is important and worth waiting for. (See Rapid Reference 4.1.)

Rapid Reference 4.1

When Establishing Rapport with a Client, Remember the Following:

1. Create a comfortable setting that might include items of interest to that population (e.g., toys), appropriate attire for the therapist, privacy, minimization of distractions, and accessibility.
2. Use language that is appropriate and effective. This would include a minimization of professional jargon and use of the client's own words when appropriate.
3. Convey empathy, congruence, and unconditional positive regard. The therapist should also display respect, openness, availability, and a nonjudgmental attitude.
4. Feel free to use personal experiences as a therapist. However, use them sparingly to establish a sense of understanding and hope for the client.
5. Upon initial contact with the client, provide direction, comfortableness, and hope.
6. Other skills that are useful in establishing rapport might include using humor, allowing for silences in the session, respecting the client's physical body and boundaries, maintaining comfortable eye contact, and keeping an appropriate seating distance between the client and the therapist.

ESTABLISHING RAPPORT WITH SPECIAL POPULATIONS

Young Children

Understand that when you interview a child, you will most likely also be interviewing an adult (e.g., parent, caretaker, school personnel). Allow yourself enough time to hear from everyone and think carefully about who you want to have in the room at the same time. Some therapists opt to meet with the child and adult(s) together, establishing the sense of a team effort, particularly since working with a young child necessitates the involvement and cooperation of the parents. Additionally, meeting as a group allows the therapist the opportunity to observe family dynamics and interactions. Other therapists, however, prefer to meet with the child and the adult individually, or both individually and together. Older children may feel more comfortable discussing issues when the parent is not present and likewise. Also, there are family and marital issues that would not be appropriate to discuss in front of a child. Whatever your preference is, keep the child in mind as you establish rapport. You may do this by introducing yourself to the child first upon your initial meeting with the family and also by engaging the child in small talk around issues they are familiar with, such as sports or activities. When meeting with the family, remember to ask the child his or her opinion and give him or her an opportunity to present what the child thinks is the problem or what needs to change.

Children respond best to adults who show them respect and friendly interest. When working with children, therapists should also be active (e.g., taking the lead, generating ideas, being involved in the child's activities), upbeat, and demonstrate a liking for the child. When working with very young children, try to place yourself so that your face is level to the child's face. It can be quite intimidating to the child to have a stranger tower over while demanding a response.

As mentioned earlier, there are some unique considerations with young children when it comes to clothing and office space. The therapist, to enhance rapport with a child, should dress comfortably, not formally. The office should be designed to be appealing to a child. Have a few current and popular items visibly present around the office since it lets the child know that you are in touch with children's interests. Keep some comfort items, such as stuffed animals, colorful children's books, clay, paper and crayons, and perhaps even a choice of snacks and drinks in the office. Children prefer to do something in therapy rather than sit passively and talk. Allow them the opportunity to engage in activities while simultaneously sharing information with you verbally and nonverbally. For example, you might ask questions about their play or have the child role-play a character (real or fantasized) while the therapist participates to the extent that the child directs. It is also helpful to engage the child (or sometimes just the therapist) in storytelling. Stories can be used to teach a

DON'T FORGET

Deciding Who Attends the Session

When working with children, the therapist needs to determine who will be invited and involved in the session. This decision is based on theoretical considerations as well as knowing what types of information need to be gathered. Options include seeing the child only, parent(s) only, child and parent(s), the entire family residing in the home, or the inclusion of other significant people in the child's life such as school personnel or daycare providers.

lesson or skill, elicit information, or allow the child to practice problem solving in a nonthreatening manner.

Finally, it is important to understand the principles of child development. This gives the therapist a great starting point for knowing what is expected or normal for children at various stages of development. Logan (1997) points out that childhood problems may reflect appropriate child developmental issues, whether they are common, transitory reactions to specific life circumstances or more severe difficulties. It is important for the therapist to look at the extent to which the disturbances are significantly interfering with play, learning, and interpersonal relationships and are slowing or impeding the development of important capacities.

Abused Populations

Karp, Butler, and Bergstrom (1998) note that the therapeutic relationship, with an authority figure whose role puts him or her in charge of the therapeutic situation, may trigger a sense of being dominated for the client. Clients who have been abused are especially vulnerable to this type of relationship. The therapist should work at creating a relationship with the client that shares decisions and control. These same authors also note that for this population there is an ongoing impairment in their ability to trust. Keeping this in mind, a therapist

Putting It Into Practice

Child-Oriented Activities

It is more effective to allow a child to engage in activities during a therapy session. For example, the therapist may let the child play with building blocks. After the child has constructed something, the therapist might say the following:

- "Is the place you built safe?"
- "What makes it safe?"
- "How is it different from (or the same as) your home?"
- "Who would live in your building?"
- "Tell me about them."
- "Do they remind you of anyone in your family?"
- "What kind of place would you build for your family?"

would be well advised to maintain consistency in how he or she behaves, demonstrate follow-through, and respect the fact that trust does not come easily or quickly. When activities are used therapeutically or the client is requested to do something as part of his or her therapy, the therapist should allow the client to engage in it only to the degree to which he or she feels comfortable. The therapist should check with the client about his or her level of comfort for the activity, be willing to discuss any discomfort, and subsequently negotiate, modify, or omit the activity. This gives the client permission to have boundaries, maintain a sense of control in therapy and also indicates that the therapist trusts the client's judgment.

Horne and Kiselica (1999), in discussing young clients who have been sexually assaulted, note that the key to rapport is simply to wait until the child is ready to talk. They also point out that boundaries, which have been so horribly violated for them, must be clear, consistent, and rehearsed; the client should be rewarded for maintaining boundaries and understand the consequences of transgressing them. Trust can be enhanced by beginning and ending sessions on time, using extreme caution about touch of any kind without the child's permission, and only inviting others into the session with the child's permission. Other issues that require consideration on the part of the therapist include the use of videotaping (again, only with the client's permission and as they feel comfortable), honesty at the beginning of therapy regarding who has access to this information and what might be done with it, and the nature of the role of the therapist (e.g., not acting as law enforcement or as a parent, but only to assist the child in feeling and doing better).

Older Adults

The key to working with older adults is to become informed regarding how their experiences are the same and different from other age groups. Elderly individuals are more likely to attribute their problems to physical health or aging rather than psychological factors. They are more likely to be seen by

CAUTION

Working with Abused Populations

A critical factor in working with an abused population is to believe the client and try to understand him or her. The therapist must be willing to feel the emotions with the client or else the client endures it alone.

physicians than mental health professionals. Physicians are less likely to identify psychological problems in older adults and more likely to attribute symptoms to age (Hays, 1996). Thus, older adults (and their families and caretakers) need to be educated about the nature of mental health problems that can occur for this population and where to obtain appropriate help.

Hays (1996) notes that elderly individuals have lower rates of affective disorders than younger adults, although anxiety disorders are approximately the same as the general population. Only a minority of elderly persons has dementia and most remain mentally sharp. Be aware of alcohol abuse and abuse of prescription drugs for this population. Because of the increased number of prescription drugs for this age group, the chance of negative drug interactions or reactions with alcohol increases dramatically. Often these reactions resemble psychological or organic conditions.

Older adults have to deal with issues such as the loss of friends and other significant individuals, cultural devaluation of their group, health and physical problems, forced isolation, and more limited financial resources. Social contacts are important, and engaging in either paid or volunteer work enhances the self-esteem and life satisfaction of older individuals (Acquino, Russell, Cutrona, & Altmaier, 1996). Other issues that face older adults may also include chronic illness and disability, caregiving for a loved one, and change of roles (e.g., retirement, loss of spouse).

When counseling older adults, consider engaging in the following: obtaining medical assessments for your client, establishing support systems for them in the community, engaging in a life review in which the older adult discusses the positive aspects of their experiences (such as having met and survived challenges), helping couples negotiate issues regarding time spent alone and together (especially after retirement), and helping adults close to the end of their lives resolve a sense of attachment to familiar objects by having them decide how heirlooms, keepsakes, and photos will be distributed and cared for (Hays, 1996).

Older Youth

Horne and Kiselica (1999) suggest that the therapist be more flexible and open to nontraditional methods of interaction in establishing rapport with older boys. For example, consider meeting at the boy's residence, a recreational center, or some other familiar place where the adolescent feels comfortable. This conveys that the counselor is willing to enter the boy's world and comprehend its realities. They have also found it helpful to develop a relationship with a boy while taking turns shooting baskets, walking side by side down the street, or sharing a snack at a fast food restaurant. The therapist should also create a male-friendly office environment by displaying sports magazines, posters of athletes or musicians, and offering the young man a soft drink or snack. Likewise for older girls, the therapist may want to include posters that are appealing to this population and items of interest throughout the office.

CAUTION

Adolescents and Privacy

Adolescents are very concerned with privacy. Discuss the issue of confidentiality at the beginning of the session and be clear on who has access to what information. Remember to cover such areas as substance use, sexual activity, and harmful behavior to self or others. Check out your state's policy on confidentiality with minors.

Horne and Kiselica (1999) also feel that it is a good idea to have flexible office hours so that the client doesn't have to wait until the scheduled appointment time in order to talk with the therapist. Older youth respond well to people they feel are available to them and whom they feel are helpful. Upon the initial meeting, engage in nonthreatening, casual conversation, perhaps about what music they are listening to or anything interesting that might have happened in school that day. In order to be most helpful, therapists may need to initially help with practical concerns, such as finding employment or helping them work out a conflict with a peer.

Families and Couples

While interviewing often focuses on an individual, it may be the case, especially when working with children or those clients who are not competent, that you are meeting with several people at once. When establishing rapport in a family or group context, you may want to keep the following in mind. First, there will be more people wanting an opportunity to provide their viewpoint so you may need to schedule more time for gathering information (either as additional sessions or a longer session). Additionally, with more people providing the therapist with information, there is more opportunity for disagreements and inconsistencies to occur, and yet validation of factual information by other individuals can be obtained.

CAUTION

Having an understanding and empathy for each member of the family, as well as an understanding and empathy for the relationships between family members, is not only complex and difficult but is sure to increase the possibility of the therapist becoming influenced by his or her own unresolved family issues and beliefs.

Triangulation may pose additional problems. It takes place when one person in the group tries to obtain support or sympathy from the therapist, and by aligning with the therapist gains more power than the other members of the group. To avoid triangulation (or at least limit it), the therapist should make a conscious effort to treat each person in the group with equal warmth and interest. Introduce yourself to each family member as you make your initial contact and check in with each member throughout the session.

It is important to discuss and clearly explain confidentiality policies. The therapist must clearly state how the members within the session should handle personal information outside of the session. During the session the therapist will also need to set limits regarding putdowns and criticisms directed toward other members. This is not only nonproductive; it is destructive and diminishes the family's confidence in the therapist's ability to work with them.

Finally, thank each member for coming in. To coordinate such a group effort requires commitment on everyone's part. Let them know that you take it as a sign that they are involved and care about what happens to that particular member. With family members present, it is easier to obtain a commitment from everyone that they will be involved in the treatment.

Gay Men and Lesbian Women

The therapist should be careful to assess all factors in the problems presented by lesbian women and gay men so as not to pay an inordinate amount of attention to sexual orientation. Therapists should remember to address possible societal issues and their role in the problems faced by lesbians and gay men. Garnets, Hancock, Cochran, Goodchilds, and Peplau (1998) agree that the therapist has the responsibility to display accurate information about gay and lesbian issues. Therapists must be sensitive to the degree of prejudice and discrimination faced by this population and yet not attribute the cause of all their problems to societal pressures and prejudice. Do not focus on sexual orientation when it is not relevant, because the problems may be completely unrelated to sexual orientation.

Garnets et al. (1998) note that the biases of the therapist may influence diagnostic impressions and treatment. They warn therapists, for example, to not assume that children of gay men and lesbian women have problems that are a result of their parents' sexual orientation (or that gay men and lesbians cannot be good parents because of their sexual orientation). They also remind therapists to respect the importance of privacy for gay men and lesbians and be aware of the consequences of "coming out." The decision to publicly reveal one's sexual orientation can only be made after a careful and realistic discussion of the pros and cons of disclosure. Therapists must be aware of the impact that negative societal pressures (perhaps internalized) and homophobia have on identity development and respect sexual orientation without attempting to change it or trivialize it. (See Rapid Reference 4.2.)

≡ Rapid Reference 4.2

Establishing Rapport with Special Populations

1. For young children, decide with whom you will meet, show respect and friendly interest, make the office child-friendly, allow children to engage in activities while in the session, and be knowledgeable about child development.

2. For an abused population, share decisions and control with the client. Develop trust through consistency, follow-through, honesty, and respect for the client, and respect boundaries both physically (as in touching) and emotionally (as in allowing the client to talk when they are ready).

3. For older adults, be knowledgeable regarding issues faced by older adults, be aware of substance abuse (including prescription drugs) and drug interactions, and check for issues of loss, negative stereotyping against the elderly, limited finances, health problems, and social isolation.

4. For older youth, be flexible regarding meeting places and office hours, create a friendly office environment geared toward their age, and help with practical concerns such as finding a job or resolving a school conflict.

5. For families, establish rapport with each member, avoid triangulation (e.g., siding consistently with one member of the family), discuss how confidentiality will be handled outside of the session, and set limits on put-downs and harsh criticisms.

6. For gay men and lesbian women, address societal issues and their effects, assess all factors involved in the problem without limiting it exclusively to sexual orientation, be aware of the consequences of "coming out" and discuss it with the client, and utilize community resources.

CULTURAL CONSIDERATIONS

African Americans

When working with African Americans, a therapist should be aware of the importance of extended family. This is accomplished by acknowledging and respecting the role of extended family members but also by gathering information about who is living in the home, who helps out, who is considered a family member, and what their relationship is to the family.

In terms of other family dynamics and practices, physical punishment is more likely to be used by African American parents than Caucasian parents as a source of discipline (Sue & Sue, 1999). However, while some types of physical discipline have been related to more acting-out behavior in Caucasian children, this was not found in African American children. Physical discipline should not be seen as an indication of a lack of parental warmth.

Communication styles are different for African Americans as compared to their Caucasian counterparts. For example, Sue and Sue (1999) note that African Americans communicate nonverbally more than Caucasian individuals and place more emphasis on nonverbal messages, believing them to be a more accurate indication of one's true feelings and beliefs. African Americans have learned that verbal interactions may be less trustworthy. Additionally, African American styles of communication are often emotional, animated, heated, interpersonal, and confrontational. There is a difference, however, between using this style to debate a position and discover where the other person stands versus an argument that expresses anger and hostility. Caucasian therapists may not be aware of the difference in intent when they experience this type of interaction.

African American clients are often distrustful of Caucasian counselors based on a history of injustice and minority status. It becomes very important for the therapist to establish a trusting relationship. African American clients will try to get a feel for the therapist and test the relationship, perhaps by directly challenging the therapist or acting in a very guarded and aloof manner. For some African American clients, establishing an egalitarian relationship with the therapist is of primary importance before beginning the therapeutic work. Only then will the client feel free to engage in introspection and personal disclosure. The therapist can facilitate the therapy process by establishing trust, engaging in conversations about events in the client's community, sharing some of his or her own background, and demonstrating interest in the client's unique cultural experiences.

Lower socioeconomic status (SES) clients who are concerned with survival or making it through the day expect advice and suggestions from the therapist and prefer a therapist who is active and directive. Appointments made weeks in advance with short, weekly 50-min contacts are not consistent with the need to seek immediate solutions. Additionally, Sue and Sue (1999) point out that many lower SES people operate under what is called "minority standard time," which is the tendency of poor people to have a low regard for punctuality. They have learned that endless waits are associated with medical clinics, police stations, and governmental agencies. The therapist will need to be flexible and available for these clients if he or she wants to be effective.

Counselor variables that are barriers to counseling an African American population include racism and prejudice (e.g., feeling superior over another group), which Sue and Sue (1999) feel is often a subtle evaluation of the client's behaviors such as lifestyle, parenting methods, and family practices as they compare to the therapist's own values and experiences. Another barrier to working with this population is color blindness, believing that African American clients are the same as any other client. This prevents the therapist from examining possible influences of culture and racism on the problem. On the other hand, paternalism, which leads the therapist to interpret the client's problems as always stemming from racism or prejudice, is equally a barrier to effective intervention. Finally, Horne and Kiselica (1999) recommend that therapists utilize community-based group-oriented programs administered by African Americans as an effective way to serve this population.

Asian Americans

Sue and Sue (1999) write that Asian American families follow a hierarchy of status with men and elders at the top. The oldest son in the family has the obligation to care for his parents and carry on the family name. It is important for the therapist to recognize that even when married, the culture expects the son to show primary allegiance to the family of origin. Children's roles are to be obedient and not argue, and because children's behaviors, good or bad, reflect on the family, shame and guilt are used to control and train the children. In fact, it is a very strong emotion in children. Children are taught to be sensitive to the reactions and evaluations of others, again because their behavior reflects on the family. Girls are expected to be passive and occupy a less important role in the family (as they are expected to adhere to the expectations of their husbands' families upon marriage). Because the child directly reflects on the family, there is a great deal of emphasis on academic success. Not only do Asian American students have the highest levels of academic achievement, but also the highest fear of academic failure compared to other ethnic groups (Eaton & Dembo, 1997).

The father maintains an authoritative and distant role and is less emotionally involved with his children. The father's decisions are not questioned. Mothers are more responsive to the children but use less nurturance and more verbal and physical punishments than Caucasian mothers. They often serve as the intermediary between father and children. Asian American parents are more restrictive, protective, and emotionally unresponsive to their children than Caucasian parents. Care is shown not by displays of affection, but by doing for the family.

In terms of communication, Asian Americans tend to discourage strong expressions of emotions because they are disruptive to family order and are self-centered (e.g., focusing attention on the individual's needs and desires versus focusing on the good of the community and family). Maturity and wisdom are associated with one's ability to control emotions and feelings, and this applies not only to expressions of anger and frustration but also love and affection.

Children in traditional Japanese culture have been taught not to speak until spoken to and patterns of communication tend to be vertical, flowing from those of higher status and prestige to those of lower. Many Japanese clients, to show respect for a therapist who is older, wiser, and occupies a position of higher status, may respond with si-

CAUTION

Intimate revelations of personal or social problems may not be acceptable in Asian American cultures, because they reflect on the whole family and there is pressure from the family not to reveal personal matters to strangers or outsiders. This reluctance should be viewed by the therapist as a cultural factor, not resistance. Additionally, emotional restraint, which characterizes many Asian immigrants, may be viewed incorrectly by Caucasian therapists as a defense mechanism or indicating some underlying psychopathology or developmental problem.

lence. Many Asian cultures are characterized by deference to authority. For many traditional Asian American groups, too much eye contact is uncomfortable, and in some Asian and Moslem countries, touching anyone with the left hand may be considered an obscenity, because the left hand is viewed as unclean while the right one is considered to be clean. In Filipino cultures, a hesitant yes actually means no (Sue & Sue, 1999).

Asian American clients are less likely to utilize mental health services. Often, shame and disgrace are associated with admitting to emotional problems. Many Asian elders believe that thinking too much about something can cause problems, and the advice they give to their children when they feel frustration, anger, depression, or anxiety is to simply not think about it. Instead, they are told to keep busy. Additionally, therapy engages in self-exploration, which is discouraged by traditional Asian Americans, because it is an individual approach as opposed to a collective approach. Finally, Nguyen (1985) notes that another reason why Asian Americans may not use mental health services is that, in many Southeast Asian countries, having a psychological problem is the same as being insane or overtly admitting inferiority.

While admission of a psychological problem is unlikely, Asian Americans often present physical complaints as a common and culturally accepted means of expressing their psychological and emotional stress. Instead of talking about anxiety and depression, the therapist will often hear complaints involving headaches, fatigue, restlessness, and disturbances in sleep and appetite (Toarmino & Chun, 1997). Somatic complaints should be dealt with as real problems, and this may include the use of physical treatments such as medication.

Sue and Sue (1999) note several items a therapist should consider when working with Asian American clients. For example, due to lack of information, misconceptions, and discomfort with the concept of therapy, it is important to prepare the Asian American client for coun-

DON'T FORGET

Utilization of Services by Asian Americans

In a study by Atkinson, Ponterotto, and Sanchez (1984), Vietnamese students in the U.S. were less likely to recognize the need for mental health services, were more concerned about the stigma attached to therapy, were less open about personal problems, and were less confident that mental health professionals would be of any help.

DON'T FORGET

Interview Techniques With Asian Americans

Because of the stigma against mental illness, the norm against sharing private matters with outsiders, and the lack of client knowledge of the mental health field, the therapist should refrain from asking too many personal questions during the initial session.

seling by discussing the roles of the therapist and client and the expectations and process of therapy. Issues of confidentiality must be discussed clearly and early in the process. The therapist should also consider that asking the client to reflect on his or her feelings is viewed as intrusive. Therefore, the therapist should ask such questions sparingly, with understanding and support, since it leads to discomfort. Use restraint when gathering information but conduct a thorough analysis of current environmental concerns, including an assessment of financial and social needs.

To be most helpful to the client, focus on the specific problem brought in and help the client develop his or her goals for therapy (e.g., work within the client's framework). Sue and Sue (1999) also suggest that the therapist take an active and directive role. Because of cultural expectations and a lack of experience with mental health therapy, the clients will rely on the counselor to furnish direction. Additionally, consider intergenerational conflicts and be willing to accept the hierarchical structure of the family. Therapy should be time-limited, focus on concrete resolution of problems, and deal with the present or immediate future.

Hispanic Americans

Hispanic Americans place high value on the family. In fact, family needs are put before individual aspiration. For example, grown men are often expected to remain at home until married and afterward to be available to do the parents' bidding. Avila and Avila (1995) note that allegiance to the family is of primary importance, taking precedence over any outside concerns such as school attendance or work. Older children, for example, may be kept at home to help care for ill siblings or parents. One of the consequences of valuing the family over the individual is that divorce is much less acceptable and less often seen as an alternative to marital difficulties.

Traditional Hispanic families are hierarchical with special authority given to the elderly, the parents, and males. The father assumes the role of primary authority figure, and children are expected to be obedient and are not consulted on family decisions. Sexual behaviors of adolescent females are severely restricted whereas male children are given greater freedom. Children are expected to contribute financially to the family when possible, and older children are expected to take care of and protect younger siblings when they are away from home. Marriage and parenthood are entered into early in life and are seen as stabilizing influences.

Hispanic males are reminded continuously that their first loyalty is to their parents, siblings, and childhood friends, not to themselves or others outside the bloodline. Even though the Hispanic male tends to be much more indulged than his white counterpart, he is also expected to live more in accord with a regime of family obligation. For example, he is expected to assist the less achieving family members, even if they are undeserving. If the male achieves success, he is expected not to draw attention to his good fortune but instead to display an attitude of humility. Boastfulness and drawing attention to the self are taken as signs of disrespect or impoliteness.

When a Hispanic American male client talks about the pressure he feels from his family to go into the family business, a culturally aware and informed therapist understands that males are viewed by their elders as excessively egotistical if they were to pursue education in places remote from their homes or pursue technical careers beyond their parents' understanding (Sue & Sue, 1999). Much of the fate of the male is dictated by his ancestry (e.g., his work and associates as well as his marriage partner, where he works, and where he travels).

The Hispanic male is typically a man of his word and embraces the values of physical toughness and bravery. The ideal Hispanic male is also self-reliant, unflinching in the face of external threats, the ultimate authority of his household, highly protective of both his own reputation and that of his family, uncomplaining, and should act like a "man" (e.g., marry early, have children, and be the breadwinner as soon as possible). There is much less equality between the sexes within the Hispanic culture than in other groups. It is expected that he view women as essentially subservient but valued for their domestic abilities and physical allure. It is also demanded of him that they receive his complete physical protection.

Central to the family's configuration is the mother. She is given the virtues of saintliness and is taught that she should display the characteristics of infinite patience and understanding as well as be wholly attentive to her husband's ongoing needs. Women are socialized to feel that they are inferior and that suffering and being a martyr are characteristics of a good woman. Traditionally, they are expected to be nurturing, submissive to the male, and self-sacrificing.

The Hispanic father is usually distant and absent, especially in the earlier years of development when children evidence dependence, to which many adult Hispanic males have trouble relating. Hispanic fathers, in fact, often show impatience with helplessness or vulnerability, urging their sons to "be a man" as quickly as possible (Sue & Sue, 1999).

The Catholic religion has had a major influence and a source of comfort in Hispanic groups. There is strong belief in the importance of prayer, that sacrifice in this world is helpful in reaching salvation, that being charitable to others is a virtue, and that you should endure wrongs committed against you (Yamamoto & Acosta, 1982). The consequences of these beliefs are that many Hispanics feel that problems or events are fated and cannot be changed.

Interpersonal relationships are maintained and nurtured within a large network of family and friends. There is a deep respect and affection among friends and family. Because of these relationships and resources, outside help is generally not sought until advice is obtained from the extended family and close friends. Additionally, many Hispanic families are quite wary of disclosing private matters with strangers. Talking about or sharing views of problems with others may be seen as a sign of weakness. The male, in particular, may have difficulty interacting with agencies and professionals outside of the family, because he may feel that he is not fulfilling his role.

Although the parents may have a strong desire for their children's conduct to improve, they are prone to minimize the full extent of their domestic difficulties (e.g., the father's drinking problem, ongoing financial pressures) to outsiders. The therapist, therefore, needs to assume an active role, asking about matters that may not have been volunteered but are crucial for understanding the child's

CAUTION

Given the traditional view of the woman's role, a Hispanic American man may have a particularly tough time working with a female therapist.

living situation. These may include the family's past and present immigration status, history of police or legal encounters by any immediate family members, nature of disciplinary practices in the home, financial status of the household, psychiatric history, or medical background (Sue & Sue, 1999). Techniques should be employed that are active, concrete, and problem solving in their orientation. Behavior therapy fits client expectations of direct intervention, specific tasks, and an active, direct counselor.

In conducting an interview or ongoing therapy sessions with Hispanic clients, cultural factors must be considered. For example, closer personal space is the custom and if the therapist moves away due to discomfort, this may be interpreted as aloofness, a desire not to communicate, or even a sign of haughtiness and superiority (Sue & Sue, 1999). Latin Americans may not feel comfortable with a desk between them and the person to whom they are talking. Because of the importance of the extended family, family therapy is often recommended. In less acculturated families, interviewing the father first shows recognition of the father's authority. Also, more formal relationships are expected with more traditional Hispanic Americans. The counselor will be seen as an authority figure and should be formally dressed. Once trust has developed, the clients may form a close personal bond with the counselor. He or she may be perceived as a family member or friend and invited to family functions and given gifts (Sue & Sue, 1999). These behaviors are not evidence of dependency or lack of boundaries but a common cultural practice.

Native Americans

Horne and Kiselich (1999) note that Native Americans face many problems, including pressure to assimilate into a society that conflicts with Native values. Major issues for Native Americans include experiences of oppression and discrimination, identity crises, stereotyping, value conflicts, and suicide. They have endured social problems such as poverty, unemployed parents, inadequate health care, substandard housing, family dissolution, education that ignores their needs, and alcohol and drug abuse. Native Americans have the highest rate of completed suicide of any ethnic group, with age as a major risk factor. Specifically, youth between ages 10 and 24 have suicide rates three times as high as rates for the total population, and it is much more common among males (Horne & Kiselich).

DON'T FORGET

Navajo Indians: Therapists should keep in mind that the Navajo believe that to ponder death is to invite it. Therefore if they willingly respond to questions about suicidal ideation (e.g., as in therapy), then regardless of their answers, they are in actuality seeking help (Horne & Kiselich, 1999).

American Indian children appear to do well during the first few years of school but by the fourth grade, a pattern of decline and dropout occurs which becomes a significant drop in achievement motivation around the seventh grade. This is associated with a perception that school is not important to them for their future life plans. Schools may view American Indian children as unmotivated because there is a reluctance to compete with peers in the classroom. To compete would be seen as an expression of individuality and suggest that the student is better than the tribe (or class). Another school-related issue that may come up is that American Indian students may feel it necessary to show test answers to another tribe member. Again, this reflects the spirit of cooperation and the value placed upon giving the tribe and family precedence over the individual.

Although we are grouping all Native Americans under one heading as if they represent one culture, the optimal designation is tribal affiliation. There is considerable diversity among tribes, but some generalizations can be made of the differences between traditional Native Americans and the mainstream culture (Horne & Kiselich, 1999). For example, Native American cultures believe in harmony with nature as opposed to the mainstream cultural belief of control over nature. Native American cultures are oriented to the present, which is in opposition to the mainstream culture's emphasis on the future. Native Americans emphasize cooperation and a view of the nature of humankind as generally good; honor and respect is obtained by sharing and giving. In fact, refusing to accept an invitation to share drinks or substances with a member of the same tribe would be considered an affront to the individual making the offer and considered a violation of the value of sharing and giving. Punctuality and planning for the future may be viewed as unimportant; the American Indian culture, rather than seeking to control the environment, accepts things as they are.

For most tribes, the extended family is the basic unit. Children are often raised by relatives such as aunts, uncles, and grandparents who live in separate households (Hildebrand, Phenice, Gray, & Hines, 1996). Extended family often extends through the second cousin. It is not unusual to have youngsters stay in a variety of different households. Children learn by observing and participating, not by being lectured or hearing discussions. Open displays of affection between men and women are rare even after marriage. Some men follow the tradition of treating women as inferior and are reluctant to have close interpersonal contacts; however, they may engage frequently in same-sex social gatherings.

Traditional Native American cultures have transmitted reluctance for a family or individual in trouble to seek help (Horne & Kiselich, 1999). Many tribes believe that mental illness is a justifiable outcome of human weakness or the result of avoiding the discipline necessary to maintain cultural values. Traditional Native Americans seldom look to nonnative counseling as a means of improving their way of life. They recognize the need for professionals only when community networks are unavailable or undesirable. When a family needs help, the extended family network is the first source to be contacted. Second, a spiritual leader may be consulted to resolve problems. Third, if the problem is still unresolved, the family will contact tribal elders. Last, when all these fail, the family may seek help from mainstream options (Horne & Kiselich, 1999). Thus, the helper must recognize that the Native American family may have experienced a series of frustrated attempts to resolve the problem.

The most appropriate approach to acquiring initial information from Native Americans is a gentle, noninvasive one with few direct questions. The therapist should learn about tribal culture, because it demonstrates an interest in the client and enhances the establishment of rapport. Another way to demonstrate respect for Native American culture is to encourage the participation of the extended family in the therapeutic process. The therapist may also want to schedule appointments that allow for flexibility in ending the session; traditional Native Americans prefer open-ended sessions to ensure closure to the presenting problem without time constraints (Sue & Sue, 1999). The therapist should respect the use of silence and also be aware that some Eskimos prefer to sit side by side rather than across from one another when talking about intimate aspects of their lives.

It is important to discuss the counseling process, emphasize confidentiality, and describe a typical session. While Native American clients will experience discomfort with the demand for self-disclosure or intrusive questioning, the therapist may make them more comfortable by initially modeling self-disclosure. Confrontation is considered to be rude and should be kept at a minimum. Allow the client time to finish his or her thoughts without interruption.

Native American clients look to the healer to identify the cause of the problem and work the cures, so the therapist should consider using helping strategies that elicit practical solutions to problems. At the same time, a helping professional must demonstrate patience, exemplified by not offering advice or interpretation without being invited to do so. Sue and Sue (1999) note that American Indians work hard to prevent discord and disharmony. They may find it easier to agree with the therapist on what needs to be done but will not follow through with suggestions.

Combining services of traditional healers with traditional counseling can be very effective, because it displays respect for traditions (Horne & Kiselich, 1999). A blend of techniques using myth and metaphor may be considered as an alternative to straight talk therapy. Use of metaphors allows helpers to tap into a world of symbolic language that is familiar to Native American populations (Horne & Kiselich, 1999). Helpers may wish to use traditional spiritual dimensions in group work. For example, group sessions may begin and end with a prayer that would be acceptable to represented tribes. This acknowledges that higher powers play a role in physical and mental happiness. Another culturally appropriate technique is the use of guided imagery. Guided imagery may be used, for example, with a youth who has concerns about self-concept by asking him to visualize himself as he perceives himself to be and then visualize how he would like to be ideally.

Irish Catholic Americans

Irish Catholic families typically display a very strong mother-son bond. However, extended family relationships among Irish Catholics are often not close, because respect for boundaries supersedes concern for relatives (Sue & Sue, 1999). For this reason, Irish Catholics are unlikely to turn to extended family for support during times of crisis, especially if that crisis could be viewed as an embarrassment for the family.

Irish Catholics experience shame in seeking counseling and prefer individual and family counseling, which is limited to immediate family members. Irish Catholics view counseling as analogous to going to a priest for confession, and once they start counseling, they are able to describe their difficulties at length, but with an indirect and superficially cheerful manner. Although humor is a useful tool, Irish Americans tend to have difficulty expressing affection and anger, and avoid conflict by relying on humor and "blarney" (Sue & Sue, 1999). Because therapists are given the same sort of respect as priests, Irish Catholic clients are diligent about completing homework assignments. They prefer behavioral and solution-focused therapies because they are objectively focused on making changes in behavior. On the other hand, Irish Catholic clients tend to be uncomfortable with gestalt therapy and psychodrama, which involve highly expressive and tactile forms of expression, and psychoanalytic models that overemphasize the dark or sinful side of humans.

Jewish Americans

Family is viewed as an important feature of Jewish identity. Although parents may contribute to the problems experienced by their children, they tend to seek help when their children are troubled and commonly commit themselves to counseling once they are engaged in the therapeutic process. Jewish boys tend to be highly sensitive to, and affected by, family problems. Pressure to succeed academically can contribute to the emergence of somatic symptoms that have no organic origins. Boys who are unable to fulfill high academic expectations may be a source of shame for the family, but typically this shame is experienced by family members unconsciously and communicated to the boy implicitly. The Jewish tradition emphasizes intellectual exchange, introspection, and the discussion of problems, which allows most Jewish clients to adapt easily and respond enthusiastically to counseling, insight-oriented psychotherapy, and bibliotherapy (Sue & Sue, 1999).

CHAPTER SUMMARY

1. The therapeutic environment should be designed to provide the most comfortable environment for the client. Factors such as the furniture, privacy, use of language, accommodations, the therapist's

attire, and any other adaption based on the client's demographics should be considered.

2. To develop a positive therapeutic relationship, the therapist accepts the client as a person rather than judging him or her.

3. Therapists should be careful not to dwell on or make assumptions for clients regarding any stereotypic beliefs for a group that they may be part of.

4. The following guidelines are summarized for various ethnic/cultural groups.

   a. African Americans

      1. African Americans may need to feel a more egalitarian relationship with the therapist before disclosing personal information.

      2. Therapists should respect the importance of extended family.

      3. For clients of lower socioeconomic status, the therapist will need to be more active by providing advice and solutions, in addition to flexibility regarding scheduling.

      4. African Americans value nonverbal communication over verbal communication, so it is not what the therapist says as much as what the therapist does.

   b. Asian Americans

      1. Emotional restraint is seen as a virtue.

      2. Physical complaints are a culturally acceptable means of expressing psychological distress.

      3. Admitting to emotional problems is viewed as shameful, selfish, and an admission of insanity or inferiority for some Asian American groups.

      4. Asian Americans may view personal questions asked by the therapist as intrusive.

   c. Hispanic Americans

      1. Talking about problems is seen as a sign of weakness, leading many Hispanic American clients to minimize their difficulties.

      2. Many Hispanic Americans prefer closer personal space.

      3. Therapists should respect the importance of extended family, perhaps by even including them in sessions.

      4. Hispanic American clients, after developing trust in the thera-

pist, view him or her as a close friend or family member and treat him or her accordingly.

  d. Native Americans

    1. Native Americans tend to accept things as they are versus trying to change their situation.

    2. They often prefer open-ended sessions to ensure closure without time constraints.

    3. They believe that mental illness is due to human weakness and thinking about problems too much.

    4. Confrontation is seen as rude.

    5. Due to a strong aversion to discord, clients may agree with the therapist but not follow through on assignments.

    6. It is helpful to combine traditional therapy with Native American healing techniques and tradition (e.g., metaphors, storytelling, guided imagery, and prayer).

  e. Irish Catholic Americans

    1. Irish Catholics tend to prefer that therapy involves the immediate family members and not extended family.

    2. Although they are conscientious about therapy, they tend to use humor to avoid negative emotions and conflicts.

    3. They prefer solution-focused therapy (and are least comfortable with Gestalt and psychoanalytic therapies).

  f. Jewish Americans

    1. Jewish Americans willingly engage in therapy and respond well to insight-oriented psychotherapy.

    2. They tend to value intellectual exchanges and introspection.

🔺 TEST YOURSELF 🔺

I. The ability to see things from a client's perspective is known as

  (a) rapport.

  (b) congruence.

  (c) empathy.

  (d) unconditional positive regard.

(continued)

2. **What might a therapist do upon initial contact with a client?**
   (a) Ask for payment in advance
   (b) Engage in small talk to put the client at ease
   (c) Talk about his or her own family and their difficulties
   (d) Avoid asking questions until trust has developed

3. **For an abused client, which of the following is most likely to be impaired?**
   (a) Ability to trust
   (b) Cognitive functioning
   (c) Memory
   (d) Motivation

4. **Which group is most likely to be seen by a physician rather than a mental health practitioner?**
   (a) Children
   (b) Gay men and lesbian women
   (c) Elderly adults
   (d) Jewish Americans

5. **Which group places great value on the extended family?**
   (a) African Americans
   (b) Hispanic Americans
   (c) Native Americans
   (d) All of the above

6. **Which group is most likely to engage in heated, confrontational communication?**
   (a) African Americans
   (b) Asian Americans
   (c) Irish Catholic Americans
   (d) All of the above

7. **Hispanic males traditionally have a primary obligation and loyalty to**
   (a) the wife.
   (b) the parents.
   (c) friends.
   (d) himself.

8. **Which cultural group would be most comfortable with psychodynamic therapy?**
   (a) Hispanic Americans
   (b) Asian Americans
   (c) Irish Catholic Americans
   (d) Jewish Americans

9. **If a therapist does not feel empathy toward a client, he or she should at least pretend to show it.** True or False?

10. **Asian Americans are more likely to present with physical complaints than psychological problems.** True or False?

11. **"Minority standard time" refers to the tendency of people from a lower SES to wait, as long as it takes, to receive services.** True or False?

12. **The highest rate of completed suicide occurs in Asian Americans.** True or False?

13. **What might you do to establish rapport with a child?**

14. **What considerations go into creating a comfortable setting for a client?**

15. **As the therapist, under what situations might you discuss your personal experiences with a client?**

16. **What should a therapist keep in mind when working with an abused client?**

17. **Discuss reasons why Asian Americans are less likely to utilize therapy. What might a therapist do to make it less uncomfortable?**

Answers: 1. c; 2. b; 3. a; 4. c; 5. d; 6. a; 7. b; 8. d; 9. False; 10. True; 11. False; 12. False; 13. There are several behaviors, such as speaking at the child's level, being non-threatening, moving slowing in attaining information, and incorporating play, that will increase rapport. 14. Consider the client's usual level of comfort. For example, an adult professional might expect a more formal setting than a child. 15. Personal experiences can be helpful when it is therapeutic and when sufficient rapport has been established. 16. When working with an abused client, the therapist must be careful in developing rapport and trust. This client can be quite vulnerable and may have several difficulties opening up to another person. 17. Asian Americans may be less likely to seek professional counseling services for many reasons. One is the shame associated with having emotional problems. Another is the belief that psychological problems are equated with inferiority, as well as the idea that exploring a problem can increase it and that ignoring it is more helpful.

Five

Biopsychosocial (biological, psychological, social) information provides an understanding of a number of areas in the client's life. It goes far beyond simply forming a diagnosis, by viewing the client from several perspectives. It provides the context within which these symptoms have occurred. Merely gathering diagnostic information does not sufficiently paint a picture of the client's history and current functioning in biological, psychological, and social areas. More than any other information received in the initial sessions, the biopsychosocial information describes specific strengths, needs, preferences, and abilities (SNAPs) that can be incorporated into the treatment plan. Biopsychosocial information is not only useful for the therapist who is working with the client, but is required by the major accrediting agencies to ensure that adequate procedures and policies are followed and that the most effective treatments are provided.

The information received in the biopsychosocial assessment is typically obtained through a combination of written and verbal means. Most commonly, prior to the initial interview, the client fills out a personal history questionnaire that contains biopsychosocial material. The therapist then reviews the information and makes additional queries based on the client's written information. The therapist may also follow a structured interview format and ask these questions of the client while obtaining clarifying information at the same time. The information is then incorporated into the diagnosis and treatment.

The relationship between the presenting problem and the client's historical information is important both diagnostically and in treatment planning. For example, if someone has never received or needed mental health services but is now suicidal, treatment will be different than someone with chronic mental illness. The more chronic or cyclical the problem, the poorer the prognosis. Other factors, such as family history, further affect the etiology and prognosis

Table 5.1 Prognosis and Treatment, Considering the Etiology Mental Health Concerns

Chronicity	Situational Factors	Genetic Factors
Acute	Positive prognosis. Short-term treatment.	Moderate prognosis depending on treatment in which insight may be helpful. Multidisciplinary treatment (psychological/medical).
Chronic	Moderate prognosis. Treatment focuses on dealing with coping skills. Psychoeducational treatment is helpful.	Poorest prognosis. Long-term treatment. Highest likelihood of medications' being needed. Multidisciplinary treatment.

for treatment. Table 5.1 depicts the relationship between etiology and chronicity on prognosis. Clients with the best prognosis in therapy are those with an acute problem in which situational factors are the primary influence on their current mental health concern. When genetic factors are coupled with chronic mental health concerns, prognosis of successful treatment is much lower.

SNAPs

SNAPs, an acronym for Strengths, Needs, Abilities, and Preferences, is becoming increasingly more popular as a means of monitoring client characteristics. The collection of SNAPs begins in the initial interview and continues throughout treatment to discharge. SNAPs consider the client's input and point of view, and they are carefully assessed and monitored since outcomes may be partially based on how treatment has focused on the client's SNAPs. Like mental health symptoms, SNAPs also vary from client to client. Examples and definitions of SNAPs can be found in Rapid Reference 5.1. SNAPs information can be incorporated into each component of the biopsychosocial assessment (e.g., social, cultural, spiritual, etc.).

DON'T FORGET

Although a client's demographic information such as background and SNAPs may not be helpful in validating a specific diagnosis, the information is crucial in planning specific treatment and understanding the client's world.

≡Rapid Reference 5.1

Definitions and Examples of SNAPs

Strengths: The client's personal characteristics that can be incorporated into the treatment process to aid recovery.

Examples: Insightful, intelligent, spiritual, cooperative, creative, friendly, compassionate, willing to change, hard working, has a sense of humor, open to treatment, compromising, open minded, honest, generous, in control of impulses

Needs: Areas in the client's life or environment, which, if met, will increase the availability and prognosis of treatment.

Examples: Transportation, shelter, social support, employment, finances, health insurance, case management services, telephone, medications, food, saftey, child care, companionship, adequate clothing, heat, accessibility

Abilities: Specific learning or skills the client brings into treatment that can be incorporated to increase its effectiveness.

Examples: Social skills, resourcefulness, job skills, organizational skills, leadership, financial management, reading, writing, recreation

Preferences: Choices the client desires during and after treatment.

Examples: Group therapy, day treatment, therapist characteristics, begin college, change jobs, join AA, (weekly) evening sessions, IOP (intensive outpatient treatment), specific types of counseling, nontraditional treatment, cultural/religious/sexual considerations.

COMPONENTS OF THE BIOPSYCHOSOCIAL ASSESSMENT

The biopsychosocial assessment is composed of three types of information: biological, psychological, and social. Biological information relates to the physical condition of the client. This includes genetic information (conditions that run in the family), current physical health, medications, past health issues, and, for children, an inquiry into labor, delivery, and early development. Social information taps into how the client relates to others and includes work history, legal history, family relationships, and marital history. Finally, psychological information relates to qualities within the client and might include areas such as how the client handles stress, past psychiatric history, and personality traits such as optimism, defensiveness, or low self-confidence. This information is extremely helpful because all three aspects are related to mental health disorders in etiology, maintenance, and treatment.

The interview begins by gathering basic, emotionally nonthreatening biographical information about the client. Background material, such as name, age, ethnic and cultural background, family information, employment, and so on, are collected to plan treatment that best fits the client's needs. The biopsychosocial assessment is an excellent opportunity to build rapport. As rapport develops, the presenting problem and diagnostic information are explored with increasingly more detail and emotional intensity, as found in the next chapter.

Social Relationships

A client's social functioning can play a major role in both diagnosis and treatment. Diagnostically, most disorders can result in social impairments. For example, a depressed person might withdraw from people, an anxious person might worry excessively about what other people think, an angry person might be easily irritated by others, a person with a behavioral disorder might act out in socially inappropriate ways, and a person with paranoia might have delusional thoughts about others' motives. Each, however, represents a different type of social impairment. Social impairments may maintain or exacerbate the clinical condition. For example, a person with poor social skills may not have developed a supportive network that would have an impact on reducing (or perhaps alleviating) such disorders as depression or stress-related disorders.

An assessment of social relationships provides a rich source of information about the client in his or her social environment. Comparisons of previous versus current social functioning aid in treatment planning. Clients with a history of adequate social functioning will most likely incorporate their social strengths in treatment whereas those with a background of inadequate or dysfunctional social skills may need to emphasize social skills training or experiences in their treatment. A client's current level of social relationships can influence the level of treatment. For example, a potentially suicidal client would have a higher chance of being hospitalized if no social supports were available to function as part of the treatment team who make themselves available to the client, especially in stressful situations. (See Rapid Reference 5.2.)

Family History and Dynamics

The relative importance of compiling a family history varies between theoretical schools of thought. However, whether the clinician is from a behavioral or

Rapid Reference 5.2

Examples of Types of Information Sought in Assessing Social Functioning

- How do you generally relate to other people? For example:

Follower	vs.	Leader
Paranoid	vs.	Overly trusting
Aggressive	vs.	Passive
Affectionate	vs.	Cold
Introvert	vs.	Extrovert
Submissive	vs.	Dominant
Avoidant	vs.	Outgoing
Argumentative	vs.	Pleases others
Defiant	vs.	Cooperative
Aloof	vs.	Attentive
Despise	vs.	Enjoy

- Assessment of SNAPs
- Do you currently have supportive friendships? How many? How close/supportive?
- What are some activities you might do with your family or friends?
- Say more about your family relationships/support?
- Do you experience any social stressors?
- Have there been recent changes in social functioning/supports/stressors?
- What changes do you desire?

psychodynamic perspective, the patterns of one's upbringing are important in evaluating how or why people behave as they do. A behavioral therapist may look more at what in the family was reinforcing to the client and how punishments may have affected him or her whereas a psychodynamic therapist may pay more attention to the client's early experiences and feelings toward the family. Important factors to consider include family medical history, socioeconomic status, educational level, marital history, and cultural considerations.

Treatment factors to consider are similar to those mentioned above in Social Relationships. Therapists from a systems orientation school of thought tend to view this part of the interview as crucial in understanding client behaviors. In such cases, information such as genograms and specific relationship dynamics in the client's current family and family of origin are standard components of the initial assessment. (See Rapid Reference 5.3.)

≋Rapid Reference 5.3

Examples of Types of Information Sought in Assessing Family History and Dynamics

- Assessment of SNAPs
- Were you raised by both of your parents?
- Tell me about the family you were raised in.
- Was there anything unusual about your family?
- Is there anything you wish was different in the family you were raised in?
- What did your parents do for a living?
- How did your parents/siblings treat you as a child?
- Were you or any of your siblings ever taken away from the home?
- Do you have any history of being abused or neglected?
- Were alcohol or drugs used in the home?
- How did you parents get along?
- How do you get along with your family now?
- Does anyone in your family have a history of mental health problems?
- What changes would you like to see in how you currently relate to your family (current and family of origin)?

Cultural and Ethnic Background and Practices

Clients from a minority culture may have concerns or experiences unique to their culture that present mental health or behavioral issues. The interviewer should have some familiarity with the client's cultural background. No matter what level of cultural awareness the clinician has, it is important to ask the client whether there are concerns unique to his or her background that he or she would like to address.

Both cultural and ethnic variables are important in understanding client concerns. Although the clinician may not understand every culture and ethnic background, sensitivity, respect, and nonjudgment are not only professional behaviors but also ethical mandates. When the clinician is not adequately familiar with the client's background, he or she should inquire about any cultural and ethnic preferences, and incorporate them into treatment. Simply being aware of cultural and ethnic preferences is certainly no substitute for being immersed in a culture, but some understanding is certainly better than no understanding or

Rapid Reference 5.4

Examples of Types of Information Sought in Assessing Cultural/Ethnic Considerations

- Assessment of SNAPs
- To which cultural or ethnic group, if any, do you belong?
- What do you see as most positive about your cultural or ethnic heritage?
- Are you experiencing any problems due to cultural or ethnic issues?
- Is there anything about your cultural or ethnic background you would like me to know?
- Are there any cultural or ethnic factors you would like incorporated in the counseling?
- What are some of these factors?
- How does your culture tend to feel about counseling?

misunderstanding. See Chapter 4 for more information about establishing rapport with clients of different ethnic groups. (See Rapid Reference 5.4.)

Spiritual/Religious Beliefs and Practices

The therapist must respect the client's spiritual and religious practices, if any, of the client. As in cultural/ethnic practices, the therapist should ask clients which practices, if any, are important to them. Although the therapist may or may not agree with the client's preferences, respect for the client's beliefs is an ethical matter. If the therapist cannot or will not work within the framework of the client's belief system, a new therapist should be assigned or an adequate referral should be sought.

The term spirituality has multiple meanings from attending religious meetings to being in touch with one's self to integrating the unseen forces in one's life. Spirituality and religion are diverse terms. The term religious often refers to a set of beliefs and practices acknowledging God, or a higher power, whereas spirituality is a more individually defined term.

The therapist must take caution not to prescribe his or her spiritual or religious practices to the client. The therapist's task is to work within the world of the client, rather than "enlighten" the client with the therapist's viewpoints.

Religious beliefs, at times, may appear as aberrant behaviors from someone outside the religious practice. For example, the concept of hearing the voice of God, may appear to be evidence of a thought disorder to a clinician who is not accustomed to such religious beliefs; however, it may be a normal part of a client's religious experience. Without adequately assessing spiritual and religious beliefs, the chance of misdiagnosis increases dramatically. Nevertheless, there are instances in which delusions of a religious nature are evidence of a thought disorder, so clinicians should fully explore this area with a client.

> ## CAUTION
>
> When interviewing a client whose spiritual/religious views seem unusual to you, do not assume that they are aberrant. Ask the client to explain them to you and research the practice, experience, or belief before attributing it to psychopathology.

Clients may also have concerns or significant experiences related to their spiritual or religious background. Sometimes these experiences will be

Putting It Into Practice

Religious, but Where Do You Draw the Line?

Joe was raised in a fundamental, protestant family. His Pentecostal beliefs included practices such as speaking in tongues, belief in miracles, hearing from God, and healing. Some people in his religious circle were considered prophets, who had a close relationship with God. To say that one had heard directly from God was not at all considered abnormal, but rather a place of honor and humility. After a number of significant stressors in his life, Joe proclaimed that he was Jesus Christ and offered to heal anyone who came to him. He stopped eating to demonstrate his faith, and stated that he could not be killed because he was the son of God.

His behaviors had gone beyond what was acceptable in his religious circle to being considered aberrant, and contradictory to his religious practices. He further placed himself in physical jeopardy by refusing to eat anymore. He had gone over the line.

Teaching Point: *Simply because someone is involved in nontraditional religious beliefs or practices, which could mimic delusions or hallucinations to an outsider, does not automatically exempt them from experiencing actual delusions or hallucinations, but clinicians should take care to fully assess whether or not a client's behaviors are normal relative to their spiritual or religious beliefs.*

strengths that can be incorporated into treatment (e.g., support network, concept of forgiveness, hope, prayer, meditation), and sometimes these issues will become a focus of treatment (e.g., fear of death, isolation or detachment from spirituality, overly self-centered and entrenched in material gain, or spiritual/religious differences with partner). (See Rapid Reference 5.5.)

Legal

Legal history and current legal status may be indicative of the client's level of social judgment, impulsivity, conformity, moral development, and respect for authority. A history of legal problems may even indicate a particular disorder such as mania, kleptomania, or antisocial personality disorder. Prognosis for successful treatment generally decreases as legal problems increase. This may be due to stress, lack of motivation for change, or issues that play a role in both legal problems and mental health problems such as a lack of social support, financial problems, drug use, or exposure to violence at a young age. A client with criminal legal problems is less likely to experience positive changes in treatment than one with civil legal issues.

≡Rapid Reference 5.5

Examples of Types of Information Sought in Assessing Spiritual/Religious Considerations

- Assessment of SNAPs
- How important to you are spiritual matters?
- Were you raised within a spiritual or religious group?
- Are you currently affiliated with a spiritual or religious group?
- Are you experiencing any problems due to spiritual or religious issues?
- Stressors/supports?
- Have you recently left or joined a spiritual or religious group?
- What are some of the spiritual/religious beliefs that are important to you?
- Would you like your spiritual/religious beliefs incorporated into the counseling?
- What are some of these factors?

Clients with no history of legal problems but who are currently going through civil legal proceedings, such as divorce or taking legal action against someone, may be experiencing much stress when entering treatment. Psychoeducational treatment such as coping skills, relaxation, or referral to a group that can provide support or information, or both may be the best treatment.

The information gained by assessing legal problems in a mental health evaluation often does not focus on the specific legal issues or crimes, unless it is the reason for referral or a forensic evaluation. Information to be gathered would include concerns such as impulsivity, what circumstances or stressors lead to criminal behavior, perceived gain, and repeated mistakes. (See Rapid Reference 5.6.)

Education

Although a client's education may not accurately predict outcomes of psychotherapy, it is helpful in selecting the type of therapy most beneficial to the client. Higher levels of education are often (but certainly not always) associated with

≣ *Rapid Reference 5.6*

Examples of Types of Information Sought in Assessing Legal Considerations

- Assessment of SNAPs
- Are you involved in any active cases (traffic, civil, criminal)?
- Are you presently on probation or parole?
- Past Legal History?
- Are you experiencing any problems due to legal issues? If so, what?
- Traffic violations?
- DWI, DUI, etc.?
- Criminal involvement?
- Type of plea?
- Civil involvement?
- Prison/Parole/Probation?
- Types of offenses (civil, criminal, money, domestic, assault, etc.)?
- Repeat offenses?

a greater level of insight. For example, a client diagnosed with Mild or Moderate Mental Retardation or traumatic brain injury is more apt to benefit from concrete, behavioral interventions, which focus on specific behaviors or changes in the environment, whereas someone with higher cognitive functioning may gain from therapy through personal insight using cognitive means.

Knowledge about one's level of education is often correlated with intellectual capacity, but other factors must be considered. For example, consider two people with similar IQ's entering college. One may drop out after the first month, whereas the other completes graduate school. Factors such as motivation, ability to cope with stress, mood, self-esteem, ability to adapt to new situations or new ideas, financial status, and persistence affect one's ability to complete college. If these same factors tend to repeat themselves in areas such as employment history and relationships, the information will be helpful in setting treatment goals. (See Rapid Reference 5.7.)

≡Rapid Reference 5.7

Examples of Types of Information Sought in Assessing Education

- Assessment of SNAPs
- Years of education?
- Special circumstances (e.g., learning disabilities, special education, gifted)?
- Attendance?
- Reasons for missing school?
- Extracurricular activities?
- Highest degree?
- Major(s)?
- If left school ... reason(s) for leaving?
- History of returning to school after leaving?
- Currently enrolled in school?
- Average school grades (current/previous)?
- Stressors while in school?
- Other training?

Employment History

A client's history of employment can be an excellent predictor of stability, ability to deal with authority, coping ability, and motivation. Aspects such as reasons for changing jobs, attendance, and advancement provide a good estimate of previous functioning and help in treatment planning. A client's employment may be affected considerably by most mental health diagnoses. Just as job stressors may affect the client's mental health condition, the client's mental health condition may lead to occupational difficulties. Occupational impairment is one of the most common purposes for clients seeking or being referred for services. (See Rapid Reference 5.8.)

≡*Rapid Reference 5.8*

Examples of Types of Questions Typically Asked in Assessing Employment History

- Assessment of SNAPs
- Current employment?
- Job history?
- Usual reason(s) for leaving jobs?
- Whose decision was it to leave?
- Average length of employment?
- How often do you miss work?
- Usual reasons for missing work
- History of dealing with coworkers, supervisors, subordinates?
- Currently ___ full-time ___ part-time ___ temp ___ laid off ___ disabled ___ retired ___ student ___ unemployed
- Current stressors of the job?
- Are you experiencing any problems due to your current job? If so, what?
- Vocational goals?
- Would you like these to be addressed in counseling?
- Changes desired?

Military Experience

Although many clients have no military experience (unless the therapist works at a Veterans Administration hospital), those who do will often describe their military experience as a lifechanging event. Factors such as length of service, type of discharge, and type of training may be indicative of emotional stability, ability to deal with authority, or a medical condition. Clients with combat experience should be assessed specifically for PTSD, which is often misdiagnosed as depression, anxiety, or other diagnoses. Other factors such as how the client deals with authority may have been significantly influenced in the military. (See Rapid Reference 5.9.)

Leisure/Recreational

Leisure and recreational activities are generally associated with normal functioning. They span both physical and social realms. It is not uncommon for these activities to decline when the client is under stress or experiencing mental health problems or cognitive declines. Leisure and recreational activities are assessed to provide information of premorbid functioning and often used in treatment planning in setting goals of returning to premorbid levels or enhancing skills in which deficits may occur.

═══ *Rapid Reference 5.9*

Examples of Types of Information Sought in Assessing Military Experience

- Military experience?
- Combat experience?
- Branch?
- Length of service?
- Discharge date?
- Type of discharge?

- Rank at discharge?
- Training?
- Duties?
- Able to deal with authority figures?
- Any problems in the military?

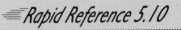

Rapid Reference 5.10

Examples of Types of Information Sought in Assessing Leisure/Recreation

- Assessment of SNAPs
- Describe special areas of interest or hobbies (e.g., art, books, music, crafts, physical fitness, sports, outdoor activities, church activities, walking, exercising, diet/health, hunting, fishing, bowling, traveling, etc.).
- How often now?
- How often in the past?
- Reasons for changes?
- How enjoyable do you find these activities?
- Desired activities?

They alleviate stress and often lead to increased social contact and possibly larger support networks. Also, they can indicate and influence disorders such as depression and anxiety. Some personality types, such as Type A personalities and obsessive-compulsive personality disorders, are less likely to engage in leisure and recreational activities. (See Rapid Reference 5.10.)

Medical/Physical/Sexual

One of the most important areas of biopsychosocial information is one's history of physical health. Client endorsement of any significant physical concerns should be referred to a physician to rule out a medical condition affecting a mental health or cognitive condition. Several organic conditions have similar symptoms as mental health disorders. Endorsement of multiple physical concerns may be indicative of a somatoform disorder. However, physical concerns may lead to mental health problems due to the stressors of coping with physical problems.

The relationship between one's physical and emotional state cannot be ignored. Just as a medical condition can influence or cause psychological problems, mental health issues can influence physical concerns. Conversion and somatoform disorders are often treated physically but ignored psychologically.

Endorsement of symptoms such as nausea, fatigue, sleeping problems, and diarrhea are similar to symptoms of Generalized Anxiety Disorder. When a client presents with such symptoms, a physical referral is suggested. Follow-up questions, such as how long they have occurred, whether the symptoms take place at certain times or in specific situations, or if they are typical responses to stress, are important both in identifying the etiology of the disorder and in treatment planning. Changes in physical functioning such as weight, appetite, sex drive, and sleep are called vegetative symptoms, which are discussed later.

Clients with a history of an underactive thyroid may experience symptoms similar to depression, whereas an overactive thyroid might be misdiagnosed as mania or hyperactivity. A health and medical history provides important referral information. Many third-party payers require that clients be examined by a physician prior to receiving mental health services. A complete physical may ascertain that one's health or a physical malady may have related psychological symptoms. Medical concerns such as chronic fatigue syndrome, underactive thyroid, and several other physical problems are often diagnosed as mental health problems. In such cases, mental health treatment is neither helpful, nor ethical (unless there are secondary mental health issues). When a client is referred to a mental health professional, the information received in the initial interview should be forwarded to the client's physician. In such cases, the client should sign a release of information form.

Many mental health clinics have a process in the intake procedures to screen for possible physical disorders. If clients endorse certain physical concerns during the intake, a physical referral may be required prior to receiving mental health services.

Although Axis III asks for medical conditions that are relevant to the presenting problem, it is still useful to gather general medical information. This type of information is useful in that physical health may be directly or indirectly connected to the client's mental health. One way in which the two are connected is that various physical symptoms may be a consequence of mental conditions. For example, physical complaints such as headaches, jaw pain, and high blood pressure may be manifestations of work-related stress. Children experiencing mental health problems such as depression are particularly likely to present with physical symptoms, including stomachaches, difficulty sleeping, and changes in eating behavior.

Physical conditions often affect one's mental health functioning. For example, weight gain may lead to an eating disorder or cancer may lead to depression. Even dealing with a physical condition requires mental skills such as coping, relaxation and stress reduction, and problem solving or information gathering. Finally, physical and mental conditions may simply co-occur, such that various physical problems may be indicators for certain mental health disorders or certain mental health disorders may have physical symptoms as part of their diagnostic criteria. For example, lack of sleep may indicate mania, or extreme episodes of hyperventilation and rapid heartbeat may indicate a panic attack.

Questions regarding sexual orientation/preferences are requirements by the major accrediting agencies. Such questions are not for the purpose of obtaining overly personal information, but rather to best meet the counseling needs of the client. Clients can decline to answer any questions posed. (See Rapid Reference 5.11.)

Putting It Into Practice

Example of Screening for Physical Examination Referral

Has there been a physical examination in the past two years (one year for age 40+)?
__Yes __ *No

Is the client complaining of any physical pain, impairment, or changes in physical condition for which no treatment is currently being received?
__ *Yes __ No

Is the client on psychotropic medications and has not had a physical exam for at least one year and under age 18 or over age 65?
__ *Yes __ No

Does the client have a substance abuse diagnosis and not had a physical exam in the past six months?
__ *Yes __ No

*If any of the above items are endorsed with an asterisk (*), refer for a physical evaluation.

Teaching Point: *Every client should be screened for possible physical health concerns. There should be organizational guidelines by which a physical evaluation is required.*

Rapid Reference 5.11

Examples of Types of Information Sought in Assessing Medical/Physical Health

- Examples of Medical/Physical Health Conditions (Indicate any problem areas the client has or has had. This type of information is generally obtained through clinical forms. It is necessary information to help rule out physical concerns with psychological or behavioral symptoms.)

AIDS	Dizziness	Nose bleeds
Alcoholism	Drug abuse	Pneumonia
Abdominal pain	Epilepsy	Rheumatic Fever
Abortion	Ear infections	Sexually transmitted diseases
Allergies	Eating problems	Sleeping disorders
Anemia	Fainting	Sore throat
Appendicitis	Fatigue	Scarlet Fever
Arthritis	Frequent urination	Sinusitis
Asthma	Headaches	Small Pox
Bronchitis	Hearing problems	Stroke
Bed wetting	Hepatitis	Sexual problems
Cancer	High blood pressure	Tonsillitis
Chest pain	Kidney problems	Tuberculosis
Chronic pain	Measles	Toothache
Colds/Coughs	Mononucleosis	Thyroid problems
Constipation	Mumps	Vision problems
Chicken Pox	Menstrual pain	Vomiting
Dental problems	Miscarriages	Whooping cough
Diabetes	Neurological disorders	Other(s)
Diarrhea	Nausea	

- Assessment of SNAPs
- Recent physical treatment?
- Upcoming physical treatment?
- Upcoming surgery?
- Sexual orientation?
- Sexual dysfunctions?
- Changes desired in sexual functioning?

Nutrition

Although mental health clinicians may not be experts in nutrition, basic information can be collected when there are possible problem areas. For example, if a client eats sugary snack foods throughout the day and rarely eats a balanced meal, a nutritional referral should be made. If the mental health clinician is not credentialed or licensed to assess and make nutritional suggestions, for ethical reasons, it must be left to others specifically trained in that area. However, questions regarding nutrition and eating patterns may be helpful in assessing an eating disorder or depression. In such cases collaborative treatment with a nutritionist, a physician, or both, is recommended. (See Rapid Reference 5.12.)

Medications

Assessing clients' previous and current use of medications helps in several areas. Previous history of medication provides a good indication of the chronicity of the client's problem areas. It is always helpful to find out why medication changes have taken place. The most common reasons for medication changes include undesirable side effects, tolerance, or that the med's were not helpful.

When a client has a history of taking a variety of types of medications at different points in time, concerns such as misdiagnosis, a personality disorder, or poor compliance should be assessed and ruled in or out.

Helpful information can be gathered about a client's medication history. If a client is currently receiving medications for reasons concordant with the diagnosis, it is helpful, and often required by agencies, to be in contact with the prescribing physician. The trend in today's mental health environment is to coordinate services in a multidisciplinary man-

═══Rapid Reference 5.12

Examples of Types of Information Sought in Assessing Nutrition

- Assessment of SNAPs
- Typical meals?
- Amounts of food?
- Nutritious?
- Frequency of meals?
- Concerns?
- Recent weight loss or weight gain?
- How much over what period of time?

ner. Correspondence among providers helps to reduce redundancies in services and aid the client by coordinating treatment.

It is not uncommon for clients to stop taking their medications even when meds are helpful. For example, a client with a diagnosis of bipolar disorder may stop taking medications when experiencing (or desiring to be) in a manic episode. Nor is it uncommon for clients with a thought disorder to discontinue taking medications, because they have had no recent hallucinations. Unfortunately, when the medications are discontinued, the hallucinations typically return.

When clients endorse taking any type of medications, the information found in Rapid Reference 5.13 can be helpful in treatment planning, client monitoring, and information sharing with the prescribing physician(s).

Chemical Use History

Clients with current chemical use concerns may have a dual diagnosis of chemical dependency and mental health concerns. Those with a substance-related

Rapid Reference 5.13

Examples of Types of Information Sought in Assessing Medications

- Names of current medications?
- Purpose?
- Name(s) of prescribing physician(s)?
- If more than one, are they in contact?
- How long taken?
- Dose?
- Effectiveness?
- Any recent changes in dose or effect?
- When last taken?
- Compliance?
- Side effects?
- Effects when not taking medication?
- Current over-the-counter meds?
- Previous medications?
- Why discontinued?
- Significant changes in types of medications? Why?
- History of medication abuse?
- History of medication overdose?
- Allergic to any medications or drugs?

diagnosis should receive appropriate, specialized treatment; therefore, an accurate diagnosis is needed. It is not uncommon for a client to receive substance abuse treatment in one setting and mental health treatment in another setting. The providers should collaborate in their treatment.

The assessment must cover topics (listed in Rapid Reference 5.14) such as history of relapse and purpose of using. The interrelation between substance use and mental health functioning cannot be ignored. Many clients will abuse substances in order to alleviate underlying mental health problems. Biopsychosocial information is very helpful in determining the client's strengths, needs, abilities, and preferences that will best increase the client's chances for successful treatment.

History of Mental Health Treatment

Usually, the more chronic the condition, the poorer the prognosis. This is not to say that people with chronic mental illness do not improve, but rather that the prognosis of an acute mental illness is better than one that is chronic. Several variables must be considered. Clients that have long-standing problems without a history of treatment may have been unaware of the extent of their mental health condition, and treatment may be quite effective. However, clients with numerous, uncompleted treatments have difficulties stabilizing and often regress to a lower level of functioning.

The historical information collected is most helpful when it accurately portrays the client's response to previous treatments. That is, if the question, "What works . . . and what doesn't work?" is answered honestly, the prognosis of successful treatment increases.

Treatment history is much more than simply writing down the client's previous counseling experiences. One of the best predictors of upcoming treatment outcome is the result of previous treatment. Helpful questions include the following items.

Have You Ever Received Mental Health Services?

If the client has received mental health services in the past, there are several possible follow-up questions to determine their effect and help determine the prognosis of upcoming treatment. Possible follow-up questions may include the following:

Rapid Reference 5.14

Examples of Types of Information Sought in Assessing Chemical Use

- Use of...?

Alcohol	Inhalants
Barbiturates	Caffeine
Valium/Librium	Nicotine
Cocaine/Crack	Over-the-counter
Heroin/Opiates	Prescription drugs
Marijuana	Other
PCP/LSD/Mescaline	

- Substance(s) of preference?
- Method of use?
- Frequency of use?
- Use in last 48 hours? ... 7 days? ... 30 days?
- Age of initial use?
- Periods of sobriety?
- Relapse history?
- Describe when and where you typically use substances.
- Describe any changes in your use patterns.
- Describe how your use has affected your family or friends (include their perceptions of your use).
- Reason(s) for use:

Addicted	Build confidence	Escape	Self-medication
Socialization	Taste	Other (specify)	

- How do you believe your substance use affects your life?
- Who or what has helped you in stopping or limiting your use?
- Does/Has someone in your family present/past have/had a problem with drugs or alcohol?
- Have you had withdrawal symptoms when trying to stop using drugs or alcohol?
- Have you had adverse reactions or overdose to drugs or alcohol?
- Have drugs or alcohol created a problem for your job?

- When were previous services received?
- How often or how many times has the client been in counseling?
- What was the average length of service or number of sessions?
- What previous diagnoses were given?
- When did services first take place?
- When were the most recent services received?
- What levels of treatment were received (e.g., outpatient, inpatient, day treatment)?
- What worked (didn't work)?
- Why were services terminated?
- How frequently did the client miss appointments?
- What were the reasons for missing appointments?
- What is the history of relapse?
- Why is the client now returning for additional services?
- What was addressed in previous sessions?
- What does the client want to be different in upcoming sessions?
- What collateral services are not being used?
- Is the client currently in treatment (for chemical dependency, mental health)?
- What is different now?

The main point is to gather information that will most clearly define the client's response to treatment. All attempts should be made to clarify what works and what doesn't work therapeutically for the client. Whether or not the client has received previous mental health services, take time to explain the purpose of the interview. One of the most helpful sessions in counseling can be the initial interview. Specific problem areas and strengths are identified, integrated, and placed into perspective. At the same time, an effective intake counselor will stay on target, motivate the client, and lead the client on the road to recovery.

Clients who have not received previous services are likely to be reticent to receive services because they may be unaware about what takes place in a mental health session. Adequate education or orientation of the process of treatment, treatment planning, agency policies and procedures, and what to expect from treatment help to ethically and emotionally prepare the client for services. Clients should know up front that counseling is intended to have both a beginning and an ending point. The treatment plan, which is usually written shortly after the initial interview, estimates the number of sessions.

How Do You Usually Handle Stressful or Difficult Situations?

Some clients have never received mental health counseling but have experienced significant mental health problems, trauma, or situational crises. It is helpful to determine their means of coping. At times they may have found adaptive means to deal with their problems that may be helpful in their treatment. For example, incorporating significant others or social supports may be useful. The therapist can help increase these skills. However, some clients have learned maladaptive means of coping such as substance abuse, avoiding problems, lashing out, and so on that need to be addressed in treatment. Client strengths and weaknesses should always be carefully assessed in order to incorporate them into treatment planning and discharge planning.

Do You Have Any History of Related Treatment?

Certain clients who have received supportive services, such as assertiveness training, family counseling, group therapy, pain counseling, rehabilitative therapy, chemical dependency counseling, or other supportive services, may not endorse that they have had previous counseling specifically for mental health. In any of the above examples, significant underlying symptoms may not have been directly addressed but may nevertheless exist (e.g., substance abuse counseling may not have addressed depression, although depression may be a primary cause for substance abuse).

Include information assessed in Item 2 to predict prognosis and incorporate the client's strengths in treatment. If the client is currently receiving related treatment, it is suggested to incorporate the other treatment providers into a treatment team, sharing and incorporating each other's information. Sharing information can also prevent duplication of services, which can become conflicting to the client.

Have You Ever Been Hospitalized for Psychiatric Reasons?

A number of clients will not endorse any history of mental health counseling although they have been hospitalized for mental health reasons. For example, a person who has experienced previous 72-hour holds in a hospital setting may have simply been observed but did not follow up with prescribed mental health treatment. Some people regularly check in at the emergency room when they are under extreme stress. Their stay becomes a breather and is therapeutic in itself. This person is apt to deny any treatment history.

Typical reasons for psychiatric hospitalizations include suicidal behavior, chronic mental illness, and difficulties coping with specific ongoing stressors. The history of hospitalizations and response to treatment are important elements of history gathering. Include information such as compliance to treatment after the hospitalization and changes that occurred as a result. Also, assess how current conditions may be similar to those at times of hospitalization.

Some clients will seek services immediately after a recent psychiatric hospitalization, because it has been suggested to them to receive follow-up care. They may or may not inform the clinician of the recent hospital stay. Sharing the previous treatment information will benefit all parties, especially the client. Other clients have previously been referred for psychiatric services but have never followed through or terminated prematurely.

Do You Have Any History of Suicidal Behavior Such as Ideas, Threats, or a Plan?

Each client should be assessed specifically for the potential danger to self or others. Accreditation agencies require that mental health clinics have specific policies and procedures that depict actions to take when the client has the potential for harm.

Some clients will endorse a long history of suicidal issues but have never been in treatment. Although this question may or may not be posed this early in the interview process, it must be addressed for every client. Failing to assess and document suicide is an error in judgment and ethics that can become a malpractice issue.

Suicide is permanent for the client and his or her loved ones. Neglecting to identify potential suicidality may pose serious problems legally, ethically, and professionally for the clinician. It is never acceptable to assume that a client does not have the potential for suicide. The therapist must take all precautions to document that all efforts were made to assess suicidal risk. Chapter 6 focuses on suicide assessment. (See Rapid Reference 5.15.)

Items Covered in the Biopsychosocial Assessment

- Family History and Dynamics
- Social relationships
- Cultural and Ethnic Background and Practices
- Spiritual/Religious Beliefs and Practices
- Legal
- Education
- Employment History
- Military Experience
- Leisure/Recreational
- Medical/Physical/Sexual
- Nutrition
- Medications
- Chemical Use History
- History of Mental Health Treatment
- Suicidality

Putting It Into Practice

Suicidality

A young woman attended an intake session and set up future counseling sessions after a court required that she receive counseling due to a history of illicit and aggressive behaviors. The day after the intake, a local hospital called the clinic to state that the woman had attempted suicide. The clinic owner immediately reviewed the client's file and consulted with an attorney to determine if the clinic was in legal jeopardy for failing to identify her intent.

The counselor was questioned about why the suicide risk was not determined in the interview. The counselor reported that the client, attending the session on a court order, was noncompliant and simply wanted a report for the court. Her record reflected that the counselor had inquired about suicide intent, and the client had denied ideations, threats, or a plan. Further, she did not claim to be depressed, appear depressed, or claim any history of suicidal behavior.

It is not uncommon for an individual to deny suicidality and soon make an attempt. It can be a form of control or power, or it can take place out of anger or revenge. In this case, after the interview the client became drunk and, as she had done on a number of past occasions, gestured suicide.

Teaching Point: *No one can predict the suicide of others. Although there may be some behaviors suggesting suicidal potential, sometimes there are not clear signs. Nevertheless, the clinician should assess suicidal risk for every client and clearly document the results.*

CHAPTER SUMMARY

1. The biopsychosocial assessment provides historical and current information about a wide range of areas in the client's life. It provides specific, client-focused areas of strengths, needs, abilities, and preferences (SNAPs), aiding in treatment planning and monitoring.
2. A client's social history aids both diagnostically and in identifying social strengths to aid in specific treatment strategies.
3. Assessing the specific types of crimes or offenses in a client's legal history can provide a fairly accurate prognosis of the success of treatment.
4. Education is often a good predictor of the type of counseling most helpful to a client. The client's educational attainment experiences (grades, absenteeism, motivation, drop out experiences) may be indicative of other life experiences, thus useful as targets in treatment.
5. Several physical disorders have similar symptoms as mental health disorders, therefore a physical examination is suggested.
6. Information about the client's other treatment (physicians, mental health, substance abuse) should be integrated into current treatment planning with a coordination of services. Accrediting agencies and third-party payers stress a multidisciplinary approach.
7. Previous diagnoses and treatment in mental health and substance abuse may significantly affect the prognosis of current treatment.

🪶 TEST YOURSELF 🪶

1. **The purpose of the biopsychosocial assessment is to**
   (a) provide a diagnosis.
   (b) determine why the client behaves the way he/she does.
   (c) provide additional background information helpful in assessment and treatment.
   (d) select the best type of therapy.

2. **Assessing cultural and ethnic background may affect the**
   (a) diagnosis.
   (b) treatment.
   (c) understanding of the nature of the presenting problem.
   (d) All of the above

(continued)

3. **Reviewing the client's medical history may result in**

   (a) misdiagnosis.

   (b) preventing misdiagnosis.

   (c) malpractice if the clinician is not a physician or nurse.

   (d) None of the above

4. **As the chronicity of a mental disorder increases, the prognosis**

   (a) remains the same.

   (b) decreases.

   (c) increases.

   (d) does not change.

5. **A client's religious beliefs and practices**

   (a) have nothing to do with mental health diagnosis and pathology; therefore, they should not be considered.

   (b) may significantly affect the interviewer's perception of the client's psychopathology.

   (c) are personal and should not be part of therapy, especially when funded by a third-party payer.

   (d) should be similar to those of the therapist.

6. **Which of the following questions is a mental health therapist most likely not to ask a client regarding medications?**

   (a) Side effects

   (b) Compliance

   (c) Effects without medication

   (d) Medications desired

7. **All clients must be referred for a physical evaluation.** True or False?

8. **All suicidal clients are depressed.** True or False?

9. **A history of depression is a good predictor of future depression.** True or False?

10. **Behaviors that may be considered pathological in one culture may be acceptable in another culture.** True or False?

11. **Discuss how SNAPs can be incorporated into all aspects of mental health treatment.**

12. **Discuss how aspects such as assessing a client's history of leisure activities can help in treatment planning.**

13. **How might it be considered a violation of ethics if a mental health clinician does not attain a physical history?**

**14. How might it be considered a violation of ethics if a mental health thera-
pist discovers that a client is physically fatigued and gives the client an exercise regime to follow?**

Answers: 1. c; 2. d; 3. b; 4. b; 5. b; 6. d; 7. False; 8. False; 9. True; 10. True. 11. SNAPs provide measures of several aspects of the client's life. By evaluating SNAPs regularly, the client's needs are considered on an ongoing basis. 12. Leisure activities are often one of the first aspects of a client's life to decline when mental health problems increase. Including historical leisure activities in treatment planning may help restore the client to premorbid functioning. 13. There are physical disorders in which the symptoms are similar to mental health disorders. It is unethical to treat a client for mental health problems when physical interventions are the proper solution. 14. Unless a mental health therapist is professionally qualified to prescribe a physical exercise regime, any physical interventions should be referred to someone with adequate training and experience. Professionals should only treat what they are competent to treat.

Six

SUICIDE ASSESSMENT

OVERVIEW

No single chapter in a text can cover all aspects of suicide assessment. This chapter provides introductory training in the issues involved, risk management, and legal concerns. Because this text focuses on interviewing and assessment, it will not cover treatment of suicidal clients.

Evaluating the risk of suicide potential is extremely difficult. This is probably due to the high level of ambivalence and uncertainty of those considering suicide. Dorpat and Ripley (1967) note that many persons simply do not know what they want the outcome of their action to be, but they do know that they want to do something to themselves or communicate something to someone else.

Every mental health interview should include a suicide assessment. Suicide is the ninth leading cause of death for adults in the United States and is the third leading cause of death for people ages 15 to 25 (Shea, 1999). Even if there is no hint of suicidal ideas during any portion of the interview, therapists must ask about suicidal behavior. If not, they risk ignoring potentially life-threatening ideas and behaviors in a client who may be too ashamed or too embarrassed to mention them spontaneously (Morrison, 1995). In cases of little or no risk, the evaluation may be brief, with only a few questions. However, if mental health services are being sought for behaviors such as depression, substance abuse, impulsivity, mental disorders secondary to physical health problems, or pain, the risk of suicide increases. For cases in which there is increased risk, documentation of each step of the assessment, including the rationale for determining the level of risk, is essential.

Knowledge of effective suicide assessment procedures and the legal aspects of suicidality are the clinician's greatest tools in suicide prevention. Although most mental health therapists do not receive much training in suicide assessment in graduate school, it does not excuse ignorance of the law or the application of appropriate procedures. Effective risk management involves providing a level of clinical treatment that is concordant both with the therapist's training and the client's level of risk. A therapist who agrees to see a client whose problem areas are beyond the therapist's level of competence is placing him or herself in legal and ethical jeopardy. Rosenberg (1999) states that regardless of mental health discipline, specific training in the assessment and prevention of suicide is inadequate. Rosenberg further adds that lack of training is a great concern since the average professional psychologist involved in direct client care has a one in five chance of losing a client to suicide.

Sommers-Flanagan, Rothman, and Schwenkler (2000) state that therapists should be trained to help suicidal clients focus on and talk about their current resources, strengths, and reasons for living within the context of the clinical interview. Therapists must receive clinical supervision when gaining experience in additional areas of competence, including suicidal clients. The clinical supervisor qualifies to provide supervision by having extensive training and experience in suicide prevention. For example, if a clinician needs supervision in treating a depressed, suicidal client, proper supervision would be from a supervisor competent in both depression and suicide. The legal chain does not stop with the therapist. The clinical supervisor shares part of the responsibility for therapeutic decisions. Simply holding a higher academic degree or being in the field longer than the person receiving supervision are not sufficient criteria for conducting clinical supervision.

Documentation of all actions taken (and not taken) by the therapist, including clinical decisions and consultations, is a critical element in risk management. Guetheil (1984, p. 3) states, "clinicians who make bad decisions but whose reasoning has been articulated clearly and whose justification for the intervention is well documented often come out better than clinicians who have made reasonable decisions but whose documentation leaves them vulnerable." Bongar (1991) adds that clinical records must be explicit in explaining why a patient is or is not hospitalized, stating, "Each significant decision point should also include a risk-benefit analysis that indicates all actions that one considered, the reasons that led one to take an action, and the reasons that led one to reject an action. The record must indicate specifically why consultation and supervision were or were not employed and include a written record of the consultant's recommendations" (pp. 171–172). (See Rapid Reference 6.1.)

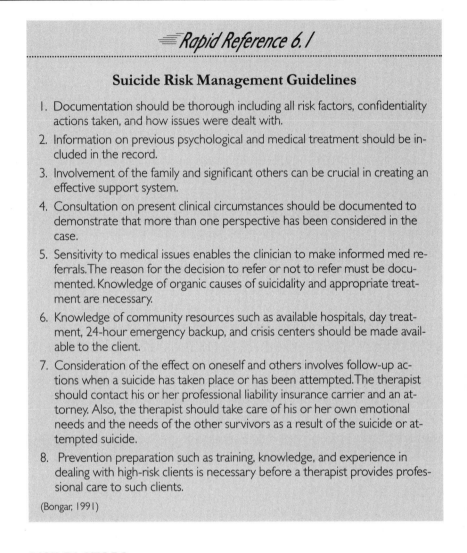

Rapid Reference 6.1

Suicide Risk Management Guidelines

1. Documentation should be thorough including all risk factors, confidentiality actions taken, and how issues were dealt with.

2. Information on previous psychological and medical treatment should be included in the record.

3. Involvement of the family and significant others can be crucial in creating an effective support system.

4. Consultation on present clinical circumstances should be documented to demonstrate that more than one perspective has been considered in the case.

5. Sensitivity to medical issues enables the clinician to make informed med referrals. The reason for the decision to refer or not to refer must be documented. Knowledge of organic causes of suicidality and appropriate treatment are necessary.

6. Knowledge of community resources such as available hospitals, day treatment, 24-hour emergency backup, and crisis centers should be made available to the client.

7. Consideration of the effect on oneself and others involves follow-up actions when a suicide has taken place or has been attempted. The therapist should contact his or her professional liability insurance carrier and an attorney. Also, the therapist should take care of his or her own emotional needs and the needs of the other survivors as a result of the suicide or attempted suicide.

8. Prevention preparation such as training, knowledge, and experience in dealing with high-risk clients is necessary before a therapist provides professional care to such clients.

(Bongar, 1991)

RISK FACTORS

Suicidal behaviors or intent may be categorized into five levels, including (a) ideations, (b) threats, (c) gestures, (d) planning, and (e) attempt. A client's risk factor increases as the levels in these categories increase. For example a client with no suicidal ideations and no history of suicidal behavior, no significant current stressors, or other mental health or substance abuse problems is considered a low risk. However, someone with a current suicide plan, previous suicide attempts, and who is currently under much stress is at a high risk for suicide.

Suicidal ideations are not uncommon for people with or without mental health issues. Thinking about what it would be like not being around, at times, is generally not a suicidal risk. But, as more time is spent thinking about suicide or death, and one becomes preoccupied with such ideations, risk increases. Therefore, if a client endorses thinking about death or suicide, the therapist must not dismiss ideations as commonplace. Specific questions such as the history, frequency, content, and duration of the ideations must be documented.

Suicidal threats are a client's means of verbalizing and demonstrating a potential suicide. Threats are not, in themselves, life threatening. A threat is a statement to others of a possible intent of suicide. All suicidal threats must be taken seriously and acted upon as if the intent is genuine. Threats are common in Borderline Personality Disorder as attention-seeking behavior.

A *suicidal gesture* is a presuicidal act such as a slight cut on the wrist or acting as if one will pull a trigger, jump into traffic, or related behaviors. Although it may be performed for the sake of receiving attention, this cannot be known for certain, therefore it must be acted on immediately by the clinician.

A *suicidal plan* is defined as the client having a course of action such as a predetermined time and place for suicide. If the clinician uncovers evidence of a plan, immediate action to notify family, police, county mental health, and others is required, depending on state laws and ethical principles. Planning and preparation are usually associated with more serious attempts. Writing or revising a will, giving away property, taking out life insurance, and writing a suicide note are all indications of planning (Morrison, 1995). Another gray area is if clients state that if or when they commit suicide, they will go about it in a planned manner, but they have no specific time in mind. In most cases, this is not considered a plan, because a time, place or both has not yet been planned. Nevertheless, such statements should not be ignored or viewed as inconsequential.

A *suicide attempt* is an action with suicide as the goal. Attempts may range from violent acts (more common in men), such as using a weapon, to passive ones (more common in women), such as overdosing on medications. It may be conducted without a specific plan when the attempt is impulsive. Most completed suicides are conducted by people with previous attempts. Suicide attempts can be rated as to their lethality or level of risk. Morrison (1995) notes that if someone was with the client when they made an attempt, this may indicate that the client had arranged a means of rescue, which is somewhat of a lower risk than if the client was alone. An attempt is considered more serious when the client follows it up by doing nothing (e.g., not calling for help) or reports feeling angry after being rescued. However, Yufit (1989) states that all suicide attempts should be considered serious. Multiple attempts, even if less lethal, reflect the inadequacy of coping and adaptive skills for dealing with stress. Many completed suicides occur because the client miscalculated the degree of lethality or combined two minimally lethal means into a high-risk method.

Along with the above-mentioned level of suicidal behaviors, the client's level of intent must be assessed. In other words, is it the client's intent to seek attention, engage in a lesser degree of self-harm as punishment, get others to change their behaviors, or to die? For example, suicidal gestures with a low intent for suicide but aimed more at obtaining attention or sympathy are at a much lower risk than suicidal gestures with high intent, which actually demonstrate a desire to cease living. The client's level of intent to commit suicide must be determined prior to continuing the interview. If a client has a history, especially a recent history, of suicidal behaviors, a medical referral should be made immediately. An opinion of the client's level of risk should be documented in the clinical record each time there is client contact. All therapeutic actions and suggestions regarding suicidal behaviors must be clearly documented. (See Rapid Reference 6.2.)

In every assessment, suicidal factors must be ruled out. The greater the risk of suicide, the higher the need for inpatient treatment. Generally, if the risk is below a moderate level, outpatient treatment is appropriate. A risk factor above moderate requires hospitalization. Whether to hospitalize someone at the moderate level of suicidal intent requires a careful decision process, which should be conducted through professional consultation. It is always better to err on the side of caution than to risk undertreatment. One life saved due to a hospitalization, is certainly greater than a few clients, who would not have attempted suicide, being upset for being hospitalized.

Kleespies and Dettmer (2000) advise that the clinician approach all situations of alleged suicide or violence risk as potential emergencies until convinced otherwise. They note that it is important to have a predetermined deci-

═Rapid Reference 6.2

Five Levels of Suicidal Risk

1. **Nonexistent:** No suicidal ideation or plans exist.

2. **Mild:** Suicidal ideation but no specific or concrete plans exist. Few risk factors are present.

3. **Moderate:** Suicidal ideation and a general plan exist. Self-control is intact; client knows several "reasons to live," and client does not "intend" to kill him- or herself. Some risk factors are present.

4. **Severe:** Suicidal ideation is frequent and intense. Plan is specific and lethal, means are available, and nearby helping resources are few. Self-control is questionable, but the client does not really "want" to kill him- or herself; intent appears low. Many risk factors may be present.

5. **Extreme:** Same description as Severe, except that the client expresses a clear intent to kill him- or herself as soon as the opportunity presents itself. Many risk factors are usually present.

(Sommers-Flanagan & Sommers-Flanagan, 1999, p. 259)

sion tree for managing a client's suicidality. Having an emergency-intervention strategy saves valuable time, reduces stress, and improves the clinician's ability to maintain control over a situation that could become chaotic. The therapist must be alert to the individual whose diagnosis and related risk factors suggest a profile of someone who could easily develop suicidal ideation or a suicidal state.

When there is a risk of suicidal behavior, a suicide assessment becomes the focus of the interview. Changing the focus of the intended purpose of the interview to a suicidal assessment is the ethical procedure. The course of the client's life may now be significantly affected by the actions taken from the interview results. The OF AID Technique, which is described in Chapter 7 of this text, requires that the following information be collected for all clinical symptoms, including suicidal behavior.

Onset:	"When did you begin feeling suicidal?"
Frequency:	"How often do you feel suicidal?"
Antecedants:	"What events or stressors bring on suicidal thoughts?"
Intensity:	"How severe or intense are your suicidal thoughts?"
Duration:	"How long do these thoughts last?"

Putting It Into Practice

One Upset Parent, One Live Client

A parent brought her adult son (age 28) into a crisis counseling session because, on the previous night, he told his coworkers that he wanted to die and held a knife to his wrist. During the assessment, the client was despondent, stating that he wanted to die and was seriously considering taking his life, "perhaps at work, tonight." He further endorsed several suicidal risk factors.

The mother was told to take her son to the hospital, immediately, because outpatient treatment was not an appropriate level of care at this time. She took him to the hospital, where he was determined to be a high suicidal risk; he was given medications and placed on a 24-hr watch. For five days, he remained an inpatient and was then referred to the hospital's intensive day treatment program.

About two weeks into the day treatment, the mother phoned the initial intake therapist complaining that the son lost his job and the treatment wasn't helping. She vehemently complained that the medications were making him "a zombie, but weren't helping." She noted much frustration with the intake therapist who referred her son to the hospital. She blamed him for her son losing his job, stating that her son was now worse off because of the hospital bills and his unemployment. She even suggested malpractice, because, "My son only threatened suicide for attention . . . He wouldn't have done it." She even refused to pay the bill.

Although the therapist simply listened to the mother and made no negative or defensive remarks, his thoughts were, "What if she hadn't taken him to the hospital and he had taken his life . . . How would she be feeling now?"

Teaching Point: *It is difficult to predict suicide. A therapist will never know if a suicide is prevented when a client is sent to the hospital. That is, it may or may not have taken place if there had been no hospitalization. The consequences of hospitalization may negatively impact the client's life, leading to ill feelings toward the therapist making the referral. But it is still better to err on the side of caution than to risk a completed suicide.*

No matter what the client's history of threats and gestures is, always take them seriously. For example, although clients with diagnoses such as Borderline Personality Disorder may find reward in the attention received in making threats and gestures and may never intend to commit suicide, it does happen. Threats and gestures are a gray area in reporting suicidal behavior. Some agencies have a policy that unless the client has a definite plan for suicide, it is not reported to county or legal authorities. Others observe policies on the safe side of caution. A conservative move is to treat all threats and gestures equally to a plan for suicide. Although a number of clients who may not have actually attempted suicide may end up in the emergency room or the psychiatric ward, the possibility of saving any lives makes it worth it. Although people with a history of receiving attention for nonserious threats and gestures may receive secondary gain, they also may suffer the natural consequences of spending a few days in the hospital, which may or may not be rewarding.

Most clients will not immediately discuss their suicidal intentions with a therapist to whom they have just been introduced. Adequate rapport must be developed. A safe and trusting atmosphere must be in place before most clients will disclose a suicidal plan. Careful attention must be given in assessing a client's plan for suicide. Miller (1985) suggests that four areas of a suicidal plan should be investigated.

1. *Specificity of the plan.* The interviewer should inquire whether the client has a specific plan for suicide, or occasional ideations about death or suicide. When clients have a specific plan, such as a time and place, the risk increases significantly. Vague plans, such as sometimes wondering what it would be like not to be around, are not considered a suicidal plan. However, the interviewer must take all measures to insure that the client is being straightforward. Difficulties may arise in client disclosure when the interviewer initially warns the client that if information is given that there is a suicidal plan, it must be reported, and confidentiality broken. In such cases, clients may deliberately withhold information due to fear of immediate hospitalization. Information provided about suicidal behavior may vary among clients, depending on the level of rapport with the therapist and disclosure. Suicidality may be one of the most difficult items for some clients to discuss, especially to a therapist they have recently met.

2. *Lethality of the method.* When the client has a plan for suicide, the risk increases more quickly as the method becomes more lethal. For example, a method of overdosing on aspirin is less lethal than a gunshot to the head. Although each method can result in death, the gunshot to the head is generally instantaneous, whereas the overdose allows more time for medical intervention. A less lethal plan,

however, may be based on a miscalculation (e.g., medication dosage), and death may result. It should still be given serious attention. Yufit (1989) notes that degree of lethality is determined by the actual behavior (e.g., gunshot to the head versus aspirin overdose), the likelihood that the plan will be carried out, the degree of ambivalence based on intention (e.g., bid for attention versus self-punishment versus death), the probability that the result will be death, and the methods available and finally chosen.

3. *Availability of the proposed method.* Clients should be assessed as to what means are available to them in their proposed method of suicide. Clients under a 24-hr watch in a hospital have fewer available means of suicide than those allowed to go home. When toxic chemicals, weapons, drugs, or other immediate means are readily available to the client, the risk increases. If the proposed method is not practical, such as jumping off the Empire State Building, when the client lives in Iowa, the immediate risk decreases. However, a suicidal client may change methods. Thus, if the stated proposed method is not available, other risk factors should be considered.

4. *Proximity of social or helping resources.* The client's social resources, such as friends and family living in the area or with the client, are important in determining who is available to the client when he or she is suicidal. Risk increases as availability of social resources decrease.

Suicidal behavior is significantly more common among the mentally ill population compared to the general population. Among psychiatric emergencies, suicide is the most common behavior, and it is the most stressful to deal with as a clinician. Suicidal potential increases when the client is seen as an inpatient. Causes are complex and interrelated, leading to no typical suicidal client. Bongar (1991) states that the central issue in suicide is not death or killing, but rather, it is the stopping of consciousness of unbearable pain, which unfortunately requires the stopping of life.

Assessing and dealing with suicide is clearly one of the most difficult tasks the clinician faces. Bongar (1991) emphasizes that there are numerous studies and guidelines available to clinicians, such as the psychological, psychodynamic, epidemiological, social-relational, and other risk factors, plus available tests and scales, but they are yet not adequate to answer the question, "Is the

Putting It Into Practice

Examples of Questions Assessing Suicidal Behavior

Note: In the beginning of the assessment, the therapist discussed the limits of confidentiality in which informed consent takes place regarding actions the therapist is required to take when a client appears to be in danger of harm to self or others.

Therapist: "Have you ever attempted suicide?"

Client: "No."

Therapist: "Most people, at some time in their lives, have some thoughts of death or suicide. Do you ever have thoughts of suicide or death?"

Client: "Yes, I do ... especially in the past month."

Therapist: "Are these ideas about suicide ... are you considering taking your life?"

Client: "When I'm really down, my thoughts are quite serious. I haven't done anything yet, but sometimes it scares me."

Therapist: "What do you mean?"

Client: "I mean that sometimes it seems like no one would even care if I was gone. Look at all the trouble I've caused other people. My troubles would be gone."

Therapist: "Have you ever threatened that you would harm yourself?"

Client: "No, When I do it, no one will be warned."

Therapist: "Have you ever made a plan for suicide?"

Client: "I've thought about it. I certainly want my family to receive the insurance, so I would make it look like an accident."

Therapist: "Have you ever tried to go through with any plan?"

Client: "That's why I'm here. Yesterday, I came close. I almost 'accidentally' slipped into traffic as a pedestrian. I knew what I was doing. I planned it in my head for a few days. I just chickened out, I guess. Last night I thought that I should have gone through with it."

Therapist: "It seems like you are in danger of harming yourself."

Client: "I know."

Teaching Point: *Some clients initially provide vague answers to suicidal questions. The therapist should clarify any vague responses. Answers such as, "I am not suicidal," are not sufficient to rule out suicidal potential. If the client appears to be at high risk, such as having a suicidal plan and strong intentions, protective actions must be taken immediately.*

patient sitting with me now, about to commit suicide" (Maltsberger, 1988, p. 47). In a summary of several suicidal studies Hillard (1995) concludes, ". . . none of these studies has identified factors that successfully predict suicide by an individual." While it is difficult to predict suicide, there are risk factors and demographic variables correlated with suicidality.

There are multiple potential causes of suicide and few clear predictors whether the client intends to complete suicide, to gain attention, or to achieve some other objective. Dorpat and Ripley (1967) state that we do not clearly know when the client's suicidal behaviors are aimed at self-harm or communication to others. Yufit (1989) describes suicide assessment in two phases, (a) screening and (b) assessment of the degree or intensity of the ideation. Suicidal screening explores whether factors indicative of suicidal potential are present. Assessment investigates the degree of potential.

There are a variety of suicidal behaviors to explore, from subtle to explicit. Subtle behaviors are those such as drug abuse, dangerous behaviors, behaviors leading to poor health or injury, and unsafe eating. Explicit behaviors such as direct suicidal attempts and self-injury are more obvious. Nevertheless, suicide indicators are not always overt.

When a suicide has been attempted, or if there is a plan, Yufit (1989) suggests that the degree of lethality must be considered. Lethality is defined as the degree or level of intent in the suicide.

DON'T FORGET

The Basis of the Degree of Lethality

1. Degree of reversibility of the act (for example, jumping from a high place versus superficial wrist cutting)
2. Probability of rescue (Was the timing of the attempt geared to coincide with being discovered?)
3. Method chosen in light of methods available (for example, taking several pills from a bottle of 100 while at home in a 10th floor apartment)
4. Degree of medical injury resulting from the behavior. (The more serious the injury, the greater the likelihood that lethality intent was high. The patient's physical health and intellect also must be considered.)

Kleespies and Dettmer (2000) note that it is not possible to predict accurately rare events such as suicide, in which the base rate is about 12 per 100,000 in the general U.S. population and about 60 per 100,000 in the psychiatric population. They also hold that only certain psychiatric diagnoses are associated with a risk of suicide that is significantly higher than in the general population. In order of prevalence, depression is first, which is present in an estimated 50% of suicides; alcohol and drug abuse is second, which is present in an estimated 20–25% of suicides; and schizophrenia is third, which is present in an estimated 10% of suicides. However, a significant lifetime risk of committing suicide for those afflicted with depression is only 6% (and 7% for alcohol dependence and 4% for schizophrenia). That is, the majority of depressed clients do not commit suicide, but many who commit suicide were depressed. Other diagnoses associated with significantly elevated rates of suicide include combat-related PTSD and certain personality disorders in the impulsive spectrum (especially Borderline Personality Disorder).

Yufit (1997) notes that suicidal clients appear to have a unique time profile, different from that of the nonsuicidal person. Most suicide-prone individuals have a minimal involvement in the future and the present while the majority of their time perspective is in the past. This preoccupation with the past usually takes two forms: one is nostalgia for the good old days that cannot be recaptured, usually with a focus on a key person or coveted environment that they believe to be permanently lost, and the second form is the obsession or preoccupation with a poor decision made in the past, along with an apparent irreversibility of that decision. In other words, the client wishes to go back into the past and undo the poor choice he or she made. The nonsuicidal individual has minimal involvement in the past and tends to be more involved in the future.

Neuringer (1964) states that suicidal patients tend to have rigid cognitive styles, in which there are difficulties finding alternative strategies or coping styles. The less options a person perceives him- or herself as having available, the greater potential for suicide. Other factors that increase suicidal potential include, poor impulse control, feelings of helplessness and hopelessness, lack of autonomy, low motivation, perfectionism, lack of outside supports available, a history of attempts, and sudden, unexpected loss or failure. Rapid Reference 6.3 details Pope and Vasquez's (1991) suggestions of the signs of a potential suicide attempt.

Signs of a Potential Suicide Attempt

1. **Direct verbal warning:** One of the best indicators is the client making suicidal statements. Never dismiss a suicidal statement as unimportant.

2. **Plan:** The more detailed, lethal, and feasible the plan, the greater the risk.

3. **Past attempts:** Most completed suicides were preceded by a prior attempt.

4. **Indirect statements and behavioral signs:** Suicidal people often provide subtle remarks and behaviors suggesting that they may no longer be around.

5. **Depression:** Depressed people have a 20 times greater rate of suicide than the general population.

6. **Hopelessness:** A feeling of hopelessness is perhaps the strongest indicator of suicidal potential.

7. **Intoxication:** Alcohol contributes to about one-third to one-half of all suicides.

8. **Clinical syndromes:** Suicide rates are highest among those with Mood Disorders, Alcohol Abuse, organic brain syndrome, Delusional Disorder, Panic Disorder, Schizophrenia, and Borderline Personality Disorder.

9. **Gender:** The suicide rate for men is about three times greater than for women.

10. **Age:** Suicide risk and completed attempts increases with age.

11. **Race:** In the United States, Caucasians have the highest suicide rate.

12. **Religion:** As a person's degree of religious commitment increases, suicidal risk decreases.

13. **Living alone:** Suicide rates decrease for clients living with a spouse, children, or someone else.

14. **Bereavement:** Bereavement increases suicidal potential.

15. **Unemployment:** Unemployment increases suicidal potential.

16. **Health status:** Physical illness and complaints increase suicidal potential.

17. **Impulsivity:** Suicidal potential increases for those with poor impulse control.

18. **Rigid thinking:** Suicidal people often experience rigid, all-or-none thinking.

19. **Stressful events:** People experiencing several undesirable events with negative outcomes have a greater risk for suicidal behavior.

20. **Release from hospitalization:** Suicidal risk increases on weekend leaves and shortly after discharge.

(Pope & Vasquez, 1991)

Murphy (1984) indicates that the three most common mental health diagnoses associated with suicide are affective disorders, alcoholism, and schizophrenia. Jacobs, Brewer, and Klein-Benheim (1999) note that those with affective disorders increase their risk of suicide if they also experience exacerbating panic attacks or abuse alcohol. Schizophrenia high risk factors are increased if the patient was formerly high functioning. Those suffering from substance abuse increase their chances of suicidal behavior if they have recently gone through interpersonal loss or comorbid depression.

Rudd and Joiner (1998) conceptualize the factors that may have a bearing on suicidal ideation in three domains: predisposing factors, risk factors, and protective factors. Predisposing factors are long standing and invariable (e.g., gender, family history of suicide, high-risk diagnosis). Risk factors consist of acute symptoms, stressors, or conditions (e.g., anxiety during a depressive episode, a recent loss for a chronic and actively drinking alcoholic). Protective factors, if weak or absent, may increase risk (e.g., lack of a social support network, absence of children under the age of 18 in the home). Based on the weight or number of factors in each of the above-mentioned domains, the authors propose a gradation of suicide risk ranging from nonexistent to extreme.

WHAT TO DO WHEN THERE IS SUICIDAL RISK

If the therapist believes that the client is at risk for committing suicide it is common to arrange for an immediate hospitalization. The client remains with qualified staff until a relative, another responsible party, an ambulance, or police pick up the client and drive him or her to the hospital. The therapist phones the hospital and asks for a return call to verify that the client has checked in. If the client does not check in, the therapist phones the client, family, or both to verify what took place. If the client still does not check into the hospital, the therapist phones the police to go to the client's residence or known whereabouts. A county social service worker is contacted to visit the client if sufficient follow-up has not taken place. The therapist documents all actions taken to obtain a higher level of care for the client. Not all clients, families, or government agencies will comply with a therapist's reporting of a client's suicidal risk.

Depending on specific services, requirements, and relationships, the client's psychiatrist and primary physician are contacted. In many cases, the client's insurance company requires that they choose the hospital in order to authorize payment for services. Although the client's life receives the highest priority, a significant hospital bill to the client could be avoided if the insurance company first authorizes the emergency treatment at the hospital. A brief phone call could prevent this problem.

There are instances in which hospitalization is not the best option because it increases the client's level of stress, thus increasing suicidal potential. A care team may be assembled to adequately monitor the client's behaviors and provide appropriate support. When caring friends or family members are not available to provide continuous observations, hospitalization is the best choice in protecting the client.

In the aforementioned scenario, if the client had significant suicidal ideas, but no plan, gestures, or threats, the clinician must clearly establish that the client is not in danger of personal harm at this time. The content of the interview must be documented. In cases of potential suicide, documentation of consultation with other mental health professionals is important.

SUICIDE CONTRACTS

It is common to write a suicide contract with clients in which the client agrees that certain steps will be followed when suicidal ideations or behaviors are taking place. It serves as a two-way contract in which both the therapist and the client list their obligations to each other. Common actions include phoning the therapist, calling a crisis center, talking with family, or going to the hospital. Although the contract is obviously not a legal document, it lists levels of treatment available to the client in tough times. Most contracts contain a number of readily available sources' phone numbers.

Suicide contracts are generally not made if the client's risk is minimal (e.g., the client states that he or she has no more than occasional thoughts of death or suicide). Clinical judgment is crucial in assessing potential suicidal situations. An overeager therapist could easily offend a nonsuicidal client, by overreacting to statements such as "I have thought about death at times." On the other hand, an undercautious therapist might refrain from acting upon a true, potential suicide by not wanting to offend the client, therefore doing nothing.

ETHICAL/LEGAL CONSIDERATIONS WHEN A CLIENT ATTEMPTS OR COMMITS SUICIDE

Few would disagree that once a therapist-client relationship exists, the therapist possesses a legal, moral, and ethical duty to protect the client, provide adequate care, and take reasonable precautions to prevent suicide. When a client attempts or commits suicide, malpractice flags may be raised. The clinical documentation could be scrutinized by any number of sources. When a doctor-patient (or therapist-client) relationship exists, records must indicate what precautions were taken to assess and prevent the suicide.

Simon (1988) describes several situations in which a doctor-patient relationship may be considered to exist. These include (a) giving advice, (b) making psychological interpretations, (c) writing a prescription, (d) supervising treatment by a nonmedical therapist, (e) having a lengthy phone conversation with a prospective patient, (f) treating an unseen patient by mail, (g) giving a patient an appointment, (h) telling walk-in patients that they will be seen, (i) providing sample medications, (j) acting as a substitute therapist, (k) providing treatment during an evaluation, (l) upholding special relationship duties to nonpatient third parties that are created by a treatment relationship with a patient (e.g., *Tarasoff* duty), and (m) providing psychiatric opinions to neighbors and friends. (See Rapid Reference 6.4.)

Few malpractice suits against therapists are successful in proving negligence, but the ratio is gradually increasing. A small portion of the malpractice insurance claims filed ever go to trial (Bongar, Maris, Berman, & Litman, 1998).

Bongar (1991) describes a *tort action*, or civil suit, as "a request by the plaintiff for compensation for damages that have occurred" (pp. 34–35). Civil suits may take place for a number of reasons; however, in mental health, a lawsuit against a therapist is generally for negligence for either omission of reasonable duties or commission of improper actions. Bongar (1991) and Simon (1988) provide excellent discussions, details, and examples of the legal aspects of suicide.

Rapid Reference 6.4

Tarasoff v. Regents of California

The California Supreme Court of California ruled that the interest of public safety held more weight than therapeutic confidentiality. The court defined the obligation that a psychotherapist has toward a third person whom a patient threatens to injure or kill.

Although suicide is difficult to predict, there are minimum standards typically viewed by the legal system. Knapp and VanderCreek (1983) state, "Courts usually consider two fundamental issues: (a) Did the professional adequately assess the likelihood that a patient was suicidal? And, (b), If an identifiable risk of harm was determined, did the professional take sufficient precautions to prevent suicide?"

CHAPTER SUMMARY

1. Every clinical assessment should include a suicide assessment.
2. Lack of knowledge in the legal aspects of suicide could lead to significant ethical, moral, and legal issues.
3. Although it is difficult to predict suicide for an individual, there are risk factors associated with suicidal behaviors.
4. When suicide is possible, the therapist must determine the client's level of risk to determine what level of care is needed.
5. Although a suicide contract will not guarantee suicide prevention, it provides the client with several options for receiving help when contemplating suicide.
6. Once a client-therapist relationship is established or implied, the therapist holds a responsibility to the client for assessing and following up on suicidal behavior.

TEST YOURSELF

1. **At what point is suicidal behavior always reportable to civil authorities?**
   (a) Severe depression
   (b) Ideations
   (c) Threats
   (d) Planning
2. **In mental health assessment, when should suicidal potential be assessed?**
   (a) Every assessment
   (b) When there is a history of suicidal behavior
   (c) When the client states there is suicidal ideations
   (d) Whenever a client appears to be depressed

3. **A suicidal gesture**
   (a) Is not to be taken seriously unless the client has a plan.
   (b) Should be ignored if the client has a long history of attention-seeking behavior.
   (c) Should be treated like an attempt.
   (d) Is no more than a cry for help.

4. **A therapeutic relationship may be legally in place in which of the following:**
   (a) Giving advice to someone
   (b) Providing supervision
   (c) Treating a client only once
   (d) All of these

5. **Which of the following is not considered to be a significant risk factor for suicide?**
   (a) Alcoholism
   (b) Mood Disorder
   (c) Obsessive-Compulsive Disorder
   (d) Borderline Personality Disorder

6. **Which of the following statements represents the greatest suicidal risk?**
   (a) "I'll kill myself if she continues to treat me that way."
   (b) "If she doesn't call me by 3:00, I'll make her feel guilty about what I did to myself."
   (c) "I often think about suicide."
   (d) "I've tried to kill myself in the past, so I'm afraid it could happen again."

7. **When a client claims to have suicidal ideations the therapist should**
   (a) Immediately refer the client for hospitalization.
   (b) Investigate what kind of ideations the client is having, then proceed.
   (c) Dismiss it as a normal behavior, unless the client states that there is a plan.
   (d) Phone the client's family to form a treatment and monitoring team.

8. **Which of the following best represents a suicidal gesture?**
   (a) A slight cut on the wrist
   (b) Overdosing on medications
   (c) Thinking about what the world would be like without oneself
   (d) Telling your fiancé that if you break up you couldn't live without her

(continued)

9. **Suicide is difficult to predict.** True or False?

10. **Suicidal risk factors can be assessed.** True or False?

11. **Men and women in the United States have an equal rate of suicide.** True or False?

12. **People recently released from the hospital have a higher rate of suicide.** True or False?

13. **What factors must be considered in assessing the risk of suicide?**

14. **What steps should a novice clinician take when a client appears to be a moderate risk for suicide but is not clearly suicidal at the time of the interview?**

Answers: 1. d; 2. a; 3. c; 4. d; 5. c; 6. b; 7. b; 8. a; 9. True; 10. True; 11. False; 12. True; 13. The major factors of suicide risk to consider include specificity of the plan, lethality of the method, availability of the proposed method, and proximity of social or helping resources. 14. A novice clinician should seek immediate supervision and consultation whenever there is any risk of suicide. If the potential is too high, the case should be transferred to a more experienced therapist.

Seven

DIAGNOSTIC INTERVIEWING

Clients desiring mental health treatment seek services at different stages in their illness and for different reasons. Whereas some people wait until their functioning is severely impaired, others seek therapy at the onset of any stressor disrupting their lives. Nevertheless, when a client seeks services, there is an underlying reason that he or she is asking for help at that time.

Many people wait for months or years before finally admitting that they need professional help. Especially in the case of a self-referral, an immediate response to a client may be the best window of opportunity for counseling to be effective. Delays in services or being placed on a waiting list may lead to the window of opportunity's closing. Other clients enter treatment not from personal desire but as a result of family pressures, legal obligations, job requirements, or any other number of reasons. Thus, in the initial session, it is important to ask the client "why now?" Some set of circumstances, events, stressors, or conditions led the client to seek help at this time. The clinician must be cognizant of why the client is requesting services and the client's motivation to receive such services. The higher the motivation to change, the better the prognosis; thus, a client's reluctance to be in counseling (e.g., court ordered or any situation in which the client did not initiate services) holds a less positive prognosis.

PRESENTING PROBLEM

The first significant information to uncover during the interview process is the client's presenting problem. The *presenting problem* is the client's stated reason that services are being sought at this time. It is not a diagnosis or the therapist's opinion as to the nature of the client's problem areas. The best way to elicit this

Putting It Into Practice

Proper and Improper Statements of a Presenting Problem

Example 1: Voices

Improper Presenting Problem Statement: The client is schizophrenic and may be in danger of harming herself.

Proper Presenting Problem Statement: The client is seeking services because she has been increasingly hearing voices for the past six months. She has quit her job because she can no longer concentrate. She fears that she will listen to the voices and harm herself or others.

Example 2: Mood

Improper Presenting Problem Statement: Mr. Jones is suicidal and suffers from Major Depression.

Proper Presenting Problem Statement: Mr. Jones states that he no longer has a will to live. He "constantly" thinks of ways he could die without making it appear to be a suicide. He no longer talks with his friends or loved ones, and hasn't left the house more than a few times in the past two months. Symptoms began when he ran out of money to pay for medications about six weeks ago.

Example 3: Partner Relationship Problems

Improper Presenting Problem Statement: Pat needs marriage counseling.

Proper Presenting Problem Statement: Pat presents with several complaints about her marriage, such as feelings of "guilt about an affair," "intense anger from being yelled at constantly," and "frustration from him spending all of the money every paycheck." Although she states that she wants to remain married, she thinks that she spends too much time crying, yelling, or avoiding her spouse.

Example 4: Child Behavior Problems

Improper Presenting Problem Statement: Lyle has a conduct problem and may become a criminal.

Proper Presenting Problem Statement: Lyle is being brought to counseling by his mother because he constantly argues with his teachers, has been suspended from school 12 times in the past two months, regularly punches his siblings, and was arrested last week for shoplifting.

Example 5: Alcoholism

Improper Presenting Problem Statement: Jan is an alcoholic.

Proper Presenting Problem Statement: Jan is being evaluated for counseling services because of increasing problems with binge drinking, black-outs, drinking on the job, and a recent DWI.

Teaching Point: *The presenting problem is stated in terms of the client's reason for being evaluated or receiving therapy. A description of symptoms and impairments is most helpful. It is never the clinician's opinion or a diagnosis.*

information is by asking the "why now?" question: What brings you here to-day? The wording of the presenting problem never looks at it as a conclusion, nor is it a diagnosis, because such decisions may not be made until after the diagnostic interview has ruled in and ruled out several possibilities. Although the presenting problem is not a diagnosis, statements are generally similar to the *DSM-IV-TR*'s descriptions of diagnoses and impairments. It is the first information used in the formulation of a diagnosis. This information is later clarified and incorporated into the treatment plan. The client describes the problem, then the therapist requests clarification, which leads to a differential diagnosis and appropriate treatment planning.

In addition to asking the client about the presenting problem, a number of other information sources are available to the clinician (e.g., medical history, prior mental health services history, family history, etc.) in formulating a diagnosis. These other information sources will be covered in depth later in the chapter.

INCONSISTENCIES IN THE PRESENTING PROBLEM

The presenting problem rarely perfectly matches information obtained from the client's history, testing, background information, and observations. Discrepancies tend to be the rule rather than the exception. Factors such as poor client insight, denial, malingering, distorted thinking, characterological concerns, changing situational factors, incomplete interviewing, and invalid or unreliable testing may lead to inconsistencies. As the science of interviewing becomes more reliable and knowledge of psychopathology increases, discrepancies will continue to decrease.

Nevertheless, the current knowledge level in psychopathology is sophisti-

Putting It Into Practice

Integrating Inconsistent Diagnostic Material

Lance presented as a very friendly, cooperative, and somewhat ingratiating client. He stated that he was very interested in receiving counseling because he knew others who had received successful therapy from the clinic. During the initial session, he seemed to enjoy talking about himself but rarely brought up any problem areas. When told that he exhibited no evidence of impairment and that his insurance would not cover further sessions, he asked the therapist to write a report to his probation officer that he had completed therapy.

In the initial session, Lance had never mentioned that treatment was required to avoid legal consequences. The therapist assumed he was a self-referral. Perhaps if the therapist had asked Lance why he was in counseling, time would not have been wasted. After this was disclosed, Lance authorized release of his records from other sources to his psychologist. His records revealed significant antisocial behaviors and a previous diagnosis of Bipolar Disorder. An appropriate treatment plan could then be developed to accurately address Lance's needs. After six more months of weekly sessions, the letter was finally sent to his probation officer. In this case, Lance's presenting problem did not match his mental health history because of his desire to present himself in a positive light in order to end treatment quickly and avoid legal problems.

Teaching Point: *When the clinician asks the client the purpose for seeking counseling services, it is necessary to further determine if there was a referral, court order, or other reason for coming to counseling. Without obtaining this information, the true purpose of the referral may not be addressed.*

cated enough to manage most discrepancies. The clinician must be skilled in a number of areas such as interviewing techniques, psychopathology, the *DSM-IV-TR,* and testing, and must have the ability of integrating these skills to arrive at the correct diagnosis.

THE RELATIONSHIP AMONG DIAGNOSES, SYMPTOMS, DISTRESS, AND IMPAIRMENTS

Diagnoses, symptoms, distress, and impairments are interrelated. Diagnoses are defined in the *DSM-IV-TR* by symptoms. The symptoms must cause significant impairment to warrant making the diagnosis. Functional impairments may include a wide range of factors, such as the client's occupation, social life, family life, and physical health. If a person is impaired, but not for mental health reasons, a mental health diagnosis cannot be made simply because impairments exist. Distress or psychological distress includes mental factors or stressors leading to mental health problems.

Symptoms

Specific *DSM-IV-TR* mental health diagnoses are defined and differentiated by their respective symptoms. Symptoms for the different categories of diagnoses (e.g., mood disorder, developmental disorders) are generally unrelated; however, symptoms within categories may be similar. For example, although similarities in symptomology exist between Dysthymia and Major Depression, there are also distinct differences that aid in differential diagnoses. Table 7.1 illustrates the similarities and differences between the symptoms of Major Depression and Dysthymia.

In Table 7.1 the major differences between Major Depressive Disorder and Dysthymia are the length of time in which symptoms must occur and the number and degree of the symptoms. A number of the symptoms required for Dysthymia typically represent pervasive negative self-beliefs and an ongoing level of decreased energy (e.g., hopelessness, low self-esteem, over 2 years duration). Major Depressive Disorder, on the other hand, is defined by symptoms suggesting a current decreased vegetative state in which the symptomology may be more severe (e.g., suicidality, recent weight changes, psychomotor agitation or retardation).

Although a number of symptoms are not shared diagnostically between Major Depressive Disorder and Dysthymia, this does not suggest that a person diagnosed with one disorder cannot experience some of the symptoms of the other one. Clinical expertise is exhibited when the clinician accurately performs a differential diagnosis by ruling in the correct diagnosis and ruling out the diagnosis in which the diagnostic criteria have not been meet.

Sometimes a client will endorse symptoms concordant with more than one disorder. In such cases, a working knowledge of the *DSM-IV-TR* will aid the clinician in knowing whether both disorders exist or if only one (when two are possible) of the diagnoses is appropriate because one subsumes the other. For example, the *DSM-IV-TR* instructs not to diagnose Oppositional Defiant

Table 7.1 Symptoms Comparison: Major Depression and Dysthymia

Diagnostic Criteria	Major Depression	Dysthymia	Comparison Symptoms
Minimum length of time	2 weeks	2 years[a]	Different
Depressed most of time	Yes	Yes	Same
Lack of pleasure	Yes	No	Different
Weight (±)	Yes	No	Different
Appetite(±)	Yes	Yes	Same
Sleep (±)	Yes	Yes	Same
Fatigue	Yes	Yes	Same
Psychomotor (±)	Yes	No	Different
Worthlessness/guilt	Yes	No	Different
Concentration (–)	Yes	Yes	Same
Suicidality	Yes	No	Different
Hopelessness	No	Yes	Different
Low self-esteem	No	Yes	Different

Note: Yes = symptom indicated in *DSM-IV-TR* for the diagnosis. No = not a *DSM-IV-TR* symptom for the diagnosis. Different = different from other diagnosis. Same = same symptom in each diagnosis. (–) = decreases in the behavior. (±) = increases or decreases in the behavior.

[a] For children, one year.

Disorder if the child has already been diagnosed with Conduct Disorder (one diagnosis subsumes the other; *DSM-IV-TR,* p. 98). It is possible, on the other hand, to diagnose Dysthymia and Major Depression concurrently, because a person chronically suffering from Dysthymic Disorder may have bouts of Major Depression in which the client's usual level of depression becomes much worse. Rapid Reference 7.1 provides a few examples of diagnoses that are generally not given concurrently.

Symptoms that are not required for a disorder to be diagnosed but that commonly exist with the disorder are termed *associated symptoms* (see discussion upcoming in this chapter). For example, some of the symptoms for Dysthymia

≡Rapid Reference 7.1

Examples of Diagnoses That Are Generally Not Given Together

Primary diagnosis of . . .	Subsumes diagnosis of . . .
Conduct Disorder	Oppositional Defiant Disorder
Mental Retardation	Attention-Deficit/Hyperactivity Disorder; Learning Disability
Substance Dependence	Substance Abuse

may also occur with someone diagnosed with Major Depression, but they do not technically define the second diagnosis. In other words, some symptoms may be essential to a diagnosis of Dysthymia, but only associated with Major Depression and vice versa.

Impairments

Impairments differ from symptoms in that they represent areas in the client's life that are preventing the client from functioning adequately in social, occupational, legal, educational, and affective aspects of life. For example, being fired from three jobs in the past month is evidence of occupational impairment but does not clearly identify specific symptoms. Clients suffering from mental health disorders and their related symptoms may be impaired in one or more areas. A given disorder is defined not by its resulting impairment but rather by its symptoms. Impairments in any area of daily functioning can exist with almost any mental health disorder. For example, social impairment can result from almost any mental health problem area (e.g., depression, anxiety, schizophrenia, conduct, ADHD, etc.), but the symptoms of these disorders are divergent.

Distress

Distress is not as easily observed as impairments. It is a subjective psychological impairment leading to mental problems. It is common for clients to desire

CAUTION

Assigning a client a diagnosis by simply endorsing symptoms is not sufficient to warrant giving the diagnosis. Impairments or distress resulting from the symptoms also must be documented.

counseling services even when they are experiencing no apparent functional impairments. For example, a client might be keeping up at work, socializing adequately, and functioning appropriately in the family environment. However, psychologically, the client may be under much duress, worrying excessively, or feeling dysphoric most of the time. It is likely that the client is in need of counseling for the short term. Diagnoses such as Adjustment Disorder or Dysthymia are often portrayed by distress rather than impairments.

Chronic distress is also depicted by ongoing stressors such as chronic pain, disability, fear of a loss of freedom, death, or a deteriorating medical condition. Although distress of a chronic nature may lead to symptoms identical to mental disorders from other causes, treatment tends to focus on coping with the stressor rather than simply alleviating symptoms.

Psychological distress is measured differently from impairments. Measurement of impairments is listed later in this chapter. Psychological distress is typically measured by either normative or individualized psychometric tests.

ESSENTIAL AND ASSOCIATED SYMPTOMS

The *DSM-IV-TR* distinguishes between essential and associated symptoms (or features). *Essential symptoms* must be prevalent to justify a diagnosis. Thus, if every *DSM-IV-TR* symptom of a diagnosis is endorsed except the essential symptoms, the diagnosis cannot be assigned. Every *DSM-IV-TR* disorder lists at least one essential symptom. *Associated symptoms* are other symptoms that may be present in someone suffering from a particular disorder. For some disorders, several associated symptoms may be listed in the *DSM-IV-TR,* and the *DSM-IV-TR* may require that at least a certain number be endorsed along with the essential symptoms before a diagnosis can be made. Other disorders may have no associated symptoms listed in the *DSM-IV-TR.*

Unlike essential symptoms, the same associated symptoms are commonly connected with several disorders. For example, associated symptoms such as social withdrawal, impulsivity, sleep disturbance, fatigue, and decreased concentration are commonly endorsed by individuals diagnosed with a wide range of disorders. Without additional information, it is possible that clients with these symptoms could be diagnosed with an anxiety disorder by a therapist specializing in anxiety or with a depressive disorder by a therapist specializing in mood disorders.

Every mental health disorder is described systematically in the *DSM-IV-TR*. The first paragraph describing each diagnosis, titled Diagnostic Features, always lists the essential symptoms required to diagnose the disorder. Thus, a familiarity with the essential features of most disorders is crucial for effec-

DON'T FORGET

Essential Symptoms and Diagnostic Features vs. Associated Symptoms

- Essential Symptoms must be prevalent to assign a diagnosis. A *DSM-IV-TR* diagnosis cannot be given if any of the essential symptoms are not present. Further, the symptom must cause significant distress or impairment.

- Associated symptoms are helpful in determining a diagnosis but may vary between clients and are common across various diagnoses. Associated symptoms, in themselves, do not warrant giving a diagnosis.

Putting It Into Practice

Vague Interviewing Resulting From Inquiring Solely About Associated Symptoms

Therapist: "Do you shy away from other people?"

Client: "Yes"

Therapist: "Have you been experiencing increased problems concentrating?"

Client: "Yes"

Therapist: "Do you sleep adequately or too much or too little?"

Client: "I don't get enough sleep."

Therapist: "Have you been feeling fatigued lately?"

Client: "Yes"

Teaching Point: *Although the client endorsed every symptom asked, the clinician can not make a definitive diagnosis because the associated symptoms that the client endorsed could fit almost any diagnosis. In this case, it is possible that different therapists might diagnose this client with depressive disorder, anxiety disorder, personality disorder, or others.*

Putting It Into Practice

Effective Ruling-in and Ruling-out Process for Depressive Disorder

Therapist: "Do you feel depressed most of the time?"

Client: "Yes"

Therapist: "How long have you been depressed?"

Client: "About three months ... ever since my fiancé left me."

Therapist: "How severe is your level of depression?"

Client: "It is very severe. I can't do anything any more. I'm getting confused and my concentration is gone. I feel this way all the time. There is no letup. It couldn't get any worse."

Therapist: "How is your appetite?"

Client: "I eat only when I have to. I no longer have any appetite."

Therapist: "Has your weight been changing recently?"

Client: "Yes, I've lost almost 20 pounds in the past month or two."

Teaching Point: *Yes/no responses to symptom endorsement provide little information. However, when the clinician seeks further information about symptoms that are endorsed, its quality is enhanced and much more helpful in treatment.*

---

tive clinical interviewing and arriving at a clear differential diagnosis. To save time, the clinician should focus the ruling-in and ruling-out process of the clinical interview on essential symptoms rather than associated symptoms. If the clinician begins by trying to rule in or rule out associated symptoms (which may be endorsed for a number of different disorders), the interview process will suffer from a lack of direction.

VEGETATIVE SYMPTOMS

Vegetative symptoms refer to symptoms regarding body functions such as increases or decreases in appetite, weight, or sleep, or decrease in level of energy and sexual interest, or libido. As the degree of mental impairment increases, vegetative symptoms are also generally more prominent, especially with depressive, anxiety, and psychotic disorders.

Vegetative symptoms are not specifically noted in the *DSM-IV-TR* as a category of symptoms, but have a long history in psychopathology terminology.

Clinicians typically inquire about changes in clients' vegetative symptoms compared to their premorbid functioning (the client's personality and behaviors prior to mental health impairment). Increased vegetative symptoms coincide with general health decreases.

DSM-IV-TR DIAGNOSTIC CRITERIA

Each *DSM-IV-TR* Axis I diagnosis is made by going through a specific set of procedures in which the client's symptoms, impairments, and other factors are investigated. Other causes such as medical and cultural factors are also considered. *DSM-IV-TR* diagnoses are divided into the following headings to help rule in and rule out the disorder.

Diagnostic Features

The Diagnostic Features section first lists the essential feature(s) of the diagnosis. As noted earlier, the essential feature is a symptom that must be prevalent in order to warrant assigning the diagnosis. If it is not present, the diagnosis cannot be given. Wiger (1999) refers to this as the *primary essential feature(s)*. The diagnosis further describes other symptoms that must be prevalent. This secondary list often notes various symptoms, in which a set minimum must be endorsed to make the diagnosis. The *DSM-IV-TR* does not give them a specific term; however, Wiger (1999) refers to these as *secondary essential features* for clarity.

In cases in which there are not sufficient secondary essential features, the *DSM-IV-TR* allows for clinical judgment, ". . . the exercise of clinical judgment may justify giving a certain diagnosis to an individual even though the clinical presentation falls just short of meeting the full criteria for the diagnosis as long as the symptoms that are present are persistent and severe" (p. xxxii). Also, the *DSM-IV-TR* allows for a diagnosis followed by NOS (Not Otherwise Specified) when endorsed symptoms are inconsistent or below the diagnostic threshold.

DSM-IV-TR *Example (paraphrased):*
300.02 Generalized Anxiety Disorder

    A. (Primary Essential Features) Excessive anxiety and worry (apprehensive expectation), occurring more days than not for at least 6 months, about a number of events or activities (such as work or school performance).

B. The person finds it difficult to control the worry.

C. (Secondary Essential Features) The anxiety and worry are associated with three (or more) of the following six symptoms (with at least some symptoms present for more days than not for the past 6 months).

Note: Only one item is required in children.

    1. Restlessness or feeling keyed up or on edge

    2. Being easily fatigued

    3. Difficulty concentrating or mind going blank

    4. Irritability

    5. Muscle tension

    6. Sleep disturbance (difficulty falling or staying asleep, or restless and unsatisfying sleep)

D. The focus of the anxiety and worry is not confined to features of an Axis I Disorder (examples given).

E. The anxiety, worry, or physical symptoms cause clinically significant distress or impairment in social, occupational, or other important areas of functioning.

F. The disturbance is not due to (other disorders listed).

Subtypes and Specifiers

Not all diagnoses have subtypes or specifiers. Subtypes receive the same diagnosis number, but additional information is given in the diagnosis to more clearly define a particular aspect of the disorder.

DSM-IV-TR *Example of a Subtype: 297.1 Delusional Disorder*
Somatic Type: delusions that the person has some physical defect or general medical condition

DSM-IV-TR *Example of a Specifier: 309.21 Separation Anxiety Disorder*
Early Onset: if onset occurs before age 6 years

Recording Procedures

Guidelines are given for reporting the name of the disorder and selecting the ICD-9-CM code. It further provides directions for applying subtypes and specifiers.

DSM-IV-TR *Example: 291.2 Alcohol-Induced Persisting Dementia*

Associated Features and Disorders

As noted earlier, associated features and disorders are symptoms, behaviors, or physical or medical findings that are not used to validate the diagnosis but often co-occur with the diagnosis. Often, they are associated with more than one diagnosis and therefore are not essential features. This section is often divided into three parts as follows: (a) associated descriptive features and mental disorders, (b) associated laboratory findings, and (c) associated physical examination findings and general medical conditions.

DSM-IV-TR *Example (paraphrased): 299.0 Autistic Disorder*
Associated descriptive features and mental disorders: mild to profound Mental Retardation, abnormalities in development of cognitive skills, hyperactivity, short attention span, lack of fear response
Associated laboratory findings: serotonegic activity
Associated physical examination findings and general medical conditions: primitive reflexes, delayed development of hand dominance, fragile X syndrome, seizures

Specific Culture, Age, and Gender Features

The client's presentation of the disorder may be affected by factors such as culture, age, or gender.

DSM-IV-TR *Example (paraphrased): 300.7 Body Dysmorphic Disorder*
Cultural concerns about a person's physical appearance may influence or amplify preoccupations. It may be equally common in men and women.

Prevalence

When information is available, prevalence data in areas such as incidence, lifetime risk, and lifetime prevalence are provided. Various settings such as community, inpatient, and outpatient are given as they relate to prevalence, when sufficient data exists.

DSM-IV-TR *Example: 301.13 Cyclothymic Disorder*
"Studies have reported a lifetime prevalence of Cyclothymic Disorder of from 0.4% to 1%. Prevalence in mood disorders clinics may range from 3% to 5%."

Course

The lifetime patterns of the disorder are described. Factors such as age of onset, mode (abrupt, insidious) of onset, cycling, and progression of the disorder are considered.

DSM-IV-TR *Example 307.46 Sleep Terror Disorder:*
"Begins with children between ages 4 and 12 years and resolves spontaneously during adolescence. In adults . . . begins between ages 20 and 30 years and often follows a chronic course . . . waxing and waning over time."

Familial Pattern

The frequency of occurrence between first-degree biological relatives is compared to the general population. Genetic transmission patterns (e.g., twin studies) are given when available.

DSM-IV-TR *Example 300.3 Obsessive-Compulsive Disorder:*
"The concordance rate . . . is higher for monozygotic twins than it is for dizygotic twins."

Differential Diagnosis

Information is provided as to how to differentiate the diagnosis with those having similar characteristics.

DSM-IV-TR *(paraphrased): Example 307.52 Pica*
"Before approximately ages 18–24 months, mouthing and sometimes eating nonnutritive substances are relatively common and do not imply the presence of Pica. . . . Eating of nonnutritivie substances may occur during the course of other mental disorders [listed]. . . . Pica can be distinguished from other eating disorders [others listed] by the consumption of nonnutritive substances."

RULE-IN AND RULE-OUT STEPS

The rule-in/rule-out method does not imply that simply selecting endorsed symptoms is all there is to making a diagnosis. Endorsement of symptoms to validate a diagnosis is a means of communication and provides clarification. Although clinical judgment in itself is not a specific step in making a diagnosis, it is part of every diagnostic procedure. Wiger (1999) suggests the following rule-in/rule-out method.

The following steps are adapted from *DSM-IV-TR* procedures for each Axis I diagnosis.

1. Rule-In/Rule-Out of Primary Essential Symptoms

Primary essential features (also called essential symptoms) are those specifically listed in the first paragraph of each *DSM-IV-TR* diagnosis. For example, in the *DSM-IV-TR* diagnosis of Paranoid Personality Disorder, it states, "The essential feature of Paranoid Personality Disorder is a pattern of pervasive distrust and suspiciousness of others. . . ." Clearly, the clinician cannot ask the client the essential features of each of the over 500 *DSM-IV-TR* diagnoses and their variations. Besides the fact that this would be extremely time-consuming, there is considerable overlap between the diagnoses; thus, more efficient means of ruling out essential symptoms are necessary.

Seventeen diagnostic categories are listed in the *DSM-IV-TR*. Prior to inquiring about specific essential symptoms for different disorders within each category, questions such as the following could be asked to help rule in and rule out disorders within these categories.

The initial inquiry of symptoms and the client's presenting problem generally eliminate most of the above problem areas. If, for example, the client states that the main concern is depressed mood, the follow-up questions should rule out the essential features of the mood disorders. However, the clinician must never assume that other diagnoses are not possible simply because the client did not claim for them to be prevalent.

If a client denies or there is evidence of the essential features of a diagnosis, it is ruled out. If the essential features are endorsed, more rule-in questions are asked. Rule-in questions generally involve factors such as the time period in which symptoms have occurred and additional symptoms listed in the *DSM-IV-TR*. For example, an adult must have certain symptoms of depression for two years in order to be diagnosed with Dysthymic Disorder, and two weeks for Major Depressive Disorder.

2. Rule-In/Rule-Out of Secondary Essential Symptoms

Secondary essential symptoms is not a *DSM-IV-TR* term. However, these symptoms are useful in further defining a *DSM-IV-TR* concept. In several of the
DSM-IV-TR diagnoses, there are additional symptoms that must be endorsed
to give a diagnosis. They are most often presented as a list of symptoms in
which at least a minimum number of them must be endorsed. When the minimum number of symptoms is not sufficiently endorsed, but impairments persist, an NOS diagnosis may be given. For example, the diagnosis of Conduct
Disorder includes an essential feature of "a repetitive and persistent pattern of
behavior in which the basic rights of others or major age-appropriate societal
norms or rules are violated." In addition, 3 or more of 15 symptoms must be
endorsed to warrant giving the diagnosis. If only 2 of the other 15 symptoms
are endorsed, but the essential symptom is met and there is clinically significantly impairment, the diagnosis of Disruptive Behavior Disorder, Not Otherwise Specified is given. All major diagnostic categories contain an NOS diagnosis for those not meeting full criteria.

This text has no intention of contradicting *DSM-IV-TR* terminology by introducing primary and secondary essential symptoms. Rather, its intent is to
further clarify the two types of essential features listed in the *DSM-IV-TR*.

3. Assess the Associated Symptoms

Some confusion in the literature exists over the term *associated symptoms*. The
DSM-IV-TR describes them as symptoms that are not essential to the diagnosis but often associated with it. Some writers describe what this text denotes as
secondary essential symptoms as associated symptoms. However, this is not
consistent with the *DSM-IV-TR;* because associated symptoms are common
across several diagnoses; they are not used to formulate a diagnosis. However,
they are helpful in understanding the individual and may be incorporated in
treatment planning. To use Conduct Disorder as an example again, the associated symptoms listed include, "little empathy and little concerns for the feelings, wishes, and well-being of others," plus several other behavioral concerns
often associated with the diagnosis. None of these, however, are to be used to
validate a diagnosis, because of the significant overlap with other diagnoses
and vagary.

4. Rule Out Other Disorders

Frequently, a client will appear to meet criteria for a diagnosis, but other factors or diagnoses that more accurately account for the symptoms also exist. The *DSM-IV-TR* disorders list several other possibilities to consider before making a diagnosis. These aspects include med-

CAUTION

Failing to either rule in or rule out the *DSM-IV-TR* diagnosis significantly increases the chance of misdiagnosing or overdiagnosis. Without conducting these procedures, both the validity and reliability of the interview are compromised.

ical problems, time factors, other mental health diagnoses, and qualifiers, such as areas of impairment that must be present.

Putting It Into Practice

DSM-IV-TR Example of Four Steps in Differentiating Between Primary Essential Symptoms, Secondary Essential Symptoms, and Associated Symptoms

Diagnosis: Dsythymic Disorder

Note: The following steps represent ruling-in symptoms only. Each *DSM-IV-TR* diagnosis must also have validated significant distress or impairments.

Step One

DSM-IV-TR Essential Feature(s) for Making the Diagnosis:

(Termed Primary Essential Symptoms in this text)

"The essential feature of Dysthymic Disorder is a chronically depressed mood that occurs for most of the day more days than not for at least 2 years." (*DSM-IV-TR*, p. 380)

Step Two

DSM-IV-TR Additional Criteria for Making the Diagnosis:

(Termed Secondary Essential Symptom in this text; termed Associated Symptoms in some texts)

"Presence, while depressed, of two (or more) of the following:

(1) poor appetite or overeating

(2) insomnia or hypersomnia

(continued)

(3) low energy or fatigue

(4) low self-esteem

(5) poor concentration or difficulty making decisions

(6) feelings of hopelessness"

Step Three

DSM-IV-TR Associated Symptoms:

The *DSM-IV-TR* states that the associated features of Dysthymia are similar to a Major Depressive Episode and states the following: "Several studies suggest that the most commonly encountered symptoms in Dysthymic Disorder may be feelings of inadequacy; generalized loss of interest or pleasure; social withdrawal; feelings of guilt or brooding about the past; subjective feelings of irritability or excessive anger; and decreased activity, effectiveness, or productivity" (p. 378).

Step Four

Rule Out Other Factors

Other criteria include (a) there have been no Major Depressive Episodes in the first two years of the disturbance; (b) there is no history of mania, hypomania, or Cyclothymic Disorder; (c) the disturbance does not occur exclusively during a chronic Psychotic Disorder; (d) the symptoms are not due to the physiological effects of a substance or medical condition; and (e) the symptoms cause clinically significant impairment in listed areas.

DIAGNOSTIC DECISION TREES

Diagnostic decision trees are an effective means of ruling in and ruling out mental health diagnoses. Appendix A of the *DSM-IV-TR* contains six decision trees that aid in differential diagnosis of (a) Mental Disorders Due to a General Medical Condition, (b) Substance-Induced Disorders, (c) Psychotic Disorders, (d) Mood Disorders, (e) Anxiety Disorders, and (f) Somatoform Disorders. The decision trees aid in understanding the organizational and hierarchical structure of the *DSM-IV-TR*.

Each *DSM-IV-TR* decision tree begins with basic clinical features in which yes/no decisions are made as to whether the feature is prominent. The process is a rule-in/rule-out method. The clinician goes through several yes/no decisions in which the final decision yields a diagnosis. However, the *DSM-IV-TR* warns not to base a diagnosis solely on a decision tree because the process is based on approximations and does not include all diagnostic criteria.

Decision trees are based on differential diagnoses. The most common means of differentiating diagnoses are found earlier in this chapter under the heading of *DSM-IV-TR* Diagnostic Criteria. Rapid Reference 7.2 provides

Rapid Reference 7.2

Example of Ruling in and Ruling out Mood Disorder Based on Time of Onset

Question: Are you usually depressed? . . . How long have you felt this way?

Client Response:	Possibilities (others such as NOS diagnoses are possible):
Less than 2 weeks	Not Major Depressive Disorder Not Dysythymia Possibly Adjustment Disorder
Two weeks to six months	Possibly Major Depressive Disorder Not Dysthymia Possibly Acute Adjustment Disorder
Six months to two years	Possibly Major Depressive Disorder Not Dysthymia Not Acute Adjustment Disorder Possibly Chronic Adjustment Disorder
Two or more years (adults 2+ years; children 1+ year)	Possibly Major Depressive Disorder Possibly Dysthymia Most likely not Chronic Adjustment Disorder

Next Question: Does this cause significant impairment or distress to you in areas such as your social, occupational, or other areas of functioning?

If no is the answer it is not a defined as a mental disorder. However, counseling may be helpful.

If yes is the answer, the therapist must know the *DSM-IV-TR* well enough to determine the next rule-out possibilities. Because depressive disorders are primarily distinguished diagnostically by time of onset and specific symptoms, it is suggested that questions regarding symptoms and impairments are now queried.

an example of ruling-in and ruling-out mood disorders based on time of onset.

Given the time period and diagnostic possibilities, the clinician now would query the symptoms of possible disorders. For example, yes/no responses to various symptoms indicative of depressive disorders would be asked (e.g., for Major Depressive Disorder, the clinician would ascertain whether five out of nine defined symptoms have been present in the same two-week time period and represent a change from previous functioning; at least one of the symptoms must be either depressed mood or loss of interest or pleasure).

__ Yes __ No	Depressed most of the day, and/or
__ Yes __ No	Diminished interest or pleasure, plus a total of five out of nine, including
__ Yes __ No	Weight loss or gain (5% in a month)
__ Yes __ No	Insomnia or hypersomnia most days
__ Yes __ No	Psychomotor retardation or agitation most days
__ Yes __ No	Fatigue or loss of energy most days
__ Yes __ No	Feelings of worthlessness or inappropriate guilt
__ Yes __ No	Decreased concentration or indecisiveness most of the time
__ Yes __ No	Recurring thoughts of death or suicidal ideation

Whether or not Major Depressive Disorder has been ruled in or ruled out, the clinician would query symptoms of other depressive disorders, because they can co-occur. For example, clients with both Major Depressive Disorder and Dysthymia are commonly described as having "Double Depression."

It is a significant time saver to avoid redundancy when querying symptoms that occur in more than one diagnosis. For example, if the symptoms of insomnia or hypersomnia are endorsed when ruling in Major Depression, there is no need to ask about it again when ruling out Dysthymia, which has some of the same symptoms.

CAUTION

To assign any given *DSM-IV-TR* diagnosis, minimally the essential feature(s) must be prevalent. If not, the diagnosis is ruled out. In addition, there may be additional symptoms required.

The *DSM-IV-TR* Appendix A provides decision trees for seven categories of diagnoses to aid the clinician's understanding of the organizational and hierarchical structure of the *DSM-IV-TR* classification system. In each of the diagnostic categories, a series of questions about symptoms are answered either yes or no. As the clinician goes through the process of several rule-outs of essential features, it ends with a tentative diagnosis. Although this method is not intended to be the sole means of obtaining a diagnosis, it is an excellent learning tool in understanding the *DSM-IV-TR*. Individual features of the diagnosis must first be ruled in before giving a diagnosis.

An accurate mental health diagnosis requires much more than simply endorsing that certain *DSM-IV-TR* symptoms exist. For example, it is doubtful that anyone can say they never feel dysphoric, or that they never withdraw from others, or never suffer from appetite or sleep problems. As humans we do not operate on an even keel all the time. When we are stressed, there is generally an emotional reaction. But normal responses to stressors do not indicate a mental health disorder.

In order to diagnose a mental health disorder there must be an appropriate endorsement of symptoms and significant impairments or distress due to the mental illness. Rapid References 7.3–7.8 provide examples of various types of mental health impairments.

As noted, symptoms, in themselves, do not provide much information about a particular client's problem. Although symptoms are the primary means of defining a diagnosis, different clients with the same diagnosis may have little in common in terms of the severity of their condition. It is extremely difficult to quantify symptoms. For example, stating that a client has 7 units of social withdrawal has little or no meaning. Likewise, a client described as moderately depressed does not give the clinician all that is needed to customize an effective treatment plan.

A simple way to record the specificity of a client's symptoms is to remember the acronym "OF AID" (Onset, Frequency, Antecedents, Intensity, and Duration). Most mental health symptoms can be described in all or some of these terms. Later, treatment planning can incorporate these descriptors by providing a measurable baseline and specific treatment objectives.

Putting It Into Practice

Using the OF AID Technique During the Interview

Symptom: Dysphoric Mood

I. Poor technique

Therapist: "Are you usually sad?"

Client: "Yes."

Narrative: Client is sad.

2. OF AID technique.

Therapist: "Are you usually sad?"

Client: "Yes."

Therapist: "How long have you felt sad?" **(Onset)**

Client: "It all started when my spouse passed away two years ago." (This answer rules out certain affective disorders due to *DSM-IV-TR* time factors.)

Therapist: "How often do you feel this sad?" **(Frequency)**

Client: "I would say at least four to six days per week."

Therapist: "Is there anything that seems to bring on or increase your feelings of sadness?" **(Antecedents)**

Client: "I'm almost always sad, but things like holidays, watching couples holding hands, and just being alone make things much worse."

Therapist: "How severe or intense are your feelings of sadness? (*Note:* descriptors such as Mild, Moderate, or Severe could be used, or the client can use rating scale, e.g. 1–100)." **(Intensity)**

Client: "I'd say they're moderate to severe. On a scale of 1–100, I'd rate it as a 75, but it's getting worse over time. That's why I'm here."

Therapist: "How long do your bouts of sadness last?" **(Duration)**

Client: "When I get depressed, I feel down for at least three days at a time ... sometimes more."

Narrative: The client has felt increasingly more dysphoric for the past two years, since her spouse passed away. She remains depressed for about three days at a time, an average of 4–6 days out of the week. Events such as holidays, being alone, and viewing couples holding hands exacerbate and increase symptoms. She describes symptoms as "moderately severe" or "75 out of 100" on a Subjective Unites of Distress (SUD) scale.

Teaching Point: *The OF AID technique can be used both diagnostically and in treatment planning. It incorporates a medical model of measuring and quantifying mental health symptoms and behaviors.*

Rapid Reference 7.3

Social Impairments: Interview Questions and Documentation of Impairments

Interview

Therapist: "Do you spend any time with friends or family?"

Client: "No, not really."

Therapist: "Was there a time when you did?"

Client: "Oh, yes . . . I used to be with my best friend regularly. We went bowling and you couldn't keep us away from ball games. Now I just avoid everybody."

Therapist: "What about your family?"

Client: "Well, they care about me, but I think I turned them off when I told them to mind their own business. Now, I'm too embarrassed or ashamed to call them."

Therapist: "Are you involved in any social activities at this time?"

Client: "No, none at all."

Therapist: "What were some of your activities before things changed?"

Client: "I used to go bicycling with my neighbor every Saturday. My best friend and I went to every sporting event you can think of. On Sunday afternoons, I was always at our family gathering. I haven't done any of these in at least two months."

Documentation of Social Impairments

Social impairment, as evidenced by (a) no longer spending recreational time with best friend, and (b) avoiding family activities. Previously enjoyed each of these social activities.

Treatment Goals and Objectives

Goal: Increase social activities to premorbid level of functioning

Objective 1: Reestablish going bicycling with neighbor on a weekly basis

Objective 2: Contact family and attend a Sunday afternoon function

Objective 3: Attend at least one sporting activity with best friend in the next two weeks

⟨Rapid Reference 7.4

Occupational Impairments: Interview Questions and Documentation of Impairments

Interview

Therapist: "Are you employed now?"

Client: "Yes, but I just received my last warning slip because I miss so much work. Actually, I've been fired from my last four jobs for poor attendance."

Therapist: "Do you know why your attendance has been a problem?"

Client: "Yes, I do. I have terrible panic attacks. I'm so afraid that I'll have one at work. I'd rather get fired than have them see me in that condition. Now, I'm just going to get fired again. They just think I'm lazy."

Therapist: "Are there any other problems at work?"

Client: "Where should I begin? My sales are at 40% of quota. I'm two months behind in productivity reports, and I avoid everybody."

Therapist: "When did these problems begin? You told me before that you used to be a top salesperson."

Client: "Yes, I was. But I started having panic attacks about three years ago, when my divorce was final. Since then, it's been downhill."

Documentation of Occupational Impairment

Occupational impairment as evidenced by (a) danger of being fired from job, (b) poor attendance due to panic attacks, (c) failure to meet quota, (d) arrears in productivity reports.

Treatment Goals and Objectives

Goal: Increase social activities to premorbid level of functioning.

Objective 1: Establish contract with employer to list steps to take to remove impending termination from job

Objective 2: Increase attendance at work from currently working an average of 20 hr per week to 40 hr per week

Objective 3: Incrementally increase sales at work from meeting 40% of quota to 100% of quota

Objective 4: Catch up on paperwork on job by June 10th

≡Rapid Reference 7.5

Legal Impairments: Interview Questions and Documentation of Impairments

Interview

Therapist: "I see that you have been referred for counseling by your attorney. Tell me what brings you here for services."

Client: "I have been charged with assault. This is my third offense. I just keep on having bouts of rage. I start fights at least once every week ... for no reason. I could go to prison this time."

Therapist: "What do you want to do about it?"

Client: "I want to learn to control my anger and never pick another fight."

Documentation of Legal Impairments

Legal impairments as evidenced by (a) upcoming court appearance for third assault charge and (b) possible incarceration

Treatment Goals and Objectives

Goal 1: End behaviors that have resulted in harm to others

Objective 1: Med referral

Objective 2: Learn and implement at least three means of managing anger

Objective 3: No incidents of aggression toward others during the course of treatment, currently involved in at least five physical fights per month

---

Some symptoms cannot be described using each of the items in the OF AID technique. For example, it is difficult to clearly describe a symptom such as low self-esteem in terms of duration, but it can easily be described in terms such as intensity. In such cases, examining the client's behavior as it relates to the symptom may be beneficial. For example, behaviors indicative of low self-esteem are easier to define than the symptom itself. Stating the frequency of self-deprecating behaviors is more helpful than estimating someone's level of self-esteem. Without measurability, the treatment progress cannot be clearly demonstrated.

Impairments are related to but not the same as symptoms. As noted earlier, they are specific problems the client is experiencing that interfere with functioning in a number of areas. Impairments are often caused by the symp-

Rapid Reference 7.6

Physical Impairments: Interview Questions and Documentation of Impairments

Interview

Therapist: "Why do you want to stop drinking alcohol?"

Client: "Although I enjoy drinking, it has ruined my body. I'm experiencing liver failure, I can't stop shaking when I don't drink, and my brain is mush."

Documentation of Physical Impairments

Physical impairments as evidenced by (a) liver failure, (b) withdrawal symptoms of DTs, and (c) decreased concentration

Treatment Goals and Objectives

Goal 1: Abstain from use of alcoholic beverages

Objective 1: Undergo physical examination by May 4th

Objective 2: Enter treatment for alcoholism

Objective 3: Avoid environments in which temptation to drink alcohol increases

Objective 4: Develop positive support system by socializing with friends and family activities that do not involve consumption of alcohol

---

toms the client exhibits; however, different symptoms (and different disorders) can result in similar impairments.

CHAPTER SUMMARY

1. The client's presenting problem is stated in the client's wording. It is not a diagnosis or the clinician's opinion of the areas of concern.
2. A diagnosis may be given when it can be demonstrated that both symptoms of the diagnosis and functional impairments or significant distress exists. Symptoms are mental health and behavioral concerns that define the *DSM-IV-TR* diagnoses. Impairments are specific areas in the client's life that are being affected due to the mental health or behavioral problems. Distress is the psychological distress experienced leading to problems functioning.
3. Most clients' statements and clinical records will have inconsisten-

≋Rapid Reference 7.7

Distress (or Affective Impairments): Interview Questions and Documentation of Impairments

Interview

Therapist: "Tell me how you usually feel."

Client: "I cry at least five times every day for no reason at all. I feel so sad. Life is just hopeless. There is nothing to look forward to. I'm a loser."

Therapist: "I would like to evaluate how severely you view the problem. On a scale of 1–100, in which 100 is being totally stressed and incapacitated, and a 1 is free of any problem, where do your rate your sadness?"

Client: "Definitely at least a 95. Like we went over before, sometimes I just want to die."

Therapist: "How long have you felt this way?"

Client: "Ever since I failed out of college."

Therapist: "How were things before this happened?"

Client: "I thought I did fine in high school. My life was normal."

Documentation of Affective Impairments of distress

Affective distress, as evidenced by (a) crying at least five times per day, (b) feelings of hopelessness and dysphoria, (c) low self-esteem

Treatment Goals and Objectives

Goal: Increase affective level to premorbid functioning

Objective 1: Decrease crying spells to no more than 2 per day by October 9

Objective 2: Raise Subjective level of distress (SUD) for sadness from current level of 90 to 60 by October 17

Objective 3: Sign suicide contract immediately

cies. Rather than ignore the information, the clinician should integrate the information. Such information is often extremely important in understanding the client.

4. A client's personal and mental health history is very helpful in estimating the prognosis of treatment.
5. Documentation of impairments should be in measurable terms.
6. Mental health symptoms can be described, measured, and tracked using the acronym OF AID (Onset, Frequency, Antecedents, Intensity, Duration).

Rapid Reference 7.8

Examples of Mental Health Disorders (With Dissimilar Symptoms) for Which Similar Impairments May Be Cited

Impairment 1: Avoiding responsibilities at home, work, and socially

Depressive Disorders	Adjustment Disorders
Anxiety Disorders	Behavioral Disorders
Thought Disorders	Organic Disorders
Personality Disorders	Substance Abuse

Impairment 2: Fatigue

Eating Disorders	Somatoform Disorders
Depressive Disorders	Anxiety Disorders
Organic Disorders	Substance Abuse

Impairment 3: Legal problems

Mania	Behavioral Disorders
Substance Abuse	Thought Disorders
Personality Disorders	

7. The clinician must be very aware of the differences and similarities in the *DSM-IV-TR* diagnoses; otherwise misdiagnosis is likely to occur.

8. Different mental health diagnoses can lead to similar functional impairments.

9. Each diagnosis has one or more Essential Symptoms, which must be prevalent in order for a diagnosis to be made. Most diagnoses also contain associated symptoms, which further define the client's areas of concerns but in themselves are not sufficient to assign the diagnosis.

🐾 TEST YOURSELF 🐾

1. **Which of the following best represents a client's presenting problem?**
   (a) The client is neurotic.
   (b) The client has symptoms suggesting neurosis.
   (c) The client states that she is overwhelmed with stress and depressed and has suicidal ideations.
   (d) The client's symptoms suggest that she is quite stressed.

2. **How long should a diagnosis which has been qualified as In Remission remain in a client's clinical record?**
   (a) Until there is no longer functional impairment due to the diagnosis
   (b) Until insurance payments cease
   (c) Until it has been established that relapse is not likely
   (d) There is no clear answer to the question

3. **Which of the following best represents mental health impairment?**
   (a) Decreased appetite, sleeping five hours per night, low self-esteem
   (b) In danger of being fired from work due to panic attacks
   (c) Drinks one case of beer each weekend
   (d) Depressed, anxious, and fatigued

4. **A client has endorsed experiencing every *DSM-IV-TR* symptom of Generalized Anxiety Disorder. In order to assign the diagnosis, what additional information is necessary?**
   (a) The resulting functioning impairments due to the disorder
   (b) Evidence that the symptoms limit the client from being a fully functioning person
   (c) The client must feel anxious
   (d) No additional information is necessary

5. **Which of the following defines essential symptoms?**
   (a) Symptoms that are causing the most impairment
   (b) Symptoms that must be alleviated to improve
   (c) Symptoms that must be present to warrant giving a diagnosis
   (d) Symptoms that affect the client's emotions the most

(continued)

6. **Give an example of a mental health symptom in which all or some of the OF AID acronym can be used both diagnostically and in treatment planning.**

7. **Discuss the pro's and con's of knowing the client's previous diagnosis.**

8. **What factors must be considered when a client endorses several vegetative symptoms.**

Answers: 1. c; 2. d; 3. b; 4. a; 5. c; 6. Example of "crying spells." Onset: 2 months ago (fired from job). Frequency: 8 or more times per day. Antecedents: Any reminders of previous employment (e.g., tasks, people). Intensity: Severe. Duration: 10–30 min. 7. Being aware of a client's previous mental health diagnoses is helpful in examining patterns of client behaviors and response to previous treatment. However, if the clinician overrelies on previous information there could be drawbacks such as if the previous diagnosis was incorrect or if the diagnosis is now changed. 8. As the degree of mental impairment increases, vegetative symptoms are also generally more prominent, especially with depressive, anxiety, and psychotic disorders.

Eight

THE MENTAL STATUS EXAM (MSE)

A mental status exam (MSE) is a combination of questions and observations intended to provide an objective snapshot of the client's current mental, cognitive, and behavioral condition. Like a physical exam, which explores various physical symptoms, the MSE monitors the client's psychological functioning. The goals of a mental status examination are to help (a) establish a provisional diagnosis and differential diagnoses, (b) develop an etiological formulation that traces the biological, psychological, and social factors that have predisposed, precipitated, and now perpetuate the client's current condition, and (c) establish each client's capacity to function (Silver & Herrmann, 1991).

The MSE described in this text is comprehensive, covering an array of client behaviors. The MSE is not a separate component in the interview, but rather a series of observations throughout the interview. Both verbal and nonverbal aspects are evaluated. Rapid Reference 8.1 outlines important elements of the mental status exam.

CLINICAL OBSERVATIONS

Clinical observations are a crucial part of any interview and should be carefully taught to therapists in training. Although psychometric techniques do not exist to compile the observations, client behaviors often suggest the degree of normal or abnormal functioning. Observations demonstrating problem areas such as depression, anxiety, mania, hyperactivity, and others are easily documented in the MSE through verbal and nonverbal means. The following areas of clinical observations are helpful in describing client behaviors.

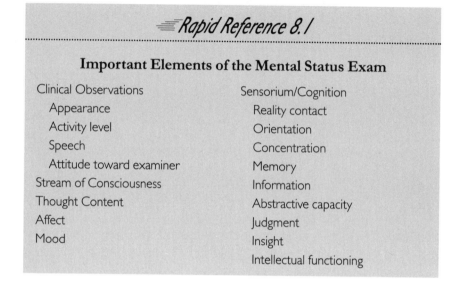

Rapid Reference 8.1

Important Elements of the Mental Status Exam

Clinical Observations
   Appearance
   Activity level
   Speech
   Attitude toward examiner
Stream of Consciousness
Thought Content
Affect
Mood

Sensorium/Cognition
   Reality contact
   Orientation
   Concentration
   Memory
   Information
   Abstractive capacity
   Judgment
   Insight
   Intellectual functioning

Appearance

Common observations of appearance include any aspects in which behavioral, affective, and physical observations are noted. Although such observations, in themselves, may provide little clinical information, when they are integrated with other clinical information, it helps validate a diagnosis and further define client concerns. A client's physical appearance (e.g., clothing, makeup, facial expressions, cleanliness, accoutrements, and observed versus actual chronological age) are often characteristic of his or her mental condition; however, consider the client's cultural, socioeconomic, and situational factors when noting physical appearance.

Pipes and Davenport (1990) state that the examiner should include whether the clients' dress and appearance are consistent with their age, occupation, and socioeconomic status when assessing appearance as part of a mental status exam. Cultural and situational factors also must be considered. Clients with problem areas such as chemical dependency, depression, mania, and various personality traits, such as promiscuity or low self-esteem, often have a physical appearance affected by the manifestations of their diagnosis. (See Rapid Reference 8.2.)

Rapid Reference 8.2

Typical Observations of Appearance

Observation:	Examples:
Apparent age	Looks 10 years older than chronological age, 5 years younger, appears chronological age
Posture	Slumped, erect, shifting
Grooming	Soiled clothing, immaculate
Health	Excellent, poor, fatigued
Hair	Disheveled, greasy, neatly combed
Nails	Bitten, long, dirty, trimmed
Odor	Strong body odor, alcohol on breath

Example of Narrative Description of Appearance:

Edward, age 32, appeared at the interview looking at least 15 years older than his chronological age. He was observed as having a slumped posture and wearing soiled clothing. He was unwashed and unshaven, with disheveled hair, nails bitten very short, and a strong odor of cigarettes and alcohol. His health seemed to be poor, as evidenced by difficulties breathing, frequent coughing, and the appearance of fatigue.

Activity Level

A client's activity level can be suggestive of several possible clinical concerns that are evidenced by physical activity or movement. An atypical activity should lead to additional observations and inquiries into areas such as substance abuse, hyperactivity, manic behavior, tics, anxiety, medication side effects, and others with related symptoms. Activity level may be influenced by the client's physical condition, medications, ability to relate, and affect.

Psychomotor behavior refers to both the quality and quantity of motor behavior. Psychomotor retardation is depicted by slow movements, speech, and cognitive processes. It becomes more prominent as depression and/or organic factors affecting the client's condition increase. Psychomotor agitation, such as increased speed of responses, increases with mania and anxiety. Medications or drugs may increase or decrease motor movement, depending on the reaction. Repetitive behaviors may be indicative of obsessive-compulsive

Rapid Reference 8.3

Typical Observations of Activity Level

Observation:	Examples:
Mannerisms	Shifted posture often, stood up often due to pain
Gait	Shuffled gait, normal gait and station, walked slowly and deliberately
Eye contact	Stared, little/no eye contact
Distractibility	Easily distracted, alert, often stared out the window
Vigilance	Hypervigilant, preoccupied
Kinetic level	Hyperactive, fidgety, restless, normal, limp

Example of Narrative Description of Appearance:

Candy entered into the interview, walking slowly and deliberately, with a notable limp in her left leg. After she sat down, she shifted her body position at least every 5 min, stating that her injury was bothering her. She maintained adequate eye contact. No concerns were noted in distractibility, vigilance, or kinetic level.

behavior or a developmental disorder. Several other observations of movement are noted in Rapid Reference 8.3.

Speech

A client's speech is perhaps one of the richest areas for mental status observations. Speech is observed throughout the entire interview. It can provide an estimate of social behaviors, organic conditions, cognition, intellectual functioning, affect, unusual thoughts, obsessions, and almost any other means of client communications or behaviors. Unusual statements should be quoted verbatim as evidence of client concerns. Speech is typically regarded as the gateway of thought. That is, one's thoughts are expressed through speech. (See Rapid Reference 8.4.)

Attitude Toward Examiner

A client's attitude toward the examiner directly influences the validity of the interview and can be indicative of the prognosis of treatment. Factors such as

≡ *Rapid Reference 8.4*

Typical Observations of Speech

Observation:	Examples:
Vocabulary	Limited vocabulary, suggested borderline IQ, advanced, within normal limits, concordant with age
Details	Excessive, concordant with diagnosis of OCD, lack of details
Volume	Loud, soft, varied with mood, normal
Pace	Rapid, normal, slow
Reaction time	Delayed, suggested depressed mood
Hesitancy	Hesitant, a further indication of malingering
Tone	Monotonous the entire interview, normal
Pronunciations	Poor, adequate, succinct
Understandability	Approximately 90% understandable, normal pronunciations, pronounced th's like s's
Other	Slurred, stuttered, mumbled, high pitch, choppy, deliberate, echolalia, neologisms, rambled

Example of Narrative Description of Speech:

Pat's speech was very loud the entire interview. She spoke with excessive details, rapid pace, and high pitch. Such observations are concordant with previous observations of mania. Her speech was clear and easily understood, with normal vocabulary and pronunciations, suggesting at least average intellectual functioning.

defensiveness, level of cooperation, and the seriousness of the client in providing information must be carefully monitored to prevent misdiagnosis. The interviewer must take careful measures to avoid making incorrect assumptions about the client's attitude. Varying interpersonal styles, cultural norms, level of physical attractiveness, misreading of nonverbal behaviors, and any other factors that may potentially distort subjective observations must be considered. It is not uncommon for a client's attitude to be described quite differently by different therapists.

The client's relatedness during the interview is an important subject of investigation, but a difficult dimension of affect to measure and describe. Relatedness involves the client's capacity to interact emotionally, to establish rapport with the examiner, and to express warmth toward the examiner (Taylor, 1981). The unrelated client appears blunt, cold, or labile.

Personality disorder (Axis II of *DSM-IV-TR*) characteristics are often evident in the client's attitude. A common characteristic of personality disorders involves problems in interpersonal relationships. While one client may overly brag, another will avoid most questions. (See Rapid References 8.5 and 8.6.)

STREAM OF CONSCIOUSNESS

A person's stream of consciousness is a measurement or indication of how one's speech reflects thought processes. These factors are observed throughout the entire interview rather than identified through direct questioning. It reflects one's patterns of thoughts, not specific content. Problem areas are often

---

≡ *Rapid Reference 8.5*

Typical Observations of Attitude Toward Examiner

Observation:	Examples:
Attentiveness	Attentive, distracted
Cooperation	Answered all questions, noncompliant, friendly, indifferent
Interpersonal	Cordial, demeaning, friendly, manipulative, aloof, intense, passive
Defensive	Open, guarded, evasive
Quality	Poor historian, history conflicted with records
Interest level	Minimal interaction, interested

Example of Narrative Description of Attitude Toward Examiner:

Throughout the interview Harry was easily distracted, often looking out the window. He refused to answer about half of the questions, responding, "None of your business." He made several comments such as, "What right do you have to get into my head?" He denied having any mental health or behavioral problem areas. When discussing his reason for admission, he blamed the "system" and became quite defensive and provided a poor history. At times he was defiant and sarcastic. Current observations make the validity of the information received in the interview marginal. However, observations were helpful in assessing attitudinal factors noted in the referral. Prognosis is poor at this time.

≡ Rapid Reference 8.6

Personality Factors Affecting Quality of the Interview

Axis II Diagnosis or Features:	Client Characteristics Affecting Quality of the Interview:
Antisocial	Irritable, blaming, deceitful, poor historian
Avoidant	Inhibited, easily embarrassed, many questions must be asked for adequate answer
Borderline	Inconsistent information, stressed, inappropriate anger
Dependent	Lack of initiating information, advice seeking, easily led
Histrionic	Dramatic, seductive, shallow, exaggerates stressors
Narcissistic	Exaggeration, arrogant, blames others
OCD	Rigidity, excessive details, easily frustrated
Paranoid	Suspicious, distrustful, guarded
Schizoid	Aloof, detached emotionally, poor social skills
Schizotypal	Socially anxious, peculiar, suspicious

Putting It Into Practice

Is the Evaluation a Valid Sample of Typical Behavior?

A client presented for an evaluation because of a work injury. Relatively recent records indicated normal intellectual, memory, cognitive, and mental health functioning. Because no apparent problem areas were identified in the previous evaluation, the client was seeking a second opinion. The second testing indicated significantly impaired memory and intellectual functioning, incongruent with the recent evaluation. Malingering did not appear to be evident.

When it was apparent that the testing was well below the previous testing, the client was asked if anything had changed since the last interview one month earlier. He denied any changes since that time. After more questions, the client stated that he was in a hurry to get finished because he had to be at another appointment soon; therefore, he was trying to get through with the tests quickly. He was subsequently re-tested at a more convenient time with similar tests. Later results were concordant with the initial evaluation.

Teaching Point: *The clinician should monitor any factors that would decrease the validity of the interview. Any significant changes from earlier observations must be carefully explained and integrated rather than solely accepted or ignored.*

Rapid Reference 8.7

Typical Observations of Stream of Consciousness

Observation:	Examples:
Speech	Spontaneous, inhibited, blocked, illogical, vague, pressured, slowed, disorganized, rambled, derailed, coherent, cause/effect, neologisms
Thinking	Relevant, coherent, goal directed, loose
Thought processes	Number of ideas, flight of ideas, hesitance

Example of Narrative Description of Attitude Toward Examiner:

Ronita's speech was illogical and disorganized. She often rambled and changed topics midsentence. On two occasions, she decompensated and became incoherent. During most of the interview she expressed an extreme number of unrelated ideas. Current observations are concordant with her previous diagnosis of Schizophrenia, Disorganized Type.

associated with thought disorders but may also be found in severe mood disorders. (See Rapid Reference 8.7.)

THOUGHT CONTENT

Unlike Stream of Consciousness, assessing thought content can be made through direct questioning, rather than observations. It provides a sample of both affective and cognitive areas of concern. Thought content describes thought patterns or topics of concern that the client is experiencing. It is important to note whether problems in thought content are relatively recent or chronic. If chronic, a thorough history of treatment and its results are important. If problems have occurred only recently, a physical evaluation is necessary to rule out organic factors.

Other information, such as when problems occur (e.g., under stress, only when severely depressed, anytime, when not taking medications, when using alcohol, etc.) is needed for adequate diagnostic specificity. For example, a client does not have to be schizophrenic to experience hallucinations. They may occur due to depression, severe stress, organic factors, chemical use, and other causes. Misdiagnosis can occur with insufficient information or with insufficient knowledge of psychopathology, or both. (See Rapid Reference 8.8.)

≡Rapid Reference 8.8

Typical Observations of Thought Content

Concern:	Examples:
Preoccupations	Obsessions, compulsions, phobias, homicide, antisocial
Suicidality	Current status and history of ideas, threats, gestures, plan, attempts
Hallucinations	Voices, visions, content, setting, sensory system, illusions
Delusions	Persecutory, somatic, grandeur
Ideas of reference	Controlled, broadcasting, content, moody, bizarre, antisocial

Examples of Questions Posed in Assessing Aspects of Thought Content:

Therapist: "Do you have thoughts that bother you or do not seem to go away?"

Client: "No."

Therapist: "Are there any situations, places, or events that cause you to become quite fearful, anxious, or panicky?"

Client: "No."

Therapist: "Have you ever heard voices or seen things that no one else hears or sees?"

Client: "Yes, I hear voices very often, but I don't have any visions."

Therapist: "How long have you been hearing voices?"

Client: "For about three years ... since I first started college."

Therapist: "Are they voices ... like now, hearing my voice ... or are they thoughts."

Client: "Definitely voices. It's a man with a low voice ... sometimes it is an old woman."

Therapist: "What do they say?"

Client: "They tell me how bad I am ... and to hurt myself ... sometimes they tell me to do bad things."

Therapist: "Are there certain times when you hear them. ... like when you are under much stress ... or depressed ... or after using drugs or alcohol."

Client: "No ... I hear them any time ... when I feel good or bad. ... They just come. I can't control it. I think they control me."

Example of Narrative Description of Thought Content:

Erik denies any intrusive thoughts but notes significant concerns of hearing voices for the past three years. He denies concerns with anxiety or depression.

AFFECT

Affect refers to clinical observations at the time of the interview. It represents the interviewer's observations of the client rather than the client's endorsement. Observations such as eye contact, facial expressions, crying, smiling, and other nonverbal body language signify a client's affect. The client is not queried about affect; it is based on the client's presentation throughout the interview.

Emotional observations are expressed in terms of sadness, happiness, anxiety, anger, or apathy (Taylor, 1981). These various types of affective messages indicate the quality of mood. The amplitude is measured by the client's intensity in expressing a particular mood, whereas the variability of these expressions over a period of time is the range of affect. Inappropriateness of mood, constriction in range of affect, or lability of affect may be signs of psychopathology. Common types of observations of affect are as follows (see Rapid Reference 8.9).

≡ *Rapid Reference 8.9*

Typical Affective Observations

Observations:	Examples:
Range	Full range, expansive, restricted, blunted, flat
Appropriateness	Concordant vs. discordant with observations
Mobility	Normal, decreased (constricted, fixed), increased (labile)
Intensity	Normal, mild, strong
Psychomotor	Normal, retardation, agitation
Predominant mood	Neutral, euthymic, dysphoric, euphoric, manic
Level of anxiety	Fidgety, restless, overanxious, calm
Anger expression	Irritable, explosive, composed

Example of Narrative Description Thought Content:

Affective observations included expansive affect such as laughing when discussing a recent death of a loved one and a recent diagnosis of cancer. It was not concordant with speech and behaviors. Mobility was labile, with psychomotor agitation most of the interview. Predominant mood was manic. The client did not appear to be anxious, irritable, or angry.

MOOD

Mood is defined as emotional symptoms that typically persist over time. Unlike affect, which relies on clinical observation, mood is typically endorsed by the client. An efficient means of ruling in and ruling out diagnoses and symptoms of mood is to begin with Essential Symptoms, then query associated symptoms. Rapid Reference 8.10 represents the typical areas assessed for mood.

SENSORIUM/COGNITION

This portion of the interview is not a formal part of the MSE, but MSE observations continue throughout the interview. It assesses a number of cognitive variables such as memory, concentration, general information, and others. Sensorium refers to the client's senses accurately perceiving the world. Disorientation in sensorium may result in problem areas such as unusual smells, sounds, visions, tastes, or touches. In addition, sensorium refers to one's level

≡*Rapid Reference 8.10*

Typical Areas Assessed for Mood

Concern:	Examples:
Anger problems	Property damage, explosive behaviors, assaultive behaviors
Panic attacks	Palpitations, chest pain, difficulty breathing, sweating, trembling
Anxiety	Excessive worrying, irritability, tenseness
Depression	Depressed mood, withdrawal, decreased concentration, suicidal thoughts
Mania	Grandiosity, impulsivity, decreased need for sleep, excessive ideas

Example of Describing Symptoms Using *DSM-IV-TR*:

Roger endorses symptoms suggestive of Panic Disorder with the following symptoms: abrupt development of palpitations, sweating, shortness of breath, chest pain, derealization, and hot flashes. He has had panic attacks for at least five years with no known antecedents. Currently, he has at least two panic attacks per day, lasting an average of about 10 min. He rates their intensity as 85 out of 100.

of consciousness, level of arousal, and level of confusion, possibly reflecting an organic brain dysfunction or psychosis (Groth-Marnat, 1970). Cognitions involve concepts such as thinking, intelligence, and memory.

Reality Contact

Throughout the interview the clinician assesses the degree to which the client is in touch with reality. This is accomplished by evaluating the quality of conversation, the reality of answers given, and the flow of conversation. Although there are no specific tests, clinical judgment is sufficient. For example, the following statement demonstrates reality concerns: "Thelma did not appear to be in touch with reality, as evidenced by referring to this therapist as her mother, asking for a 'pass to the mass of the glass,' and stating that the table was a giant microphone, because microphones are also round like flying saucers."

Orientation × 3

Orientation × 3 (times three) refers to the client's orientation to time, place, and person. Some time during the interview, it is common to ask clients the approximate time of day, where they are (or why they are there), and their name. Incorrect, incomplete, or vague information is indicative of cognitive concerns. As cognition declines, or decompensation takes place, orientation to time usually decreases first, then orientation to place, then to person. The less oriented the client is, especially to person, the higher the likelihood of decreased cognitive ability or functioning, or psychosis.

Concentration

Concentration is defined as sustaining one's attention. Concentration is typically assessed by presenting novel numerical or verbal tasks that require certain calculations or manipulation of letters or numbers. Few norms are available in tasks of concentration; however, the Wechsler adult and children's intelligence tests (WAIS-III and WISC-III) offer age-related norms for repeating random digits forward and backward from memory.

When assessing tasks of concentration, important clinical observations include timing, number of errors, pauses, level of anxiety, perseverance, recognition of errors, and how quickly one gives up. Although the actual estimate of concentration may be important, the specific clinical observations can be quite revealing.

Overall, most adults can repeat about five to seven digits forward and four to six digits backward from memory. Children's scores improve with age. Although significant departures do not provide specific diagnostic information, in themselves, they can help point out potential problem areas. For example, an adult who repeats only three digits forward and two digits backward could suffer from a wide range of problem areas such as depression, organic brain dysfunction, anxiety, low IQ, an amnesic disorder, active substance abuse, a thought disorder, defiance, boredom, poor hearing and others. As the interview progresses and the specific problem areas are discovered, the client's level of concentration helps define the degree of impairment.

Older adults often feel more threatened when asked to respond to tests that involve numbers or arithmetic. The serial sevens subtraction test, for example, is more dependent on a client's premorbid intellectual capacity and education than on an underlying impairment of concentration. A simple test to assess attention consists of reading a series of random letters to clients and asking them to indicate every time they hear the letter A (Silver & Herrmann, 1991).

Before a final opinion is made regarding the client's level of concentration, the therapist should assess whether the client's mental and physical condition at the time of the interview are a representative sample of the client's normal functioning. Always remember to ask the client questions such as whether they are feeling well, have a headache, or any information that may lead to invalidating the quality of the interview. (See Rapid Reference 8.11.)

Memory

Memory tasks focus on a longer period of time than concentration tasks. The mental health interview often assesses both remote (long-term) and recent (short-term) memory. It is not unusual for clients with mood disorders to have temporary problems with short-term memory. Significant cognitive declines are often picked up when problem areas in remote memory are present.

When memory issues are noted, it is important to assess previous memory functioning, which may require collateral informants. That is, someone who has never had very good memory functioning may be misdiagnosed as having

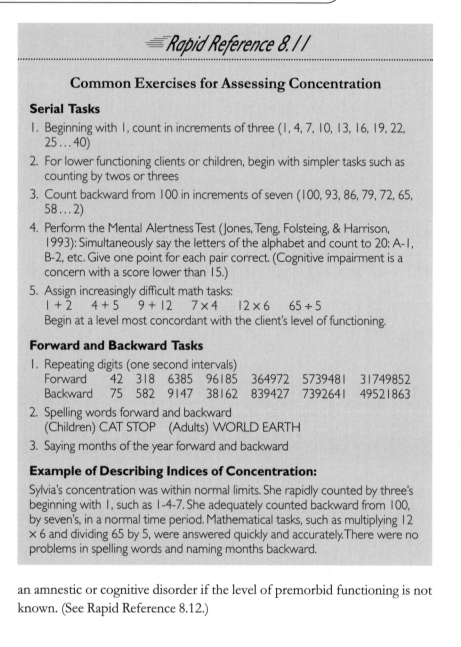

≡Rapid Reference 8.11

Common Exercises for Assessing Concentration

Serial Tasks

1. Beginning with 1, count in increments of three (1, 4, 7, 10, 13, 16, 19, 22, 25…40)
2. For lower functioning clients or children, begin with simpler tasks such as counting by twos or threes
3. Count backward from 100 in increments of seven (100, 93, 86, 79, 72, 65, 58…2)
4. Perform the Mental Alertness Test (Jones, Teng, Folsteing, & Harrison, 1993): Simultaneously say the letters of the alphabet and count to 20: A-1, B-2, etc. Give one point for each pair correct. (Cognitive impairment is a concern with a score lower than 15.)
5. Assign increasingly difficult math tasks:
   $1 + 2$ $4 + 5$ $9 + 12$ 7×4 12×6 $65 \div 5$
   Begin at a level most concordant with the client's level of functioning.

Forward and Backward Tasks

1. Repeating digits (one second intervals)
Forward	42	318	6385	96185	364972	5739481	31749852
Backward	75	582	9147	38162	839427	7392641	49521863
2. Spelling words forward and backward
   (Children) CAT STOP   (Adults) WORLD EARTH
3. Saying months of the year forward and backward

Example of Describing Indices of Concentration:

Sylvia's concentration was within normal limits. She rapidly counted by three's beginning with 1, such as 1-4-7. She adequately counted backward from 100, by seven's, in a normal time period. Mathematical tasks, such as multiplying 12 × 6 and dividing 65 by 5, were answered quickly and accurately. There were no problems in spelling words and naming months backward.

an amnestic or cognitive disorder if the level of premorbid functioning is not known. (See Rapid Reference 8.12.)

Information

A client's knowledge of ongoing events and general environmental information often reflect cognition, contact with reality, social alienation, affect, or a

≡ Rapid Reference 8.12

Examples of Memory Areas Assessed

Type of Memory:	Examples of Items Queried:
Remote memory (weeks to years)	Previous schools and teacher's names
	The street one grew up on
	Activities on most recent holiday
	Historical events in one's life (e.g., describe what you were doing when Kennedy was shot; or, for people born after 1970, refer to the Space Shuttle Challenger or other significant historical events occurring during the client's life.
Recent memory (minutes to few weeks)	Most recent meal
	Activities over past few days
	Remembering three words given after 5 and 30 min
Immediate memory (less than one minute)	Repeating digits
	Copying designs after a brief viewing.

Example Describing Memory Functioning:

Although long-term memory seemed to be intact, concerns were noted in Linda's short-term memory, as evidenced by forgetting recent meals and activities. She states that she has had no physical trauma, but since her divorce, she has been much more forgetful. She stated, "I'm too depressed to want to remember what I'm doing."

combination of these factors. Although factors such as intelligence and opportunity to acquire knowledge affect one's level of information, an estimate based on these factors is helpful. The questions asked should reflect information that is available to everyone, of relevance to the client, and not affected by schooling. (See Rapid Reference 8.13.)

Abstractive Capacity

Abstractive capacity is the ability to differentiate between concrete and abstractive meanings. Cognitive developmental theorists, such as Piaget, view abstractive thinking as a step in cognitive development. For example, when considering the proverb, "The early bird catches the worm," an 8-year-old child

Rapid Reference 8.13

Examples of Information Areas Assessed

Type of Information:	Examples:
Current information	"Do you read the newspaper, watch or listen to the news? . . . Describe a recent news event."
	"Who is the current president?"
	"Who is the current governor of the state?"
	"Name three large cities."
Historical information during the client's life	"Can you name the past five presidents of the United States?"
General historical information	"Who was Martin Luther King?"
	"Who was the first president of the United States?"
General factual information	"What country is north of the United States?"
	"What is the capitol of this state?"
	"How many months are in a year?"
	"How many days are in a leap year?"

Example of Describing a Client's Level of Information:

"Kirsten regularly reads the newspaper and watches the news on television. She was in touch with current events and knew the name of the current and past five presidents. Her fund of information appears to be within normal limits."

might interpret it concretely, such as, "Birds eat worms," whereas an adult would most likely interpret it abstractly, such as, "People who get up early are more likely to get ahead."

Abstractive capacity may be affected by intelligence, an organic brain disorder, level of comprehension or judgment, cognitive delays, or any concerns that may lead to a lower quality of response. The quality of the client's response goes beyond simply whether it was abstract or concrete. The client's reaction to questions that require more thinking than usual may be anxiety provoking, or may lead to giving up, without responding. For example, a client with low self-esteem may not venture an attempt to interpret the proverb for fear of making an error in front of someone.

Some clients answer "I don't know," or they remain quiet. Common inter-

≡ *Rapid Reference 8.14*

Assessing Abstractive Capacity by Interpreting Proverbs

Examples of Proverbs:

"The early bird catches the worm."

"A rolling stone gathers no moss."

"Strike while the iron is hot."

"Don't cry over spilled milk."

"Don't judge a book by its cover."

"Two wrongs don't make a right."

"Don't count your chickens before they hatch."

Example: "The early bird catches the worm."

Assessment:	Response:
Normal, Abstractive	"Those who get up early get the best things."
Normal, Concrete	"Birds eat worms."
Unusual	"Its never too early in life to go bird hunting."
Bizarre	"The whirly bird wormy whirls."
Defiant	"None of your business." or "That's stupid."
Passive	"Whatever" or "I've never heard of that before."
Obsessive	"It could mean a lot of things ... for example ..."

pretations of this behavior may include low self-esteem, depression, and little exposure to models of abstract thinking. Also consider cultural or language barriers when assessing abstractive capacity.

Unusual responses, such as interpreting the maxim "Don't cry over spilled milk" as "It means that milk is meant to make you happy . . . because it's from your mother," must be interpreted in the context of the entire evaluation. In this case, the clinician is advised to look for themes or other unusual patterns. (See Rapid Reference 8.14.)

Judgment

Several clinical areas such as a thought disorder, antisocial traits, organic brain disorders, affective level, or other characterological factors can affect a client's level of judgment. One must carefully consider background information, such as education level and experiences with parents as well as current behavioral issues such as impulsivity, in that they may influence judgment. When concerns are noted, such as a history of severe impulsivity, the quality of the response is helpful in determining the client's level of awareness of social norms and mores, or if the client knows socially appropriate responses but has not demonstrated such a history. Usually, the best indicator of judgment is the client's behavioral history. The use of collateral informants may be more reliable than that of the client when there is a history of poor judgment.

When assessing judgment in older adults, traditional tests that ask clients what they would do in imaginary situations are not very helpful, because these tests are not sensitive to the subtle alterations in judgment seen in many geriatric disorders. More subtle alterations in judgment include the inability to make and carry out plans and inappropriate behavior in social situations (Silver & Herrmann, 1991). (See Rapid Reference 8.15.)

≡ Rapid Reference 8.15

Examples of Questions Requiring Judgment in the Response

"What would you do if you found a person's wallet?"

"What would you do if you were in a movie theatre and were the first one to see smoke and fire coming from under one of the exit doors?"

"What would you do if you saw someone breaking into your neighbor's house?"

Example: "What would you do if you were in a movie theatre and were the first one to see smoke and fire coming from under one of the exit doors?"

Assessment:	Response:
Normal	"I'd tell the manager."
Normal, but lacking in judgment	"Yell 'fire'."
Antisocial	"Get out and let them burn."
Depressive/suicidal	"Hope it's finally the end."
Passive	"Tell the person next to me."
Bizarre	"Turn up the volume."
Concrete/low functioning	"Stop, drop, and roll."

Insight

Insight is the client's level of awareness of his or her own issues. It is a crucial part of treatment planning, in that poor insight suggests a poor prognosis for treatment and is often associated with a lower quality of the information supplied by the client.

Client insight cannot be directly measured. It is an opinion, made by the therapist, regarding the client's ability to self-reflect and be aware of his or her issues. (See Rapid Reference 8.16.)

Intellectual Functioning/Education

An estimate of the client's intellectual functioning is helpful in assessing areas such as abilities, helpful modes of treatment, premorbid functioning, and potential need and access to services. Although the client is usually able to list years of education, it may not be concordant with the client's presentation or current functioning. The best predictor of both current and premorbid intel-

≡Rapid Reference 8.16

Levels of Insight Examples

Complete denial

Example: "I'm not depressed ... I have no problems."

Slight awareness

Example: "I realize that I attempted suicide a few hours ago, but I'm not really upset ... It just happened ... it meant nothing."

Awareness, but blames others

Example: "Yes, I'm depressed, but it's my family's fault."

Intellectual insight, but few changes are likely to take place

Example: "Now it all makes sense to me why I'm so depressed ... who wouldn't be down in my situation? It's normal."

Emotional insight and understanding in which changes can occur

Example: "I understand the problem, and I will change my behavior and my ways of thinking about it, otherwise I'll just stay the same."

lectual level is vocabulary. Vocabulary is one of the last cognitive functions to decline when decompensation takes place.

It is possible for a client to seemingly present with an above average vocabulary, but actually be functioning at a much lower level. Other indicators such as presenting challenging but novel tasks or increasingly more difficult math problems may help ascertain the client's current cognitive functioning level.

Education is evaluated by both formal and informal education. Informal education, or being "streetwise," can go a long way in adaptive functioning. In some environments informal education may go further than formal depending on client variables. For example, there are some professions, such as sales, in which one can become successful with or without a college degree. Information learned on the job rather than in a classroom may be the key to success.

Other predictors of intellectual level include previous school grades, occupation, socioeconomic status, occupational advancement, and level of conversation. No one predictor is entirely accurate, but when considering all factors, a more clear picture is presented. (See Rapid Reference 8.17.)

≡Rapid Reference 8.17

Examples of Describing Intelligence and Education

High Functioning

John has a master's degree in education, plus two years of military intelligence training. He views himself as having above average intelligence, which is concordant with this psychologist's opinion.

Decreased Functioning

Pat graduated from high school with average grades. Although she never attended college, she quickly advanced in her position at the post office as a supervisor until her closed head injury. During the interview she spoke rather concretely, with normal vocabulary. At times she had difficulty finding words. At present, it is estimated that her intellectual functioning is in the low normal range and significantly lower than premorbid functioning.

Low Functioning

Chuck attended school until age 18 in an adaptive education program. He never progressed academically beyond the 2nd grade level. Since high school he has worked in an enclave position with a job coach. Previous testing and his adaptive level suggest an IQ in the Moderate Mental Retardation range.

PUTTING THE MSE PIECES TOGETHER

Describing MSE observations, without integrating the various components, is like randomly gathering all of the pieces of a puzzle, but not putting them together to see the full picture. A separate description of each piece of a puzzle, with no reference or interconnections to the other pieces, is confusing. Puzzle pieces that are difficult to fit in cannot be discarded or ignored. The pieces must fit together or those viewing it will notice the missing pieces. Likewise,

Putting It Into Practice

Looking at All of the Pieces of the Puzzle

A psychiatrist and two mental health therapists had treated an 11-year-old boy for two years for Obsessive-Compulsive Disorder (OCD). He exhibited several repetitive and compulsive-like behaviors; thus, it was assumed that OCD was the correct diagnosis. Although other behavioral problems that were not characteristic of OCD existed, the diagnosis was upheld, for lack of fit with any other diagnosis observed by the providers.

Because med's and therapy were not helpful, the child was referred for another opinion. A complete diagnostic evaluation resulted in agreement that the child exhibited OCD-like behaviors, but several other symptoms were present that could not be accounted for by OCD.

After interpreting IQ, projective, and other tests, and conducting a thorough clinical interview, the diagnosis was modified to Asperger's Disorder, which contains a number of OCD-like features but differs significantly in treatment. Important diagnostic information, such as extreme deficits in comprehending social nuances and stereotypic behaviors, was not factored into the original diagnosis, but rather, these aspects were viewed as unusual OCD symptoms. The puzzle pieces now fit.

When those involved reviewed the *DSM-IV-TR* descriptions of Asperger's, there was no disagreement in the change of diagnosis. The focus of treatment changed considerably from focusing on thought and behavior patterns to working on concrete social comprehension skills. Previously, only the pieces that seemed to fit the puzzle were used for the original diagnosis, resulting in two years of unsuccessful treatment and ineffective meds.

Teaching Point: *Many disorders feature similar symptoms. It is easy to assign a well-known diagnosis, but if the correct diagnosis is unfamiliar to the clinician, it may be overlooked. An incorrect or incomplete diagnosis may lead to improper medication, ineffective treatment, or both.*

the clinician must elicit information from all of the MSE, biopsychosocial, and diagnostic areas to most ethically look at all possible aspects of client's current functioning. Information about the client that does not seem to coincide with other information about the client must never be discarded simply because it doesn't fit a preconceived model. It is often the conflicting information that aids in opening other diagnostic possibilities that have not yet been considered. Misinformation or misperceived information can do more harm than good.

CHAPTER SUMMARY

1. The Mental Status Exam (MSE) provides a current snapshot of the client's mental and cognitive condition. It is not a one-time or one-session observation; MSE observations take place every session.
2. MSE observations take place throughout the interview.
3. A client's speech is one of the best indicators of cognitive functioning.
4. Attitudinal factors during the interview may suggest similar factors outside of the interview.
5. Assessment of stream of consciousness is conducted by observing speech patterns in relation to thought processes.
6. Affect is observed by the clinician, whereas mood is described by the client.
7. Assessing sensorium and cognition involve assessing the client's level of being in touch with reality both perceptually and cognitively.
8. Both memory and intellectual functioning can be estimated by administering a few basic tasks.

🖋 TEST YOURSELF 🖋

1. What is the main purpose of the Mental Status Exam?
(a) Making a diagnosis
(b) Assessing the chronicity of one's mental health condition
(c) Providing a current view of the client's mental condition
(d) Assessing whether testing is necessary

2. **What is the essential feature of Obsessive-Compulsive Disorder (DSM IV or DSM-IV-R needed to answer question)**
   (a) Obsessions and compulsions
   (b) Obsessions or compulsions
   (c) Recurrent thoughts
   (d) Repetitive behaviors
   (e) All of these

3. **Which of the following is considered to be the best indicator of a client's premorbid intelligence?**
   (a) What the client tells you
   (b) Birth order
   (c) Vocabulary
   (d) Current IQ testing

4. **What is the most salient indicator of one's thought processes?**
   (a) Speech
   (b) Testing
   (c) Nonverbal behaviors
   (d) Family information

5. **Mood is to affect as**
   (a) Color is to green
   (b) Behavior is to personality
   (c) Climate is to weather
   (d) Attention is to concentration

6. **Which of the following best represents disorientation?**
   (a) The client has no idea what time of day it is.
   (b) The client had difficulty finding the clinic.
   (c) The client misplaced his keys in the office.
   (d) The client can't count by threes.

7. **Which of the following is the best example of assessing recent memory?**
   (a) "What is the name of the street you grew up on as a child?"
   (b) "What are the names of the past three presidents?"
   (c) "What did you have for dinner yesterday?"
   (d) "Please repeat the numbers I just told you."

8. **An unkempt appearance is always a sign of depression.** True or False?

(continued)

9. **Hearing voices means that a client is clearly schizophrenic.** True or False?

10. **An assessment of sensorium refers to a client's perceptions such as what they hear, see, smell, and so on.** True or False?

11. **Describe the relationship between client personality characteristics and quality of information received during the interview.**

12. **How might a client's abstractive capacity provide information as to what type of counseling (e.g., insight, cognitive, behavioral) may be the most helpful for a client?**

Answers: 1. c; 2. b; 3. c; 4. a; 5. c; 6. a; 7. c; 8. False; 9. False; 10. True; 11. A client's personality characteristics strongly affect the quality of information provided in the interview. Traits and behaviors such as insightfulness, honesty, and ability to disclose and to trust affect the information received. 12. Clients with concrete thinking may benefit more from behavioral interventions, while those with abstract thinking may prefer insight-oriented treatment.

Nine

This chapter incorporates aspects of the material learned in the previous chapters. No chapter Summary or Test Yourself sections are included since the material is also covered earlier in the text.

A psychological evaluation, in itself, is little or no help to the client. It must be acted upon in determining the types of services needed. The information collected in the initial interview is the basis for future services.

After the initial interview several decisions must be made regarding the information collected. Typically, a report is written in which the *reason for referral* is the primary focus of the report. Referrals made for nonspecific reasons are difficult to assess due to the many possible dimensions of mental health assessment. The following procedures are provided for incorporating the diagnostic information with mental health services and developing a plan.

Perhaps one of the greatest skills in diagnostic assessment is integrating information from all sources (i.e., the clinical interview, clinical observations, records from other sources, testing, biographical information, and collateral informants.) Although there is no standard format for psychological reports, most are similar. The following areas, already discussed in this text, will provide a format for a sample psychological assessment.

Psychological reports can be time consuming to write, especially for the novice therapist. Few third-party payers pay for the time it takes to write a report. Therefore, time efficiency is a crucial skill to learn in report writing. Although the report should be accurate, professional, and helpful, too much time spent in its writing is not cost effective. A report that includes everything the client says is often repetitious and lacks integration. If a report happens to be missing a piece of information that the reader desires to know, further details can be requested from the original data.

Psychological reports are not intended to be literary masterpieces. A typical report may be read only a few times. Many readers skim the report, primarily reviewing the diagnosis and recommendations. However, some reports are reviewed by several professionals and may significantly affect the client's life.

First, the report writer must consider who will be reading the report. A report written for a parent will differ from one written for a fellow mental health professional. The parent likely will prefer conclusions and suggestions, whereas the professional may prefer more raw data by which to form his or her conclusions.

Using a dictation service can cut down report-writing time down by at least 75%. Likewise, a structured psychological assessment form that follows the same format as the report, makes organizing the report material less time consuming. After all of the client questions are posed and background and testing materials are reviewed, the report is ready to be dictated. Then, the material gleaned from the client is reported; a section summarizing collateral information is presented; mental status observations are reported; test results (if any) are indicated; and the information is integrated, leading to a diagnosis and recommendations.

Cutting down on report-writing time is a function of efficiency; it is not a compromise of validity or quality. A thorough knowledge of the *DSM-IV-TR* also significantly decreases the time required to conduct an interview. It is a good idea to continue the interview process until a diagnosis (or lack of a diagnosis) has been determined. Simply accumulating diagnostic information, without integrating the data during the interview via rule-in's and rule-out's, can leave many questions unanswered. Once the client leaves, there may not be another chance to obtain the data needed. As the clinician becomes more experienced in interviewing and in knowledge of psychopathology, the quality of information received steadily improves and less time is needed to conduct the interview.

Novice clinicians tend to spend an inordinate amount of time gathering unnecessary or unrelated information, counseling the client, and going off on tangents that make it more difficult to integrate what has been received when writing the report. Staying on target, both during the interview and in writing the report, produces the best results. (See Rapid Reference 9.1.)

The following psychological report covers all areas of a clinical interview (excluding testing). However, different reading audiences do not require all of this information. The suggested information provided in various types of reports as needed by various referral sources is as follows.

≡Rapid Reference 9.1

Tips to Reduce Report-Writing Time and Remain Efficient

1. Write the report in the same format and order as the clinical questions posed to the client. Make all clinical forms that the client fills out in the same order and format as the questions posed to the client. These two procedures will save much time searching for information.

2. Avoid redundancies. Do not ask the client for the same information that has been requested in other forms or intake procedures. Add to information already received.

3. Write the report to the intended audience in their language of understanding. One size does not fit all.

4. Include only information that is helpful in understanding the client. Avoid irrelevant information. Be brief and to the point.

5. Integrate and summarize information, rather than saying everything.

6. Document all information required by sources such as the clinic, third-party payers, and accreditation agencies. This information is very difficult to add to a report when an auditor reviews the files. Do it right the first time. Don't cut corners.

7. Consider dictating the report, rather than personally typing it. The time spent typing a report could be used more efficiently working with another client while a clerical staff member or dictation service types the report.

Referral Source	*Contents of Report*
Other mental health professionals	Entire report
Review by accrediting agency	Entire report
Family physician	Integrative summary and diagnosis
Third-party payer	Integrative summary and diagnosis
Employer	Psychological factors affecting employability

REVIEW OF RECORDS

Previous mental health records included progress notes from previous mental health counseling, a summary of chemical dependency (CD) treatment, and physical health records.

Putting It Into Practice

Sample Psychological Report

Client: John Doe   Date of Evaluation   8-8-01
222 E. Main St.   Date of Report   8-9-01
Oxford, MI 49999   Date of Birth   8-27-62
                                   Age   39   Gender Male
Phone (999)555-1212   SSN   999-99-9999
                                   Race   African American.

Reason for Referral:

John Doe was referred by his primary physician, Wendy Ackers, MD to evaluate his level of depression and appropriateness for counseling services.

Presenting Problem:

John Doe states that he is currently experiencing difficulties coping with several ongoing stressors, including death of loved ones, not keeping up at work, marital conflict, and financial problems. He further notes having problems functioning socially, such as avoiding most friends and not answering the phone. He is feeling physically fatigued, stating that his level of energy is very low. At work, he has missed 6 out of the past 10 days at work and is in danger of being fired or suspended without pay. Symptoms include lack of pleasure, low motivation, fatigue, and frequent feelings of sadness.

Collateral Information:

Mental health progress notes received from Tony Barrellia, MA, indicated a diagnosis of Dysthymic Disorder when he received eight sessions of individual counseling in the summer of 1996. Records indicate that after eight sessions he did not desire to continue services. No significant progress was noted, as evidenced by a beginning and ending GAF of 60 and no notations of successful interventions.

A recent physical evaluation (7-18-01) from his primary physician, Wendy Ackers, MD indicated no known physical health problems explaining his level of fatigue, or a history of physical or health problems. He was referred for a psychological evaluation. He was prescribed Prozac, 20 mg.

A report from New Direction Chemical Dependency Services indicated that he received CD treatment for alcoholism between January and March 1997. Upon entering treatment, he was diagnosed with Alcohol Dependence. He graduated from the 90 day program. Records from the center indicated that he had three previous DWI's and had been in CD treatment on two previous occasions in 1992 and 1994.

History of Present Problem:

John Doe reports that he had received previous counseling, both for depression and chemical dependency. He has not consumed alcohol since his last treatment in 1997. He states that in the past he avoided dealing with stress by drinking alcohol. Since abstaining from alcohol, when he is having difficulties coping, he becomes increasingly more dysphoric. He states that his level of depression has increased over the past four months since his wife told him about an extramarital affair. He believes that his "whole world is caving in," with problem areas in marriage, social life, finances, and occupation. The bank has begun foreclosure procedures on his house, which has exacerbated his level of stress and depression.

Biopsychosocial Assessment:

All developmental milestones were met in normal time periods. He maintained appropriate childhood friendships. School attendance and behaviors indicated no problem areas. He was active in high school sports. He denies any history of childhood physical, behavioral, legal, or mental health problems.

He is quite close to his parents, whom he describes as "very supportive." They have offered him a loan to catch up on bills. He is currently going through significant marital stressors. This is his first marriage. He has been married for eight years. He has two children, with whom he reports to be very nurturing. He desires to save his marriage and resume family activities.

Currently, he has one close friend who is willing to spend time with him in social and recreational activities. Until about a year ago they used to get together on weekends for activities such as fishing, billiards, bowling, or sporting events. He describes himself as socially inferior and shy, stating that he is not able to approach new people. Recently he has avoided almost all social contacts, such as not answering the door or telephone and not accepting invitations to go out with his best friend. He describes his social goals as once again involving himself with his friend and developing new friendships.

He is proud of his African American heritage, but often feels frustrated due to "prejudice in the world." He denies any cultural or ethnic practices that he would want incorporated into counseling.

John Doe was raised in a family with strong Christian religious beliefs and practices. During the past year, he has discontinued his association with his church, stating, "God has abandoned me." Although he would like to increase his spiritual beliefs to their former level, he states that he isn't ready for such a commitment.

He has no history of criminal or civil legal problems. Prior to 1997 he had three DWI's. No divorce or separation papers have been filed to date.

(continued)

He graduated from high school with above average grades in average classes. Since high school, he has taken a few courses to further his employment opportunities. He enjoys reading and learning, stating that he has always wanted to receive some college training.

He has worked as a mechanic on the same job for the past 15 years and states that his "performance is excellent." Approximately one year ago he was passed up for a promotion that he believed he should have received. Presently, he is in jeopardy of losing his job due to excessive absences in the past few months. He served in the Army for four years and describes the experience as positive. He was not in combat. There are no current negative consequences of being in the military.

He has not been involved in any significant leisure or recreational activities for over one year. Although he misses activities such as bowling, sailing, going to movies, and golfing, he states that he has no energy at this time.

Historically, he has been in good health. He has had no history of hospitalizations or physical treatment. Over the past few months, John Doe states that he is feeling very tired and fatigued, and he has gained about 25 pounds. His most recent physical evaluation indicated no observable problem areas. He physically exercised until about two years ago. Currently, he sleeps about four to five hours per day, compared to at least seven to eight hours a few years ago.

John Doe denies any current use of alcohol, illegal drugs, tobacco products, or misuse of prescribed medications. He last drank alcohol in 1997. His relapses occurred when he was under significant stress. He denies any current cravings for alcohol. He has remained sober for the past four years.

In 1996, he underwent individual mental health counseling for difficulties coping with several stressors, which he stated was not helpful. He received four sessions of marital therapy in 1997, which he believes was successful at the time. He has been in CD treatment three times. The last treatment was in 1997. He attended weekly AA meeting until the summer of 2000.

Mental Status Exam:

He drove to the interview independently, arriving on time. He appeared to look his chronological age. His body odor suggested that his hygiene was below average. His posture was slumped. No other concerns were noted about his appearance. There were no unusual gestures or mannerisms. He was alert and relaxed. He walked slowly. Eye contact was below average. He did not appear to be preoccupied, hypervigilant, or easily distracted. At times he was lethargic, especially when discussing current stressors in his life. Observations suggested a normal vocabulary, details, pronunciations, reaction time, and sentence structure. His speech was soft at times but not slurred, stuttered, or mumbled.

He was attentive, frank, and cooperative throughout the interview, answering every question. He did not appear to be guarded, defensive, evasive, or manipulative. He seemed to be an adequate historian.

There was no evidence of a thought disorder. His speech was spontaneous and organized. His thinking appeared to be relevant, coherent, and goal directed. His thought processes did not indicate problem areas in number or flight of ideas or hesitance. Thought content indicated no problem areas in preoccupations, suicidality, hallucinations, illusions, delusions, or ideas of reference.

Affective observations during the interview included a restricted range of affect with mild intensity, and moderate psychomotor retardation. He did not appear to be anxious, irritable, or angry. Predominant mood during the interview was dysphoric.

He denied typical mood symptoms of problems with anxiety, anger management, panic attacks, mania, or PTSD. He endorsed symptoms of being depressed most of the time for at least the past year: lack of pleasure, significant weight gain, poor sleep, fatigue, psychomotor retardation, feelings of worthlessness, and social withdrawal. He attributes these symptoms to significant impairments occupationally and socially, adversely affecting his finances, employment, friendships, and marriage.

He denies current suicidal ideations and denies any history of suicidal behavior. However, he states that he will phone the clinic immediately if he becomes suicidal. He further denies any homicide or self-harm ideations.

He was in touch with reality and able to hold a normal conversation. He was oriented × 3. Memory and concentration were within normal limits. He was able to subtract serial sevens, in a normal time period, making no errors. He repeated six digits forward and four digits backward, which is within normal limits. He correctly spelled the word WORLD forward and backward. He recalled three out of three words immediately and after 5 and 30 min. He recalled recent and remote events in his life. He does not claim to have any memory problems. His fund of information was within normal limits. For example, he knew the names of four out of five of the most recent presidents, recent news events, and the names of three large cities. He abstractly interpreted various proverbs. Estimated IQ is in the normal range, as evidenced by his level of conversation, previous educational functioning, and vocational background. Overall, no problem areas are noted in memory or concentration.

His level of judgment was intact. His responses to hypothetical situations did not suggest impulsivity or poor judgment. He is aware of and has adequate insight as to how multiple stressors have exacerbated his condition, appearing to understand how changes can occur.

Interpretive Summary:

John Doe presents with several stressors in his marriage, job, and finances. He is feeling dysphoric, withdrawn, fatigued, and has low motivation to leave the house or speak with friends. Financial problems have increased over the past few years, resulting in decreased self-esteem and dysphoric mood. Marital and financial difficulties have significantly exacerbated his level of depression. He is

(continued)

currently in danger of losing his job, due to excessive absences. He received individual mental health counseling for Dysthymia in 1996 and marital therapy in 1997. The individual therapy was not helpful, while the marital therapy was considered successful at the time. He was in treatment of chemical dependency in 1992, 1994, and 1997. He reports no usage since 1997.

He is motivated to save his marriage and return to work full-time, but he states that his spouse desires to end the marriage. He has a supportive family and best friend who are willing to be involved in his treatment.

Due to a high level of premorbid functioning and positive social supports, prognosis is positive. However, potential concerns are noted in possible relapse in alcohol use, because previous relapses took place when he was under considerable stress. He has no history of suicidal behavior and does not endorse having a current suicidal plan or ideations. However, risk factors include depression, alcohol relapse potential, financial problems, marital stress, and a potential of losing his job. Each of these stressors must be addressed in treatment. He agreed to phone this clinic if he becomes suicidal.

A psychiatric referral is suggested due to his level of depression. Anticipated care will be approximately 12 sessions of individual psychotherapy and six sessions of conjoint therapy with his spouse, if possible.

DSM-IV-TR **Diagnosis**		**Code**
Axis I	Major Depressive Disorder, Single Episode Moderate	296.22
	Partner Relationship Problem	V61.1
	History of Alcohol Dependence, Full Remission	303.90
Axis II	No Diagnosis	V61.1
Axis III	Defer to physician	
Axis IV	Occupational, social, and financial problems	
Axis V	GAF = 55 Highest GAF in past year = 70–75	

Client's Signature *John Doe*		Date	*8-15-01*
Guardian's Signature N/A		Date	
Therapist's Signature *Sela Freud, CSW*		Date	*8-15-01*
Supervisor's Signature *Cynthia Victoria PhD*		Date	*8-19-01*

Appendix

Overview of Selected *DSM-IV-TR*™ Diagnoses

A diagnostic interview serves several purposes. Each treatment team member may focus on a different aspect of the assessment. A psychiatrist may be interested in information to assess the need for medications; a family therapist looks into the family relationships and dynamics; a social worker investigates the social network and supports; the psychologist investigates the formulation of the treatment plan; but each of them is interested in the diagnosis.

Some mental health professionals reject the idea of diagnosing clients. They state that the focus should be the client's treatment, not a diagnosis. Although this claim may be valid, most insurance companies require an Axis I diagnosis for treatment reimbursement. Therefore, it is in everyone's best interest to take sufficient time to carefully and ethically arrive at an accurate diagnosis.

A diagnosis is a means of communicating a general description of the client's symptomology. The client, not the diagnosis, is the focus of treatment. However, the degree of impairment typically associated with *DSM-IV-TR* diagnoses can be a moderate predictor of the types of services needed. For example, two clients who are currently experiencing psychotic thoughts may have entirely different etiologies of their problems. Their *DSM-IV-TR* diagnoses can provide clear information as to the nature of the psychotic thoughts. For example, a diagnosis of Schizophrenia paints a very different picture of a client than a diagnosis of Major Depressive Disorder, with Psychotic Features. Although both clients may have psychotic features in common, the treatment, medications, course of illness, impairments, and prognosis are quite different.

Assigning a clinical diagnosis, more than any clinical procedure, provides summary communication about the client's disorder that has been standardized in the profession. It is not based on a specific theory or opinion but rather an agreement between professionals that the diagnostic titles comprise various symptoms. It allows clinicians to differentiate among disorders using a common language. Although diagnoses do not provide individualized information about the client's specific lifestyle, coping strategies, supports, and stressors, it provides a classification system. The *DSM-IV-TR* makes a precautionary statement in noting that it does not classify people, but rather, it classifies disorders. The *DSM-IV-TR* (p. xxxi) states, "the DSM-IV (as did the DSM-III-R) avoids the use of such expressions as 'a schizophrenic' or 'an alcoholic' and instead use the more accurate, but admittedly more cumbersome, 'an individual with Schizophrenia' or 'an individual with Alcohol Dependence.'"

The *DSM* does not claim to be the final authority. It is periodically revised as the fund of knowledge increases. It is explicit in describing potential problems in classifying mental disorders. There can be much overlap between the classifications of disorders. Individuals with the same diagnosis may behave differently; therefore, additional information is needed for treatment beyond simply assigning a diagnosis. Clinical judgment is considered as more important than mechanistically checking off symptoms to make a diagnosis. The combination of clinical judgment and adherence to diagnostic criteria provide the best language for clinical communication. LaBruzza (1994, p. 88) states, "In fact, the DSM-IV diagnostic criteria are intended to serve as guidelines that always require clinical judgment and are not meant to be used in a cookbook fashion."

ORGANIZATION OF THE *DSM-IV-TR* DISORDERS

The *DSM-IV-TR* classifies disorders into seventeen categories. Chapter 7 of this text described the rule-in/rule-out process of making a clinical diagnosis. This appendix does not cover every *DSM-IV-TR* diagnosis; however, it provides an overview of selected diagnostic categories. Adequate diagnosis requires use of the *DSM-IV-TR* due to its complete descriptions, specifiers, rule-outs, and exclusion criteria.

Mood Disorders

The *DSM-IV-TR* (p. 825) defines mood as, "A pervasive and sustained emotion that colors the perception of the world . . . in which types of mood include dysphoric, elevated, euthymic, expansive, and irritable." A mood disorder is determined diagnostically by ruling in three levels of criteria, including (a) mood episodes, (b) mood disorders, and (c) specifiers of the most recent episode and recurrence of the symptoms.

Everyone has some degree of mood variation. For example, it is not abnormal to be sad when there are several stressors in one's life, such as loss of a loved one and severe financial problems. The *DSM-IV-TR* describes mood episodes as time periods in which the person is unusually happy or sad, at a clinical level of significance. There are two main categories of mood disorders, depressive disorders and bipolar disorders, as well as other mood disorders. The *DSM-IV-TR* defines a number of types of episodes, including Major Depressive Episode, Manic Episode, Mixed Episode, and Hypomanic Episode. These four are not diagnoses in themselves but serve as markers by which the diagnoses are based. The various diagnoses are delineated by level of mood, time frames, and specific symptoms. Representative mood disorders are as follows:

Depressive Disorders

Major Depressive Disorder consists of being depressed most of the time or lacking pleasure or interest for at least two weeks duration, resulting in significant stress or impairments. At least four out of nine additional listed symptoms must be endorsed.

Dysthymic Disorder involves chronic depressed mood and does not cause the same degree of impairment as that of a Major Depressive Episode. It is often life long. A diagnosis for adults requires at least two years; children and adolescents, one year.

Depressive Disorder NOS is given when the client is significantly depressed but does not meet the specific criteria of other mood disorders.

Bipolar Disorders

Bipolar I Disorder includes one or more Manic Episodes. Those with the diagnosis usually also have Major Depressive Episodes.

Bipolar II Disorder includes one or more Major Depressive Episodes accompanied by at least one Hypomanic Episode.

Cyclothymic Disorder is defined by at least two years of several episodes of hypomania and depressive episodes that do not meet criteria for a major depressive episode or manic episode.

Bipolar Disorder NOS is denoted by bipolar features not meeting criteria for a specific bipolar disorder.

Anxiety Disorders

The *DSM-IV-TR* (p. 820) defines anxiety as, "The apprehensive anticipation of future danger or misfortune accompanied by a feeling of dysphoria or somatic symptoms of tension. The focus of anticipated danger may be internal or external." A *panic attack* is a period of intense fear or dread, palpitations, chest pain, and several other possible physical and emotional symptoms. *Agoraphobia* is intense anxiety about places or situations where an individual fears help might not be available. Panic attacks and agoraphobia are not diagnoses, in themselves, but serve as the basis for describing the anxiety disorders. All *DSM-IV-TR* anxiety disorders are not listed.

> *Panic Disorder* is characterized by recurring panic attacks and worry about future attacks and their consequences. It is diagnosed as with agoraphobia or without agoraphobia. Essential feature: recurrent, unexpected panic attacks.

> *Agoraphobia Without a History of Panic Disorder* is a type of agoraphobia in which the person does not fully meet the criteria for Panic Disorder. Essential feature: presence of agoraphobia.

> *Specific Phobia* is an intense fear of specific objects or situations such as heights, animals, closed places, and so on, or situations which may lead to physical reactions such as choking or getting sick.

> *Social Phobia* is a fear of social situations in which the person believes they will become highly embarrassed in social situations such as public speaking, dining in public, and so on.

> *Obsessive-Compulsive Disorder (OCD)* is denoted by repetitious thoughts or behaviors that serve no purpose in themselves other than to alleviate anxiety about a situation.

> *Posttraumatic Stress Disorder (PTSD)* involves extreme stress due to reliving a past traumatic event.

> *Acute Stress Disorder* is simular to PTSD; however, it is experienced for less than one month and takes place during or just after the event takes place.

> *Generalized Anxiety Disorder (GAD)* is characterized by several ongoing specific symptoms of anxiety but not distinct episodes of panic.

Substance-Related Disorders

There are four types of substance-related disorders, which are further broken down into two categories: Substance Use Disorders, which includes Substance Dependence and Substance Abuse, and Substance-Induced Disorders, which includes Substance Intoxication and Substance Withdrawal. These four types are not diagnoses in themselves but are used to describe the pattern of use for various substances.

The *DSM-IV-TR* lists over 100 specific Substance-Related Disorders. They are broken down into the following substance categories: (a) Alcohol, (b) Amphetamines, (c) Caffeine, (d) Cannabis, (e) Cocaine, (f) Hallucinogens, (g) Inhalants, (h) Nicotine, (i) Opioids, (j) Phencyclidine, (k) Sedatives, Hypnotics, or Anxiolytics, (l) Polysubstance, and (m) other. Most, but not all, of the various mind-altering substances denote each of these four categories as a separate diagnosis. The *DSM-IV-TR* describes specific clinical criteria in further detail.

Substance Use Disorders

Substance Dependence is characterized by continued use of a substance, despite cognitive, behavioral, and physiological symptoms and problems. Through time the person develops *tolerance* for the substance, in which either greater amounts of the substance are desired or the same amount no longer achieves the desired effect. *Withdrawal* takes place when more of the same substance is needed to avoid or relieve withdrawal symptoms.

Substance Abuse results in recurrent negative consequences in areas such as no longer fulfilling major obligations whether occupational, social, or financial due to the use of the substance. It may also involve problems in which the person recurrently places him or herself in dangerous situations physically or legally.

Substance-Induced Disorders

Substance Intoxication involves recent ingestion or exposure to a substance, leading to maladaptive behavioral or psychological changes, or both, which are reversible. Different substances may lead to different maladaptive behaviors.

Substance Withdrawal is denoted by ending or reducing the use of a substance that had been used heavily, leading to significant stress or impairment. Symptoms vary by substances used.

Disorders Usually First Diagnosed In Infancy, Childhood, Or Adolescence

Although there is no clear distinction between adult and childhood disorders, some disorders tend to be more prevalent in childhood or adolescence. However, many may not be diagnosed with these disorders until adulthood. Further, there are several disorders listed in other sections that are common among both children and adults. All *DSM-IV-TR* diagnoses are not listed.

Mental Retardation (MR) is denoted by below average intellectual functioning (IQ of 70 or below), an onset prior to age 18, and significantly below average adaptive functioning (e.g., social, academic, communication, daily living skills). Mental retardation is classified into four codes by decreasing levels of functioning. Mild, Moderate, Severe, Profound, and Unspecified.

Learning Disorders (LD) are characterized by functioning significantly lower than one's expected level (e.g., age, level of education, tested IQ) in specific academic areas. Disorders include, Reading Disorder, Mathematics Disorder, Disorder of Written Expression, and Learning Disorder Not Otherwise Specified.

Communication Disorders are identified by problem areas in speech or language. These include, Expressive Language Disorder, Mixed Receptive-Expressive Language Disorder, Phonological Disorder, and Stuttering.

Pervasive Developmental Disorders (PDD) are described as failure to develop or severe and pervasive impairments in a child's ability to function in areas such as socialization communication, or self-expression. The most prominent features and impairments of the disorders are

Autistic Disorder:	social and communication problems, stereotypy
Rett's Disorder:	6 months normal development, then abnormal development in areas such as head growth, language, gait, hand movements

Childhood Disintegrative Disorder:	loss of acquired skills after two years of normal development
Asperger's Disorder:	significant social delays; similar to Autism, but without language delays.

Attention-Deficit and Disruptive Behavior Disorders

Attention-Deficit/Hyperactivity Disorder (ADHD) is a persistent pattern of any or all of the following behavior patterns: hyperactivity, impulsivity, inattentiveness. It is diagnosed as either ADHD, Combined Type; ADHD, Predominantly Inattentive Type; or ADHD, Predominantly Hyperactive-Impulsive Type.

Conduct Disorder is characterized by violating social norms or the rights of others. It is broken down into four types of symptoms: (a) aggression to people and animals, (b) destruction of property, (c) deceitfulness or theft, and (d) serious violations of rules.

Oppositional Defiant Disorder (ODD) is a pattern of negativistic, defiant and hostile behaviors and attitudes. It does not imply criminal activity.

Feeding and Eating Disorders of Early Infancy or Early Childhood

Pica is regular eating of nonnutritive substances (e.g., dirt, animal droppings, insects, hair).

Rumination Disorder involves regurgitation and rechewing of food already eaten.

Feeding Disorder of Infancy or Early Childhood is characterized by failure to eat adequately, resulting in weight loss or failure to gain weight.

Tic Disorders

Tic Disorders involve sudden, recurrent, nonrythmic, and stereotypic motor movements or vocalizations. The most common is Tourette's Disorder, in which there are multiple motor and vocal tics occurring frequently.

Elimination Disorders

Encopresis is repeated expulsion of feces inappropriately (e.g., in clothing, on the floor), either involuntarily or intentionally after age 4.

Enuresis is repeated urination into bed or clothing, occurring after age 5.

Somatoform Disorders

Somatoform Disorders are each characterized by the presence of physical symptoms that are not explained by a medical condition, the results of a substance, or another mental disorder. Every somatoform disorder has not been listed.

Somatization Disorder is denoted by multiple symptoms (pain, gastrointestinal, sexual, and pseudoneurological) beginning prior to age 30.

Conversion Disorder is defined by unexplained physical symptoms in which psychological factors are deemed as being associated with the symptoms.

Pain Disorder is characterized by pain being the predominant purpose of treatment. Psychological factors tend to affect the onset, intensity, and course of the pain.

Hypochondriasis involves a preoccupation or unfounded belief of having a serious illness.

Body Dysmorphic Disorder is when a person with normal physical features believes that his or her body, or body parts, are misshaped or defective.

Adjustment Disorders

Adjustment disorders are defined as when an identifiable stressor results in behavioral or emotional symptoms that lead to either marked distress or functional impairments beyond that which would be normally expected in the situation. The course of the disorder may be either acute or chronic, but is usually short lived. The diagnostic categories of an Adjustment Disorder include Adjustment Disorder, (a) With Depressed Mood, (b) With Anxiety, (c) With Mixed Anxiety and Depressed Mood, (d) With Disturbance of Conduct, (e) With Mixed Disturbance of Emotions and Conduct, and (f) Unspecified.

Schizophrenia And Other Psychotic Disorders

The term psychotic does not receive universal agreement in its definition. The *DSM-IV-TR* defines psychotic with respect to certain symptoms that cross various diagnoses. There are several specific diagnoses and specifiers in this

category. This text will comment on the most prominent, without referring to
the subcategories.

Schizoprenia is defined as endorsing two of five symptoms, lasting six or
more months, including (a) delusions, (b) hallucinations, (c) disorganized behavior, (d) disorganized speech, and (e) negative symptoms.
Positive symptoms are those symptoms which are in excess, such as
delusions, hallucinations, and disorganized speech. *Negative symptoms*
are restricted behaviors, such as lack of emotional expression, flat
speech, and lack of goal-directed activity. *Paranoid Type* is typified by
auditory hallucinations or prominent delusions, such as persecution,
jealousy, or religious themes. *Disorganized Type* involves disorganized
speech and behavior. Hallucinations and delusions are less prominent than negative symptoms. *Catatonic Type* is depicted by marked
psychomotor disturbance such as excessive or lack of mobility or
unusual movements or speech. *Undifferentiated Type* involves some
or all of the basic types, in which none dominates. *Residual Type* takes
place when psychosis has improved but behaviors, perceptions, or
speech remain peculiar.

Schizophreniform Disorder is identical in symptomology as schizophrenia,
but the time frame is one to six months.

Schizoaffective Disorder is diagnosed when the person has symptoms of
schizophrenia for at least six months and significant symptoms of
depression or mania.

Delusional Disorder involves the presence of one or more nonbizarre
delusions lasting at least one month. *Erotomanic Type* centers around
a delusion that another person is in love with oneself in an idealized
or romantic manner, rather than sexually. *Grandiose Type* involves a
belief that one has tremendous, unrecognized importance in areas
such as talent, insight, religion, or other areas in which self-
importance may be grandiose. *Jealous Type* is a belief that one's
spouse or lover is unfaithful, based on incorrect information. *Persecu-
tory Type* is a belief that one is being conspired against, cheated, spied
on, drugged, or intentionally wronged by others. Neutral or minor
impositions are exaggerated. *Somatic Type* is a delusion in which there
are delusions about body functions or sensations such as smells, in-

festations, parasites, or appearance. *Mixed Type* involves more than one type of delusion.

Brief Psychotic Disorder is a brief psychotic disturbance of psychotic symptoms for less than one month.

Shared Psychotic Disorder takes place when a person shares delusions with a relative or someone close who already has the delusion.

Personality Disorders

Personality Disorders are an inflexible, ongoing pattern of behaviors and thought patterns that are significantly different than one's culture in areas such as cognition, affectivity, interpersonal functioning, and impulse control. Personality Disorders are divided into three clusters.

Cluster A Personality Disorders are depicted by relationship problems such as lack of trust, suspiciousness, social withdrawal, and indifference.

1. *Paranoid Personality Disorder* is depicted by suspiciousness, grudges, perceived character attacks, distrust, difficulties confiding in others, and a belief that there are hidden meanings in other people's statements.

2. *Schizoid Personality Disorder* is characterized by significant social detachment, emotional coldness, lack of social pleasure, involvement in solitary activities, and lack of desire for friendships.

3. *Schizotypal Personality Disorder* is described as having significant deficits such as interpersonal discomfort, cognitive distortions, odd beliefs, paranoia, odd behavior or appearance, and excessive social anxiety.

Cluster B Personality Disorders are typified by people who are dramatic and constantly seek attention but whose emotions are often shallow. They tend to make a good initial impression, but have difficulties interpersonally.

1. *Antisocial Personality Disorder* is denoted by a disregard for social norms, and behaviors such as deceitfulness, impulsivity, irresponsibility, lack of remorse, and violating the rights of others.

2. *Borderline Personality Disorder* is highlighted by behaviors such as

recurrent interpersonal instability, moodiness, suicidal behavior, inappropriate anger, and difficulties coping with stress.

3. *Histrionic Personality Disorder* is characterized by behaviors such as extreme emotionality, not being comfortable unless they are the center of attention, self-dramatization, being easily influenced by others, and attention-seeking behavior.

4. *Narcissistic Personality Disorder* is accompanied by behaviors such as being preoccupied with fantasies of success, exaggerated feelings of self-importance, entitlement, interpersonal exploitation, and arrogance.

Cluster C Personality Disorders are typified by problem areas such as social anxiety, dependency on others, tense, and overcontrolled.

1. *Avoidant Personality Disorder* is depicted by behaviors such as avoiding activities due to fear of rejection, not getting involved unless they know they are liked, social inhibition, feelings of inferiority, and becoming embarrassed easily.

2. *Dependent Personality Disorder* is characterized by behaviors such as having difficulties making decisions, being dependent on others, being easily hurt, feeling uncomfortable when alone, often seeking nurturance, and having difficulty disagreeing with others due to fear of disapproval.

3. *Obsessive-Compulsive Personality Disorder* involves a preoccupation with perfection, details, and order. Concerns are noted in inflexibility in areas such as morals, rigidity, difficulties discarding items, and excessive devotion to work, but exclusion of leisure and friends.

References

Acquino, J. A., Russell, D. W., Cutrona, C. E., & Altmaier, E. M. (1996). Employment status, social support, and life satisfaction among the elderly. *Journal of Counseling Psychology, 43,* 480–489.

American Psychiatric Association. (1997). Practice guidelines for the treatment of patients with Alzheimer's disease and other dementias of late life. *American Journal of Psychiatry, 154,* 1–39.

American Psychiatric Association. (2000). *Diagnostic and statistical manual of mental Disorders* (4th ed., text revisions). Washington, DC: American Psychiatric Association.

Atkinson, D. R., Ponterotto, J. G., & Sanchez, A. R. (1984). Attitudes of Vietnamese and Anglo-American students toward counseling. *Journal of College Student Personnel, 25,* 448–452.

Avila, D. L., & Avila, A. L. (1995). Mexican Americans. In N. A. Vacc, S. B. DeVaney, & J. Wittmer (Eds.), *Experiencing and counseling multicultural and diverse populations* (3rd ed., pp. 119–146). Bristol, PA: Accelerated Development.

Bernard, L. C. (1991). The detection of faked deficits on the Rey Auditory Verbal Learning Test: The effect of serial position. *Archives of Clinical Neuropsychology, 6,* 81–88.

Bernard, L. C., McGrath, M. J., & Houston, W. (1996). The differential effects of simulating malingering, closed head injury, and other CNS pathology on the Wisconsin Card Sorting Test: Support for the "pattern of preference" hypothesis. *Archives of Clinical Neuropsychology, 11,* 231–245.

Binder, L. M., Villaneuva, M. R., Howieson, D., & Moore, R. T. (1993). The Rey AVLT recognition memory task measures motivational impairment after mild head trauma. *Archives of Clinical Neuropsychology, 8,* 137–148.

Bongar, B. M. (1991). *The suicidal patient: Clinical and legal standards of care.* Washington, DC: American Psychological Association.

Bongar, B. M., Maris, R., Berman, A. L., & Litman, R. E. (1998). Outpatient standards of care and the suicidal patient. In B. M. Bongar, A. L. Berman, R. W. Maris, M. M. Silverman, E. A. Harris, & W. L. Packman, (Eds.), *Risk Management with Suicidal Patients* (pp. 4–33). New York: Guilford Press.

Butcher, J. N., Dahlstrom, W. G., Graham, J. R., Tellegen, A., & Kaemmer, B. (1989). *Minnesota Multiphasic Personality Inventory–2: Manual for administration and scoring.* Minneapolis, MN: University of Minnesota Press.

Carkhuff, R. R., & Berenson, B. G. (1977). *Beyond counseling and therapy* (2nd ed.). New York: Hold, Rinehart, & Winston.

Cavanaugh, M. E. (1990). *The counseling experience.* Prospect Heights, IL: Waveland Press.

Dorpat, T. L., & Ripley, H. S. (1967). The relationship between attempted suicide and committed suicide. *Comprehensive Psychiatry 8,* 74–79.

Eaton, M. J., & Dembo, M. H. (1997). Differences in the motivational beliefs of Asian Americans. *Journal of Educational Psychology, 89,* 433–440.

Edens, J. F., Otto, R. K., & Dwyer, T. (1999). Utility of the Structured Inventory of Malingered Symptomatology in identifying persons motivated to malinger psychopathology. *Journal of the American Academy of Psychiatry and the Law, 27*(3), 387–396.

Faden, R., & Beauchamp, T. (1986) *Informed consent: History, theory and implementation.* New York: Oxford University Press.

Frederick, R. I., Crosby, R. D., & Wynkoop, T. F. (2000). Performance curve classification of invalid responding on the Validity Indicator Profile. *Archives of Clinical Neuropsychology, 15*(4), 281–300.

Fruch, B. C., & Kinder, B. N. (1994). The susceptibility of the Rorschach Inkblot Test to malingering of combat-related PTSD. *Journal of Personality Assessment, 62,* 280–298.

Gaies, L., & Kinder, B. N. (1995, March). *Detection of malingered depression with the Personality Assessment Inventory.* Paper presented at the meeting of the Society for Personality Assessment, Chicago, IL.

Garnets, L., Hancock, K. A., Cochran, S. D., Goodchilds, J., & Peplau, L. A. (1998). Issues in psychotherapy with lesbians and gay men: A survey of psychologists. In D. R. Atkinson & G. Hackett (Eds.), *Counseling diverse populations* (2nd ed., pp. 297–316). Boston: McGraw-Hill.

Goldberg, L. R. (1965). Diagnosticians versus diagnostic signs: The diagnosis of psychosis versus neurosis from the MMPI. *Psychological Monographs, 79* (602).

Greiffenstein, M., Baker, W., & Gola, T. (1994). Validation of malingered amnesia measures with a large clinical sample. *Psychological Assessment, 6,* 218–224.

Groth-Marnat, G. (1990). *Handbook of psychological assessment* (2nd ed.). New York: Wiley Interscience.

Gutheil, T. G. (1984). Malpractice liability in suicide. *Legal Aspects of Psychiatric Practice, 1,* 1–4.

Haas, L. J., & Malouf, J. L. (1995). *Keeping up the good work* (2nd ed.). Sarasota, FL: Professional Resource Press.

Hays, P. A. (1996). Culturally responsive assessment with diverse older clients. *Professional Psychology: Research and Practice, 27*(2) 188–193.

Hildebrand, V., Phenice, L. A., Gray, M. M., & Hines, R. P. (1996) *Knowing and serving diverse families.* Englewood Cliffs, NJ: Prentice-Hall.

Hillard, J. R. (1995). Predicting Suicide. *Psychiatric Services, 46*(3), 223–225.

Horne, A., & Kiselica, M. (1999). *Handbook of counseling boys and adolescent males: A practitioner's guide.* Thousand Oaks, CA: Sage.

Hutchings, D. E., & Vaught, C. C. (1997). *Helping relationships and strategies* (3rd ed.) Pacific Grove, CA: Brooks Cole.

Iverson, G. L., Slick, D. J., & Franzen, M. D. (2000). Evaluation of a WMS-R malingering index in a non-litigating clinical sample. *Journal of Clinical and Experimental Neuropsychology, 22*(2), 191–197.

Jacobs, D. G., Brewer, M., & Klein-Benheim, M. (1999). Suicide assessment: An overview and recommended protocol. In D. G. Jacobs (Ed.), *The Harvard Medical School guide to suicide and intervention* (pp. 3–39). San Francisco: Jossey Bass.

Jaffee v. Redmond, 116 S. Ct. 1923 (1996).

Jones, B. N., Teng, E. L., Folsteing, M. F., & Harrison, K. S. (1993). A new bedside test of cognition for patient with HIV infection. *Annals of Internal Medicine, 119,* 1001–1004.

Karp, C., Butler, T., & Bergstrom, S. (1998). *Treatment strategies for abused adolescents: From victim to survivor.* Thousand Oaks, CA: Sage.

Kleespies, P. M. & Dettmer, E. L. (2000). An evidence-based approach to evaluating and managing suicidal emergencies. *Journal of Clinical Psychology, 56*(9), 1109–1130.

Knapp, S., & VanderCreek, L. (1983). Malpractice risks with suicidal patients. *Psychotherapy: Research, and Practice, 20,* 274–280.

LaBruzza, A. L. (1994). *Using DSM-IV: A clinician's guide to psychiatric diagnosis.* Northvale, NJ: Aaronson.

Laplanche, J., & Pontalis, J. B. (1973). *The language of psychoanalysis.* New York: Norton.

Logan, N. (1997). Diagnostic assessment of children. In R. J. Craig (Ed.), *Clinical and diagnostic interviewing.* Northvale, NJ: Aronson.

Maloney, M. P., & Ward, M. P. (1976). *Psychological assessment: A conceptual approach.* New York: Oxford University Press.

Maltsberger, J. T. (1988). Suicide danger: Clinical estimation and decision. *Suicide and life-threatening behavior, 18*(1), 47–54.

Matarazzo, J. D. (1986). Computerized clinical psychological test interpretations: Unvalidated plus all mean and no sigma. *American Psychologist, 4,* 14–24.

Meehl. P. E. (1954). *Clinical versus statistical prediction: A theoretical analysis and a review of the evidence.* Minneapolis, MN: University of Minnesota Press.

Meehl. P. E. (1965). Seer over sign: The first good example. *Journal of Experimental Research in Personality, 1,* 27–32.

Miller, H. A. (2000). The development of the Miller's Forensic Assessment of Symptoms Test: A measure of malingering mental illness. *Dissertation Abstracts International, 60* (8-B), 4238.

Miller, M. (1985). *Information center: Training workshop manual.* San Diego: The Information Center.

Mittenberg, W., Azrin, R., Millsaps, C., & Heilbronner, R. (1993). Identification of malingered head injury on the Wechsler Memory Scale–Revised. *Psychological Assessment, 5,* 34–40.

Morey, L. C. (1991). *Personality Assessment Inventory: Professional manual.* Odessa, FL: Psychological Assessment Resources.

Morey, L. C., & Lanier, V. W. (1998). Operating characteristics of six response distortion indicators for the Personality Assessment Inventory. *Assessment, 5*(3), 203–214.

Morrison, J. (1993). *The first interview.* New York: Guilford.

Morrison, J. (1995). *DSM-IV made easy.* New York: Guilford.

Murphy, G. E. (1984). The prediction of suicide: Why is it so difficult? *American Journal of Psychotherapy, 38,* 341–349.

Neuringer, C. (1964). Rigid thinking in suicidal individuals. *Journal of Consulting and Clinical Psychology, 28,* 54–58.

Nguyen, S. D. (1985). Mental health services for refugees and immigrants in Canada. In T. C. Owen (Ed.), *Southeast Asian mental health: Treatment, prevention, services, training, and research* (pp. 261–282). Washington, DC: National Institute of Mental Health.

Othmer, E., & Othmer, S. C. (1989). *The clinical interview using DSM-III-R.* Washington, DC: American Psychiatric Association.

Othmer, E., & Othmer, S. C. (1994). *The clinical interview using the DSM-IV* (Vols. 1–2). Washington, DC: American Psychiatric Association.

Paniagua, F. A. (1994). *Assessing and treating culturally diverse clients.* Thousand Oaks, CA: Sage.

Pipes, R. B., & Davenport, D. S. (1990). *Introduction to psychotherapy: Common clinical wisdom.* Englewood Cliffs, NJ: Prentice-Hall.

Pope, K. E., & Vasquez, M. J. T. (1991) *Ethics in psychotherapy and counseling.* San Francisco: Jossey-Bass.

Rogers, C. R. (1961). *On becoming a person: A therapist's view of psychotherapy.* Boston: Houghton Mifflin.

Rogers, C. R. (1975). Empathic: An unappreciated way of being. *Counseling Psychologist, 5,* 2–10.

Rogers, R., Bagey, R. M., & Dickins, S. E. (1992). *Structured interview of reported symptoms: Professional manual.* Odessa, FL: Psychological Assessment Resources.

Rosenberg, J. I. (1999). Suicide prevention: An integrated training model using affective and action-based intervention. *Professional Psychology: Research and Practice, 30*(1), 83–87.

Rudd, M. D., & Joiner, T. (1998). The assessment, management, and treatment of suicidality: Toward clinically informed and balanced standards of care. *Clinical Psychology: Science and Practice, 5,* 135–150.

Ruffolo, L. F., Guilmette, T. J., & Willis, W. G. (2000). Comparison of time and error rates on the Trail Making Test among patients with head injuries, experimental malingerers, patients with suspect effort on testing, and normal controls. *Clinical Neuropsychologist, 14*(2), 223–230.

Sabin, J., & Daniels, N. (1994). Determining "medical necessity" in mental health practice. *Hastings Center Report, 214,* 5–13.

Shea, S. C. (1999). *The practical art of suicide assessment: A guide for mental health professionals and substance abuse counselors.* New York: Wiley.

Silver, I., & Herrmann, N. (1991). History and mental status examination. In J. Sadavoy, L. Lazarus, & L. Jarvik (Eds.), *Comprehensive review of geriatric psychiatry.* Washington, DC: American Psychiatric Press.

Simon, R. I. (1988) *Concise guide to psychotherapy and the law.* Washington, DC: American Psychiatric Press.

Scissons, E. H. (1993). *Counseling for results: Principles and practices of helping.* Pacific Grove, CA: Brooks Cole.

Skodol, A. E. (1989). *Problems in differential diagnosis.* Washington, DC: American Psychiatric Press.

Smith, K. (1986). Research-informed comments on the treatment of suicidal inpatients. *Psychiatric-Hospital, 17*(1), 21–25.

Sommers-Flanagan, J., Rothman, M., & Schwenkler, R. (2000). Training psychologists to become competent suicide assessment interviewers: Commentary on Rosenberg's (1999) suicide prevention training model. *Professional Psychology: Research and Practice, 31*(1), 99–100.

Sommers-Flannagan, R., & Sommers-Flannagan, J. (1999). *Clinical interviewing* (2nd ed.). New York: Wiley.

Sue, D. W., & Sue, D. (1999). *Counseling the culturally different: Theory and practice* (3rd ed.). New York: Wiley.

Suhr, J. A., & Boyer, D. (1999). Use of the Wisconsin Card Sorting Test in the detection of malingering in student simulator and patient samples. *Journal of Clinical and Experimental Neuropsychology, 21*(5), 701–708.

Steiger, W. A. & Hirsch, H. (1965). The difficult patient in everyday medical practice. *Medical Clinics of North America, 49,* 1449–1465.

Taylor, M. A. (1981). *The Neuropsychiatric Mental Status Examination.* New York: Spectrum.

Toarmino, D., & Chun, C. A. (1997). Issues and strategies in counseling Korean Americans. In C. C. Lee (Ed.), *Multicultural issues in counseling* (pp. 233–254). American Counseling Association, Alexandria, VA.

Wagner, L., Davis, S., & Handelsmann, M. (1998). In search of the abominable consent form: The impact of readability and personalization. *Journal of Clinical Psychology, 54,* 115–120.

Wechsler, D. (1997a). *Manual of the Wechsler Adult Intelligence Scale–Third edition.* San Antonio, TX: The Psychological Corporation.

Wechsler, D. (1997b). *Manual of the Wechsler Memory Scale–Third edition.* San Antonio, TX: The Psychological Corporation.

Wiger, D. E. (1999). *The clinical documentation sourcebook: A comprehensive collection of mental health practice forms, handouts, and records* (2nd ed.). New York: Wiley.

Wiger, D. E. (2000). *The psychotherapy documentation primer.* New York: Wiley.

Wiger, D. E., & Solberg, K. B. (2001). *Tracking mental health outcomes: A therapist's guide to measuring client progress, analyzing data, and improving your practice.* New York: Wiley.

Wiggins. J. S. (1973). *Personality and prediction: Principles of personality assessment.* Reading, MA: Addison-Wesley.

Wildman, R. W., & Wildman, R. W., II (1999). The detection of malingering. *Psychological Reports, 84*(2), 386–388.

World Health Organization. (1997a). *Multiaxial classification of child and adolescent psychiatric disorders: The ICD-10 classification of mental and behavioural disorders in childhood and adolescence.* London: Cambridge University Press.

World Health Organization. (1997b). *The multiaxial presentation of the ICD-10 for use in adult psychiatry.* London: Cambridge University Press.

Yamamoto, J., & Acosta, F. X. (1982). Treatment of Asian-Americans and Hispanic-Americans: Similarities and differences. *Journal of the Academy of Psychoanalysis, 10,* 585–607.

Yufit, R. I. (1989). Assessment of suicide potential. In R. J. Craig (Ed.), *Clinical and Diagnostic Interviewing.* (pp. 289–303). New Jersey: Aronson.

Zuckerman, E. L. (1995). *The clinician's thesaurus* (2nd ed.). New York: Guilford Press.

Annotated Bibliography

Bongar, B. M., Maris, R., Berman, A. L., & Litman, R. E. (1998). Outpatient standards of care and the suicidal patient. In B. M. Bongar, A. L. Berman, R. W. Maris, M. M. Silverman, E. A. Harris, & W. L. Packman (Eds.), *Risk Management with Suicidal Patients* (pp. 4-33). New York: Guilford Press.

This edited book provides information from well-known experts in suicidology. Topics such as psychopharmological interventions and legal considerations are well covered. Standards of care and risk management for both inpatient and outpatient settings are included.

Corey, G. (1996). *Theory and practice of counseling and psychotherapy* (5th ed.). Monterey, CA: Brooks Cole.

This is one of the most widely used texts for beginning counselors and developing basic counseling skills. It's easy to follow format provides the reader with clear examples of atheoretical aspects of the counseling process.

Craig, R. J. (1997). *Clinical and diagnostic interviewing.* Northvale, NJ: Aronson.

This book provides valuable information about specific theoretical approaches as they apply to diagnostic interviewing (e.g., psychoanalytic interviewing, behavioral interviewing) as well as guidelines for interviewing clients with specific psychopathologies (e.g., substance abuse, personality disorders).

Jacobs, D. G. (1999). *The Harvard medical school guide to suicide assessment & intervention.* San Francisco: Jossey-Bass.

This lengthy and comprehensive, edited text covers all aspects of suicide from several theoretical, practical, and diagnostic perspectives. Several special issues are reviewed, which are typically not covered in similar texts. The appendices provide easy-to-follow lists of risk factors, DSM-IV disorders correlated with suicide, and other guidelines from the Risk Management Foundation of the Harvard Medical Institutions.

Morrison, J. (1993). *The first interview.* New York: Guilford Press.

This classic, comprehensive text in interviewing covers all aspects of interviewing such as rapport building, encouraging the client, mental status exam, diagnostic interviewing, dealing with sensitive subjects, interviewing informants, making recommendations, and the psychological report.

Morrison, J. (1995). *DSM-IV made easy*. New York: Guilford Press.

Although this is not a book on interviewing skills, it provides a chapter for each of the DSM-IV diagnostic categories. Each DSM-IV diagnosis is described. Several tips and cases studies are included to aid in differential diagnosis.

Othmer, E., & Othmer, S. C. (1994). *The clinical interview using the DSM-IV* (Vols. 1–2). Washington, DC: American Psychiatric Association.

This text is written in conjunction with the DSM-IV, describing several approaches to interviewing. Several interviewing strategies to increase the rapport and ability to collect information are covered. The text focuses on the several steps involved in arriving at a clinical diagnosis within a DSM-IV framework.

Sommers-Flannagan, R., & Sommers-Flannagan, J. (1999). *Clinical interviewing* (2nd ed.). New York: Wiley.

This comprehensive, well-written text provides much practical information and examples in areas such as dealing with special populations, assessing suicide, cultural issues, and working with families. Almost one-half of the book covers the relationship and listening aspects of clinical interviewing.

Sue, D. W., & Sue, D. (1999). *Counseling the culturally different: Theory and practice* (3rd ed.). New York: Wiley.

This comprehensive and informative text provides a wealth of information and examples to prepare one for counseling people from several cultural backgrounds.

INDEX

Acute Stress Disorder, 203
Adjustment disorders, 144, 207
Affective disorders, 131, 163
African Americans, 74–75
Agoraphobia, 203
Agoraphobia Without a History of Panic Disorder, 203
Alcohol Dependence, 129, 195
Alcohol-Induced Persisting Dementia, 148
Alcoholism, 131, 139
Antisocial Personality Disorder, 40, 209
Anxiety disorder, 203
Asian Americans, 75–78
Asperger's Disorder, 205
Assessment interview. *See* Intake interviews
Attention-Deficit/Hyperactivity Disorder (ADHD), 205
Autistic Disorder, 149, 205
Avoidant Personality Disorder, 210

Beck Depression Inventory–II, 57
Biopsychosocial assessment:
  chemical use history, 108–109, 110
  components of, 92–93
  cultural/ethnic background and practices, 95–96
  education, 99–100
  employment history, 101
  family history and dynamics, 93–95
  history of mental health treatment, 109–113
  items covered in, 114
  legal history, 98–99
  leisure/recreation, 102–103
  medical/physical/sexual, 103–106
  medications, 107–108
  military experience, 102
  nutrition, 107
  overview, 90–91
  in report, 195
  social relationships, 93
  spiritual/religious beliefs and practices, 96–98
Bipolar Disorder, 108, 202
Body Dysmorphic Disorder, 149, 207
Borderline Personality Disorder, 121, 124, 129, 209
Brain injury, 100
Brief Psychotic Disorder, 208
Butterfly interviewing, 44

Canine interviewing, 44–45
Checklist interviewing, 43
Chemical dependency (CD), 16, 193–199
Chemical use history, 108–109, 110

Childhood Disintegrative Disorder, 205

Chronic fatigue syndrome, 104

Clinicians. *See* Interviewers

Communication disorders, 205

Competencies, 20–21

Computerized testing, 20–21

Conduct Disorder, 142, 152, 205

Confidentiality:
  with adolescents, 71
  with Asian Americans, 78
  overview, 17
  sample statement, 18

Congruence, 63

Conversion Disorder, 207

Countertransference, 38–39

Culture/ethnicity:
  in biopsychosocial assessment, 95–96
  interviewer's self-awareness of, 36
  in report, 196

Cyclothymic Disorder, 149, 202

Decision trees, diagnostic, 154–162

Delusional Disorder, 148, 208

Dependent Personality Disorder, 210

Depressive disorders, 49, 129, 202

Diagnoses:
  common errors in, 27
  differences in, 24
  information sources for, 21–23
  overview, 200–201
  vs. presenting problem, 137–139
  previous, 23–28
  provisional, 28
  rule-out, 28
  skills for, 3–5

Diagnostic interviews. *See* Intake interviews

Diagnostic and Statistical Manual of Mental Disorders–Fourth Edition, Text Revision (DSM-IV-TR):
  Axis I, 30, 151–154
  Axis II, 30–31, 172, 173
  Axis III, 31, 104
  Axis IV, 31
  Axis V, 31–32
  diagnostic criteria, 147–150
  essential vs. associated symptoms, 144–146
  in four-quadrant approach, 53–54
  in intake interview, 29
  medical model of, 4–5
  multiaxial classification system of, 29–32
  organization of, 201–210
  presenting problem and, 139
  primary vs. secondary essential features, 147–148
  report writing and, 192
  sample diagnosis, 153–154
  sections
    Associated Features and Disorders, 149
    Course, 150
    Diagnostic Features, 147–148
    Differential Diagnosis, 150
    Familial Pattern, 150

Prevalence, 149
Recording Procedures, 148
Specific Culture, Age, and Gender Features, 149
Subtypes and Specifiers, 148
structured questions and, 50
symptomatology, 141–143
third-party payers and, 2
use of, 25
Dissociative Identity Disorder, 48
Distress, 143–144, 163
Documentation:
for affective impairments, 163
example, 10
importance of, 9
in intake interview, 15
for legal impairments, 161
for occupational impairments, 160
for physical impairments, 162
skills for, 3–5
for social impairments, 159
for suicide assessment, 119
Double Depression, 156
Dual relationships, 19–20, 37–38
Dysthymic Disorder:
defined, 202
distress and, 144
in report, 194
rule-in/rule-out procedures for, 156
sample diagnosis, 153
symptomatology, 141–143

Education, 99–100, 196
Elimination disorders, 206

Empathy, 62–63
Employment history, 101
Encopresis, 206
Enuresis, 206
Ethics:
culture/ethnicity and, 95–96
dual relationships and, 19–20
in intake interview, 14, 16
medical history and, 104
medical necessity and, 6
religion and, 96–98
in suicide assessment, 133–135

Family history, 93–95
Feeding Disorder of Infancy or Early Childhood, 206
Functional impairments, 29

Generalized Anxiety Disorder (GAD):
biopsychosocial assessment and, 104
defined, 203
diagnostic features of, 147–148
Genograms, 94
Global Assessment of Functioning (GAF) Scale:
Axis V and, 31–32
in report, 194
scores on, 7–8

Hispanic Americans, 78–81
History:
chemical use, 108–109, 110
employment, 101

History (*continued*)
   family, 93–95
   legal, 98–99
   medical, 103–106
   medication, 107–108
   mental health treatment, 109–113
   nutritional, 107
   physical, 103–106
   prior, 25, 28
   sexual, 103–106
Histrionic Personality Disorder, 209
Hypochondriasis, 207

Impairments, 143
Information gathering, 21–23
Informed consent, 17–19
In (full or partial) Remission, 25, 28
Insurance companies. *See* Third-
   party payers
Intake interviews:
   biopsychosocial assessment in, 90
   competencies in, 20–21
   confidentiality in, 17, 18
   DSM-IV-TR and, 29
   ethical considerations for, 16
   example, 16
   history of mental health services,
     111
   inconsistent material in, 140
   information gathering in, 21–23
   informed consent in, 17–19
   medical necessity and, 9
   note taking during, 15
   overview, 13–14
   previous diagnoses in, 23–28

screening for physical disorders,
   104
   sharing results in, 23
   therapist-client relationships in,
     19–20
   time breakdown for, 14
   "window of opportunity," 137
International Classification of
   Diseases–Tenth Revision
   (ICD-10), 2
Interviews:
   butterfly, 44
   canine, 44–45
   checklist, 43
   closed-ended vs. open-ended,
     46–47, 51
   four-quadrant approach to, 51,
     52–55
   initial contact, 65
   language appropriate for, 62
   nonstructured vs. structured, 47–
     52
   vs. psychological testing, 20–21
   semi-structured, 50–52
   setting for, 61–62
   skills for, 3–5
   smorgasbord, 43–44
   structure of, 42–52
Interviewers:
   appropriate attire for, 61–62
   background of, 48
   personal experiences of, 64–65
   role of, 3–5
   self-awareness of, 35–38
   skills of, 65

Irish Catholic Americans, 84–85

Jaffee v. Redmond, 17
Jewish Americans, 85

Learning Disorders, 205
Legal history, 98–99, 196
Legal impairments, 161
Leisure/recreation, 102–103
Lethality, 125–126, 128
Listening skills, 64

Major Depressive Disorder:
   defined, 202
   interviewer's background and, 48
   rule-in/rule-out procedures for,
     146, 156
   sample statements of presenting
     problem, 138
   symptomatology, 141–143
Malingering, 22, 40–42
Med controlled, 28
Medical history, 103–106, 196
Medical necessity:
   degrees of, 7–8
   in intake interview, 29
   overview, 5–10
   sample documentation of, 10
Medication history, 27–28, 107–108
Mental Retardation:
   Axis II and, 30–31
   biopsychosocial assessment of,
     100
   defined, 205
   sample misdiagnosis of, 26

Mental status exam (MSE):
   abstractive capacity, 181–183
   activity level, 169–170
   affect, 176
   appearance, 168–169
   attitude toward examiner,
     170–172
   clinical observations, 167
   concentration, 178–179, 180
   example, 173
   information, 180–181, 182
   insight, 185
   intellectual functioning/educa-
     tion, 185–186
   judgment, 183–184
   memory, 179–180, 181
   mood, 177
   orientation × 3, 178
   overview, 167
   reality contact, 178
   in report, 197–198
   sensorium cognition, 177–178
   speech, 170, 171
   stream of consciousness, 172–174
   thought content, 174–175
Military experience, 102
Miller's Forensic Assessment of
   Symptoms Test, 42
Minnesota Multiphasic Personality
   Inventory–2 (MMPI-2), 40
Mood disorders, 155, 201–202

Narcissistic Personality Disorder,
   209
Native Americans, 81–84

New Direction Chemical Dependency Services, 194
Note taking, 15. *See also* Documentation
Nutritional history, 107

Obsessive-Compulsive Disorder (OCD):
    defined, 203
    familial patterns and, 150
    leisure/recreation and, 103
    sample interview, 187
Obsessive-Compulsive Personality Disorder, 210
Occupational impairments, 160
OF AID technique, 123, 157–162
Oppositional Defiant Disorder (ODD), 141–143, 205
Overprescribing, 6–9

Pain Disorder, 207
Panic attack, 203
Panic Disorder, 203
Paranoid Personality Disorder, 151, 209
Personality Assessment Inventory (PAI), 40
Personality disorders, 30–31, 209
Pervasive Developmental Disorders (PDDs), 205
Physical history, 103–106
Physical impairments, 162
Pica, 150, 206
Posttraumatic Stress Disorder (PTSD):
    defined, 203

questioning and, 49
remission and, 25–27
suicide risk and, 129
Presenting problem:
    biopsychosocial assessment and, 90
    example, 140
    inconsistencies in, 139–140
    overview, 137–139
    proper vs. improper statements of, 138–139
Prior History, 25, 28
Prozac, 194
Psychometrics, 2

Questions:
    for assessing suicidal behavior, 127
    closed-ended, 46–47, 51
    nonstructured, 47–48, 51
    open-ended, 46–47, 51
    rule-in/rule-out procedures, 57
    semi-structured, 50–52
    structured, 48–50, 51

Rapport:
    with abused populations, 68–69
    with African Americans, 74–75
    with Asian Americans, 75–78
    biopsychosocial assessment and, 93
    with families and couples, 71–72
    in four-quadrant approach, 52
    with gay men and lesbian women, 72–73
    with Hispanic Americans, 78–81

influence of, on data gathering, 38
in intake interview, 15
with Irish Catholic Americans,
    84–85
with Jewish Americans, 85
with Native Americans, 81–84
in nonstructured interviewing, 47
with older adults, 69–70
with older youth, 70–71
with special populations, 73
suicidality and, 125
with young children, 66–68
Reason for referral, 4, 191
Recreation/leisure, 196
Referral question, 4, 191
Reliability, 50
Reliable Digits Test, 40
Religion, 96–98, 196
Report:
    biopsychosocial assessment, 195
    example, 193–199
    history of present problem, 195
    interpretive summary, 198–199
    mental status exam (MSE),
        197–198
    overview, 191–193
    review of records, 193–195
    writing tips, 193
Resistance, 39–40
Rett's Disorder, 205
Rey Auditory Verbal Learning Test,
    42
Rule-in/rule-out procedures:
    decision trees and, 154–162
    for Major Depressive Disorder, 146
    overview, 55–57

presenting problem and, 139
of primary essential symptoms,
    151
of secondary essential symptoms,
    152
structured questions and, 50
Rumination Disorder, 206

Schizoaffective Disorder, 208
Schizoid Personality Disorder, 209
Schizophrenia:
    defined, 207–208
    sample misdiagnosis of, 26
    sample statements of presenting
        problem, 138
    suicide risk and, 129, 131
Schizophreniform Disorder, 208
Schizotypal Personality Disorder,
    209
Self-awareness, 35–38
Separation Anxiety Disorder, 148
Sexual history, 103–106
Shared Psychotic Disorder, 208
Sleep Terror Disorder, 150
Smorgasbord interviewing, 43–44
SNAPs. See Strengths, Needs, Abili-
    ties, and Preferences (SNAPs)
Social impairments, 159
Social Phobia, 203
Social relationships, 93
Somatization Disorder, 207
Somatoform disorders, 206–207
Specific Phobia, 203
Spirituality, 96–98. See also Religion
Strengths, Needs, Abilities, and Pref-
    erences (SNAPs), 91–92

Structured Interview of Reported Symptoms, 42
Structured Inventory of Malingered Symptomatology, 42
Substance Abuse, 204
Substance Dependence, 204
Substance Intoxication, 204
Substance-Induced Disorders, 204
Substance-related disorders, 204
Substance Use Disorders, 204
Substance Withdrawal, 204
Suicidality:
    assessment for, 113
        ethical considerations, 133–134
        hospitalization and, 122, 131–132
        lack of training for, 118–119
        legal considerations, 133–135
        medical necessity and, 8
        overview, 118–119
        suicide contracts, 132
    countertransference and, 38–39
    five levels of, 120–122
    lethality (*see* Lethality)
    plan, 125–126
    prediction of, 129
    risk factors for, 120–131
    sample assessment, 124
    sample interview, 114, 127
    sample statements of presenting problem, 138
    signs of potential suicide attempt, 130

Symptoms:
    associated
        assessment of, 152
        defined, 142–143
        vs. essential, 144–146
    diagnostic decision trees and, 154–162
    essential
        mood and, 177
        primary, 151
        secondary, 152
    overview, 141–143
    sample interview, 145
    vegetative, 146–147
Systematic inquiry, 49

Tarasoff v. Regents of California, 133
Testing, role of, 57
Therapists. *See* Interviewers
Third-party payers:
    Axis I diagnosis and, 30
    data collection and, 22
    documentation for, 2, 3
    four-quadrant approach and, 54
    intake interview reimbursement, 14
    medical history and, 104
    medical necessity and, 5–10
    report writing and, 191
    rule-in/rule-out procedures and, 55
    suicide and, 132
Tic disorders, 206
Tolerance, 204
Tort action, 133

Trail Making Test, 40–42
Transference, 38–39
Triangulation, 72

Unconditional positive regard, 63–64
Underprescribing, 9

Validity Indicator Profile, 42
Vocational history, 196

Wechsler Adult Intelligence
    Scale–III (WAIS-III), 40,
    178
Wechsler Intelligence Scale for Chil-
    dren–III (WISC-III), 178
Wechsler Memory Scale–III, 40
Wildman Symptom Checklist, 42
Wisconsin Card Sorting Test, 40
Withdrawal, 204

About the Authors

Donald E. Wiger, PhD, specializes in psychological assessment. He teaches courses in psychological assessment, clinical documentation, and mental health policies and procedures at Argosy University. He also conducts national seminars in clinical documentation. He has authored or coauthored three books including, *The Clinical Documentation Sourcebook, The Psychotherapy Documentation Primer,* and *Tracking Mental Health Outcomes.*

Debra K. Huntley, PhD, is a professor at Argosy University-Twin Cities campus and teaches graduate courses in the clinical psychology doctoral program. She specializes in child and family issues and cognitive-behavioral techniques. She is an active researcher, currently studying the role of women in psychology.